OH MY GODDESS!

OH MY GODDESS!
— F I R S T   E N D —

WRITTEN BY
YUMI TOHMA

WITH ILLUSTRATIONS BY
KOSUKE FUJISHIMA AND HIDENORI MATSUBARA

ENGLISH TRANSLATION BY
CAMELLIA NIEH

DARK HORSE BOOKS®
MILWAUKIE

❧ OUR CHARACTERS ❧

BELLDANDY

A Goddess First Class Type Two Unlimited and employee of the Goddess Technical Help Line, which provides aid to people in need. The middle sister, she is also the Goddess of the Present.

URD

The eldest of the three sisters, Urd is the Goddess of the Past, with a Second Class, Management Category Limited license. Half-goddess and half-demon, she is the daughter of Hild, ruler of the Demon Realm. She can't—or won't—become a Goddess First Class because of her habit of telling lies.

SKULD

The youngest of the three sisters, Skuld is the Goddess of the Future, with a Second Class Type One Limited license. She barely has any magical powers yet, but she's a wizard with machines, inventing all sorts of amazing contraptions.

KEIICHI MORISATO

A short, penniless, run-of-the-mill college student with a heart of gold. Keiichi loves cars and motorcycles and works at a motorcycle shop run by Chihiro Fujimi, the original president of the Motor Club.

PEORTH

Like Belldandy, Peorth is a Goddess First Class, Type Two Unlimited. Works for the Earth Assistance Hotline, a rival organization to the Goddess Technical Help Line where Belldandy works.

TAMIYA AND OTAKI

Upperclassmen in the Motor Club. Currently graduate students. Tend to be overbearing and pushy, dragging everyone around them into their wild schemes—particularly Keiichi.

WHAT IS *OH MY GODDESS!?*

Keiichi Morisato, a student at the Nekomi Institute of Technology, is short, poor, and a total failure with the ladies. One day, he finds himself visited by a real, live goddess. The goddess Belldandy offers to grant him one wish, and Keiichi responds, "I want a goddess like you to be with me always." His wish comes true, and before long Belldandy is joined by her elder sister Urd and younger sister Skuld. Thus begin the trials and tribulations of an ordinary college student living with three goddesses.

Book design by Scott Cook
Cover illustrations by Kosuke Fujishima
Interior illustrations by Hidenori Matsubara

English translation by Camellia Nieh

Special thanks to Carl Horn, Rachel Miller, Michael Gombos, and Riko Frohnmayer for editing consultation.

Published by Dark Horse Books
A division of Dark Horse Comics
10956 SE Main Street
Milwaukie, OR 97222

Library of Congress Cataloging-in-Publication Data

Toma, Yumi, 1966-
 [Shoshu. English]
 Oh my goddess!: first end / written by Yumi Tohma ; illustrations by Kosuke Fujishima and Hidenori
Matsubara ; [English translation by Camellia Nieh].
   p. cm.
 "First published in Japan in 2006 by Kodansha Ltd., Tokyo"--T.p. verso.
 Novelization based on Aa, megamisama by K. Fujishima. Cf. NDL-OPAC.
 ISBN-13: 978-1-59582-137-9
 ISBN-10: 1-59582-137-6
 I. Fujishima, Kosuke. II. Matsubara, Hidenori. III. Nieh, Camellia. IV. Fujishima, Kosuke. Aa, mega-
misama. V. Title. VI. Title: First end.
 PL876.O66S5613 2007
 895.6'36--dc22
                      2007028231

Dark Horse Books First Edition: November 2007
ISBN: 978-1-59582-137-9

Printed in the United States of America

10 9 8 7 6 5 4 3 2 1

❧ CONTENTS ❧

OH MY GODDESS!

✇ PROLOGUE ✇

"Uh-oh . . ."

Keiichi let out a soft exclamation and stopped what he was doing.

In a corner of the temple grounds, he'd been running the cell motor of his sidecar-equipped BMW for more than three hours. Louder and softer, louder and softer . . . its rumble had been irregular but continuous. Now, the motor stopped, gave off a few muffled pops, and was quiet.

Keiichi straightened up slightly—he'd been crouching for hours, completely absorbed in his work.

"Oops."

He let out a long sigh.

The sun shone brightly in the big blue sky, interrupted now and again by cool breezes from the east. The fan-shaped golden leaves of the ginkgo trees danced in the wind.

"I shouldn't have pushed it . . ."

He stood up slowly and began to walk with a heavy stride. The dried leaves scattered on the ground crunched underfoot.

It was a mild, sunny afternoon at Tarikihongan Temple. After glancing around the grounds, Keiichi gave the sliding door to the main building a strong shove, sending it rattling open.

Sunlight streamed into the dark interior.

Once inside the front entryway, Keiichi sighed deeply, as if to belie the vigor with which he had pushed open the door.

"Now I've done it," he lamented aloud.

Reaching back, Keiichi quietly pulled the door shut and sank listlessly onto the stoop that led up into the building. Carelessly, he wiped the sweat from his brow with his sleeve, which was rolled up to the elbow, and gazed down at his still-clenched right fist.

"Out of the way, Keiichi!"

Startled, Keiichi jumped to his feet and did an about-face.

"O-oh! Skuld!"

Where had she come from? Skuld stood with a shopping basket in hand and a sunny expression that contrasted with Keiichi's flustered one.

"Don't just sit there in the middle of the front entryway. If you're taking a break, at least come inside."

He certainly couldn't argue with that.

"Oh, uh, sorry . . . Are you going shopping?"

"Yep! The new issue of *Dobon* comes out today!"

Dobon was the manga magazine that Skuld read faithfully every month. She could always be counted on to be in a good mood the day it hit the shelves.

"Th-that's great!" That accounted for her cheeriness. As discreetly as possible, Keiichi used his left hand to cover the object he was gripping, hiding it behind his back.

"Well," he offered pleasantly, trying to match Skuld's bright smile, "take care, then!" He began to beat a swift retreat, but unfortunately, human beings are cursed with the tendency to be most obvious when they're trying hardest to hide something.

Not surprisingly, Skuld noticed.

"Just a minute, Keiichi . . . You're hiding something, aren't you?"

"!!"

Bull's-eye. Keiichi froze.

"First you act all panicked and flustered, then you turn all cool and casual . . . something's going on!"

Skuld extended her hand. Unfortunately, her first Reveal Hidden Object spell failed. Despite his despondency, Keiichi's reflexes remained intact.

"Rats!"

She attempted the spell a second time, then a third. But each time, her hand only waved impotently in the air.

"Argh!" Skuld glowered at the floor. Her rosy mood had evaporated completely, and ominous angry clouds were beginning to gather.

" . . . id, aren't you . . ."

"Huh?" Keiichi couldn't make out whatever it was Skuld was muttering. But it was plain from her trembling shoulders and clenched fists that her irritation was quickly evolving into rage.

"S-S-Skuld?" Keiichi stammered fearfully. Skuld's anger-voltage continued its steady climb.

"You're treating me . . . like a kid . . . aren't you?!"

"Wha . . . ?"

This time, her words were clear but the message caught him off-guard.

"You're blowing me off because you think I'm just a kid, aren't you!"

"Huh? No . . . I never . . ."

The unforeseen accusation and unprovoked surge of fury baffled Keiichi. But with the needle of her anger-gauge hovering in its red zone, Skuld was in no state to listen to reason.

Slowly, she raised her head. "Fine! If that's how you're going to be . . . I'm telling!"

"What?"

"I'm telling Belldandy on you!"

"What's Belldandy got to do with this?" For some reason, the sudden mention of Skuld's big sister seemed not so much surprising to Keiichi as completely absurd.

But when Skuld was set on getting her way, reason and coherence went out the window. This time, her power play was to use Keiichi's beloved Belldandy as leverage to make Keiichi cave.

"Belldandyyyy . . . Belldandyyy . . . Keiichi's hi—" Skuld began to shout toward the back rooms, her voice triumphant. This was beginning to get out of hand.

"Okay, okay! It's really not that big a deal!"

Reluctantly, Keiichi slowly brought his right hand out from behind his back.

"That's better!" A pleased smile spread across Skuld's face, both from the satisfaction of having won and the excitement of uncovering what she was after.

"I'm afraid you're going to be disappointed," Keiichi found himself muttering when he saw the curiosity glittering in Skuld's eyes.

" . . . a screwdriver?"

Skuld frowned at the uninteresting tool in Keiichi's hand. It was clear from her reaction that this wasn't what she'd expected.

Keiichi sighed. Just as he'd thought.

"I tried to tell you . . ."

"Then why wouldn't you just show it to me? You looked so suspicious—I thought it was something important!" Her interest completely evaporated, Skuld retrieved the shopping basket she'd flung to the ground.

Keiichi's expression clouded slightly at her sudden indifference.

"It *is* important. To me, anyway . . . As it happens, this screwdriver is kind of special . . . I've always done my best to take excellent care of it. But just now, I was using it, and I twisted it just a little bit too hard . . ."

"Oh?"

Skuld took the specialty Phillips screwdriver from Keiichi and examined it closely. A tiny corner was missing from the precision-formed plus-shape at its tip.

"It looks to me like it should still work."

The flaw was so small it was hardly noticeable without careful scrutiny. But a Phillips screwdriver's torque was a function of its head fitting perfectly into the grooves of the screw. Even the tiniest chip would change the tool's feel significantly, hampering its effectiveness at performing delicate tasks.

"If it really bothers you, I'll get you a new one while I'm out. A number 3, right? Until I get back, you can borrow one of mine," Skuld offered breezily.

Keiichi snatched the screwdriver back. "No, Skuld . . ."

"Why not? It's hard to use now, right?"

"That's not the point . . ."

As Keiichi gazed lovingly at his screwdriver, Skuld's face registered disappointment. Here she'd gone out of her way to be nice, and Keiichi was turning her down?

"Then what *is* the point?"

"It's just that . . ." Keiichi bit his lip. "Remember when I told you that scratches are part of a person's history? That goes for everything we use, including tools. Even when they get chipped, or worse, broken . . . when you've used something for a long time, through good times and bad, that makes that something one-of-a-kind. It makes it irreplaceable. That's how I feel, anyway."

" . . ."

Skuld listened attentively to what Keiichi had to say, but in the end she remained unconvinced.

"Yeah, but . . . it's a tool. Usability is everything, right?" She swung her shopping basket and hopped into her shoes. "Sheesh, what a waste of time! I'm off to buy *Dobon* now!" Where was her rage now? Skuld bounded off into the afternoon sun, her good cheer restored.

"I suppose that makes sense, too . . ." Keiichi smiled wryly from inside the building as he watched Skuld disappear into the distance.

"But I still prefer this old thing," he concluded, grinning.

He squeezed the Phillips screwdriver.

❦ CHAPTER ONE ❧

U T A K A T A — E P H E M E R A

Dancing gently in the breeze, the large white magnolia flowers looked almost like handkerchiefs tied to the tree's limbs. Amid the blooms, sparrows flew busily hither and thither. Twittering happily, they flitted from branch to branch as if playing hide-and-seek.

Just then, a single sparrow fluttered to the ground, abandoning its companions frolicking among the blossoms. In bouncy little hops, it advanced toward the figure that stood near the front entrance to the main building.

Vreeeeeeee.

A lens focused on the approaching sparrow, capturing the small, round black eyes peeking out from its cap of white and brown feathers.

Banpei smiled in spite of himself. Well—to be accurate, the "anti-demon tactical strike robot" built by Skuld to protect the goddesses and Keiichi day and night didn't have the capacity to actually smile. But if he did, Banpei would have been smiling right now.

He was capable of love, of offering aid . . . and even of making mistakes. Endowed with an abundance of both compassion and pathos, Banpei was more tenderhearted than a human being.

The sparrow drew fearlessly closer to Banpei, as if it could somehow read the security robot's true nature. Then it leapt into the air, coming to rest on the black conical straw hat on Banpei's head.

Immediately, the rest of the flock, having observed their companion from above, swarmed down toward Banpei. Perching on the robot's hat and arms, the sparrows amused themselves, fluttering and alighting, fluttering and alighting.

Bathed in the gentle rays of the still-dawning sun, it was a peaceful morning like any other at Tarikihongan Temple.

In a hot skillet, a pat of butter sputtered and melted, readying the pan to receive the frothy, beaten eggs. Sizzling appetizingly, the eggs cooked quickly.

Belldandy sang a lilting melody as she stirred the eggs with her cooking chopsticks, her long, chestnut-colored ponytail swaying to the tune of her song. A rosy glow flushed her pale, creamy complexion.

When they were scrambled but still moist, Belldandy transferred the fluffy eggs to a plate. Then she added the bacon she'd fried in a separate pan. There—breakfast was ready.

Belldandy smiled, satisfied with her work.

"What should I be doing?"

In the living room, an agitated Keiichi was beginning to regret having sat down at the low table so early.

"Reading the paper? No, that doesn't seem right . . . Watching TV? No, that's not right either . . ."

Belldandy's singing was faintly audible through the sliding paper doors that separated the living room from the kitchen. This was part of her normal breakfast-making routine.

On the other hand . . . the sight that had met Keiichi's eyes that morning made it clear that this was not going to be an ordinary breakfast.

The low table was adorned with a lace tablecloth. Keiichi's normal chopsticks and chopsticks rest were absent, supplanted by a carefully placed set of sparkling silverware.

"Why am I so nervous?"

Keiichi's pulse thumped loudly in his ears. He couldn't help feeling somewhat ashamed that he was so intimidated by this situation.

"This is pretty pathetic." He gave a wry little laugh and took deep breaths, doing his best to calm down.

The goddess' gentle voice greeted him cheerfully. "Keiichi, your breakfast is ready!"

The paper door slid open, and the living room was transformed by a delicious smell and Belldandy's dazzling smile. For a moment, Keiichi found himself leaning forward in eager anticipation.

"Pardon me." Belldandy excused herself demurely as she entered the room with her well-laden tray.

"Er, of course!"

This was definitely no ordinary breakfast. Flustered, Keiichi sat up as straight as possible.

In a long beige dress and white lacy apron, Belldandy almost looked like a maidservant. Keiichi was unable to look directly at her as she kneeled beside him and served him with deft, graceful movements.

First, a glass of fresh, antioxidant-rich tomato juice. A bowl of yogurt garnished with chopped strawberries and apples in the upper left corner, and a steaming cup of creamy corn soup in the upper right. A basket of fragrant, piping hot rolls on the left, and finally, the main dish—bacon and scrambled eggs—between the knife and fork.

"Wow!" Keiichi let out a sigh of wonder at the dazzling spread. But immediately, he realized his dilemma. "Um, I don't really know the proper etiquette for this kind of thing . . ."

From the waist up, the use of silverware suggested that Western table manners were in order. But from the waist down, sitting cross-legged at a low table added a definite Japanese element, making Keiichi wonder if perhaps such decorum was unnecessary. Despite this awkwardness, Keiichi racked his brains, trying to remember the correct rules for dining with a knife and fork.

"Keiichi, the most important thing is that you enjoy your meal. I'll be happiest if you just forget about proper etiquette and eat however you like."

Finally, Keiichi's tense expression softened. "Thanks, Belldandy—that's a big relief!"

He set his knife down and transferred the fork to his right hand.

"This looks delicious!"

With a look of pure joy, Keiichi started in on his scrambled eggs. Next, he applied a pat of margarine to a fresh-baked roll. The warm bread quickly melted the margarine, and Keiichi opened his mouth wide and sank his teeth into its softness. A delicious fragrance wafted up into his nostrils.

"I know you've said that rice fills you up better than bread . . . but the photo of a hotel-style breakfast in my magazine looked so lovely, I had to try it," Belldandy explained. "What do you think?"

She pulled a magazine out from under the low table, opening it to the bookmarked article about a vacation resort on some distant shore. Pictures of the cuisine at the hotel restaurant were presented next to the photos of luxurious suite rooms.

A stem of delicate Chinese Lantern Lilies arched gracefully in a small vase. The silver was buffed to a high shine, and the glasses were of sparkling Bohemian crystal. The places were set with Meissen porcelain dishes as if it were no big thing.

Though the tableware in front of him paled in comparison to that of the magazine, to Keiichi, nothing could top a meal that Belldandy had cooked specially for him.

"This is fantastic. No hotel has a better breakfast than this!" Grinning from ear to ear, he stuffed a piece of bacon into his mouth.

Belldandy's lavender eyes danced at the sight of Keiichi's

enjoyment. Nothing made her happier than watching him take pleasure in her cooking. His sincere words filled her with inexpressible warmth.

"That was a real feast."

Not the most delicate eater, Keiichi polished off his breakfast in no time flat and let out a sigh of contentment. The fact that not a single drop of food remained testified to his satisfaction.

"I'll put on some tea." Belldandy began to clear the table, her lacy apron fluttering. Just then, the telephone in the hallway began to ring.

"Who could that be at this hour?" Keiichi frowned. It was unusual for the phone to ring so early in the morning.

"I'll get it." Halfway to the kitchen, Belldandy changed direction and moved toward the hall.

As she stepped out of the living room, the chill in the air told her that spring's arrival was yet to come.

The sound of the telephone grew louder as she made her way down the corridor. But despite its insistent ringing, Belldandy was unhurried as she picked up the receiver.

"Morisato residence," she said.

"Belldandy! It's me, Skuld!"

The voice on the other end conveyed an urgency even greater than the ringing phone.

It had all begun two days ago.

Then, too, the phone had rung . . . at first, Skuld had ignored it, pretending not to hear. But she was the only one home, and eventually she reluctantly picked up the receiver.

"Yeah?" she said unenthusiastically. It violated her principles, but she was willing to use the I'm-just-a-kid act if it meant dodging a telemarketer.

"Oh, *très bien!* I'm so glad someone's home"

"Peorth?"

Like Belldandy, Peorth was a Goddess First Class Type 2 Unlimited. Her extensive skills were put to use in managing the Yggdrasil system. For that reason, unless something major was happening, they didn't hear from her often.

" . . . Er, what's going on?" Skuld asked hesitantly.

"Yggdrasil's in a state of emergency!"

Exactly as Skuld had feared. Of course things had to go wrong when her big sisters weren't home! She felt a wave of gloom at the unfortunate timing.

But up in Heaven, that was the furthest concern from Peorth's mind. Her explanation issued forth like a stormy tirade.

Setting aside the technical and mathematical details, the basic gist of it was that for several days, there had been a sudden epidemic of bugs in Heaven.

Skuld sat down and hugged her knees, listening to Peorth go on and on. After about twenty minutes, Peorth finally paused and Skuld managed to cut in, "but this is nothing new, right? Bugs are always popping up in Yggdrasil—so if you just launch a debugging program . . ."

"*Évidement.* We did that quite some time ago." Peorth interrupted, as if to rebuke Skuld for stating the obvious. The rising pitch of her voice betrayed her irritation. She let out a sigh. "But this is something different. Otherwise, I wouldn't be calling, *n'est pas?*"

"Something different?" Skuld stopped playing with the telephone cord and gripped the receiver with both hands. "Then the debugging program . . ."

"*Complètement inutile.* We executed the program and tried to run a delete, but to absolutely no avail. In fact, things are worse than ever."

Apparently, the problem was beginning to affect Yggdrasil's main system, a completely unprecedented situation. Skuld leapt to her feet. If things were this bad, she had to send her sisters to help as quickly as possible.

"Got it. I'll tell Belldandy and Urd right aw—"

"Never mind that. I want *you* to come."

"Huh? Me?" For a moment, this unexpected request caused Skuld's thoughts to completely freeze. Pointing toward herself and speaking slowly, she tried to confirm what Peorth had just said. "You want . . . me?"

"Yes. You."

The answer hadn't changed.

"Yeah, but . . . if it's a problem with the system, maybe Urd . . ."

Even though Skuld and Urd were both Goddesses Second Class, Skuld's qualifications were a far cry from Urd's Limited Administrator License. Besides, to be completely honest, Skuld wasn't at all eager to return to the celestial sphere overcome by chaos. Quickly, she began to make excuses, but Peorth remained adamant.

"Getting rid of these bugs is the number one priority right now. Who better to round them up then you, Skuld?! Return at once!"

"Eep!"

On Earth, two days had passed since then, while in the celestial realm it had probably only been a few hours. But to Skuld, it felt like a thousand years since she'd received her sudden orders to return home.

"Belldandy, listen to me . . . I don't know what to do! I . . . I'm still a long ways away from being able to come home . . . even with my brilliant talents, we're just barely able to keep things from getting any worse . . . no matter how many times I re-calculate, the numbers keep changing! I just can't keep up!"

A flood of tearful lamentations poured out of Skuld. The fact that Belldandy listened to everything with such compassion only increased the deluge.

Once she'd had a good cry, Skuld seemed to feel somewhat better, but now her wailing turned to disgruntlement over being left to handle this job all alone. For a time, Skuld's tirade of complaints flooded forth without pause.

It was then that Belldandy noticed that Urd had sidled up to the phone and was listening in on Skuld's diatribe.

"Urd . . ." Belldandy murmured.

"*Shh.*"

"But why am *I* the one who had to come out here? Systems administration is *Urd's* field. Shouldn't *she* be the one taking care of this?"

Skuld just happened to shift gears in her grousing with deadly timing, unaware that Urd was now at the other end of the line.

"So you know what, Belldandy? I was thinking . . . maybe you could tell Urd that she should come up here and help me restore the system."

It was an excellent proposal. The problem was, she was submitting it to the wrong party.

"She'll listen to you, Belldandy. 'Course, Urd lacks *my* prodigious talents, but a helping hand never hurts . . ."

"Oh, really? I think I'll pass!"

On the other end of the line, Skuld froze. Figuratively speaking, her temperature dropped to -273.15° C—a temperature at which even a rose is reduced to particles.

" . . . U-u-urd!!"

It was only then that Skuld realized just how deep she'd dug herself. At what point exactly had Urd picked up the phone? But the damage was already done.

"I'm sure we have nothing to worry about if we leave everything to your prodigious talents!"

Poor Skuld was unable to even move.

"Why, this should be a piece of cake for you! A walk in the park! I'm sure that if I were there, I'd only get in your way!"

Skuld was completely incapable of countering Urd's sarcasm-loaded attack.

"Give my regards to Peorth!"

Skuld's mouth was too dry to squeeze out a response.

"And have a nice day!"

Gently, Urd hung up the phone. Only the endless refrain of the impassive dial tone echoed in Skuld's ear.

"*Ah-ha-ha-ha-ha-ha!* That was *too* perfect!"

Meanwhile, back at the Morisato residence, Urd doubled over with uncontrollable laughter, tears welling up in her eyes.

"Urd . . . are you sure about this?" Belldandy asked her convulsing older sister in a worried tone. But Urd was completely unconcerned.

"Oh, come on, everything's fine! You really are a worrywart, you know that? Look, if things were really that bad, Peorth would contact me directly."

It was true—even though she was a Goddess Second Class, Urd's powers were tremendous. And it wasn't for nothing that she held an Administrator Limited License—when it came to Yggdrasil's system, even Belldandy couldn't hold a candle to her.

"I suppose so, but . . ." Still somewhat concerned, Belldandy stared at the phone.

Just then, she felt a tap on her shoulder.

"Belldandy, do you really have time for this right now?" Urd asked.

Oh! Urd's prompting brought Belldandy back to the present. She had to pack Keiichi's lunch before he left . . . besides, he hadn't even finished his breakfast yet!

"Oh, dear! I was going to make Keiichi's tea . . ."

Urd watched, yawning, as Belldandy hurried back to the kitchen, moving much faster than when she'd come for the phone.

"Sheesh! The human world sure is busy, too!"

Urd gazed languidly toward the living room and slowly closed the sliding paper door to her room.

Bereft of the lustrous goddesses that had inhabited it moments earlier, the corridor was restored to its chilly silence.

Just then, a dark form wriggled.

A cloudlike shape came burbling out of the telephone that had moments earlier been connected to the celestial realm. It remained motionless for a time, as if surveying its surroundings, then leapt suddenly down to the hall floor, landing silently on its eight long, spidery legs. It rolled its big, wide eyes vacantly, and its long rabbitty ears twitched incessantly.

A "bug."

This was precisely the enemy against which Skuld was currently waging a one-girl war. In the Yggdrasil system, however, the bugs were mere data errors—but down on Earth they took the form of weird, supernatural creatures. Unfortunately, they also had the inconvenient quality of being invisible not only to the human eye, but to heavenly beings as well.

Nobody knew yet that this bug was here in the human realm.

*　　*　　*

Tweet-tweet-tweet-tweet!!

Cheeping shrilly, the flock of sparrows burst suddenly into flight.

They flew over the magnolia tree and settled, all at once, on the roof above.

Vreeeeeee.

Adjusting his focus, Banpei slowly rotated his lens to locate the visitor announced by the sparrows.

Straight ahead, someone was approaching the temple, pushing a heavy-looking Kawasaki KSR II. Leaving a deep tire-groove in the sandy ground, the visitor arrived at the front door of the main building and drew a deep breath.

"Phew! I made it!"

From the looks of it, she'd come a fair ways on foot. She was breathing hard, in little puffs of white. Rivulets of sweat streamed down from her forehead, and her hair, which was cut in a short bob, clung to her face. She pushed the KSR around the side of the building and set its kickstand, caught her breath, and peered into Banpei's lens.

"Morning, Banpei! Is Kei-chan still here?"

After checking her smiling face against his database, Banpei turned to indicate the main building. *Vreeeeeeee.* It was his policy to respond quickly and politely to anyone who was a friend.

"Thanks!"

She pushed up her sleeve and glanced at her watch. After checking the time, she inhaled deeply and shouted toward the shoji-shuttered windows.

"Kei-chan! Kei-chan!!"

For a moment, there was no response.

Just as she was drawing another deep belly breath to shout again, one of the main building's external paper doors finally slid open.

" . . . Megumi?" Keiichi peered out, clearly irritated at being interrupted at such a busy time of day. "What are you doing here at this hour . . ." But when he noticed the KSR II at Megumi's side, the peevishness immediately melted from his expression. "Oh, you blew a tire?"

It wasn't obvious, since the KSR-II had tubeless tires, but there was something slightly off about the rear wheel.

"Good eye, Kei-chan. I considered just riding it like this, but, you know . . ."

True, it could still be ridden . . . but Megumi hadn't wanted to risk damaging the rims. She had a sincere affection for her vehicle.

Clasping her hands in front of her chest as if in prayer, she looked up at Keiichi beseechingly. "Kei-chan . . . are you going to the Institute today?"

"No, I work today."

"Oh . . . I was afraid of that . . ."

Just her luck. Megumi cradled her face in her hands and let out a despondent sigh.

Keiichi Morisato and Megumi Morisato were brother and sister, just one year apart in age. They both had a passion for motorcycles, and Keiichi was one year ahead of Megumi at the

Nekomi Institute of Technology.

Until last year, anyway.

Due to a minor technicality that resulted in a missing second language credit, Keiichi was forced to stay back a year at the Institute. Naturally, this also meant he'd had to pass up the job offer he'd worked so hard to secure. Fortunately, he'd been thrown a life line—by none other than Chihiro Fujimi, the founder of the Motor Club Keiichi belonged to. "After all, you don't want to waste a whole year," she'd said generously, offering him a job at her newly opened motorcycle shop. Best of all, she'd promised to take him on full-time after graduation.

That was how Keiichi had ended up with the busy task of doing a second senior year at the university and working a job at the same time.

For the entire year, the only class Keiichi had to take was his second language credit. Megumi knew that the chances were slim that Keiichi would have class that day, but she'd hoped against hope. If she'd been lucky, she could have gotten a ride with him to campus. But unfortunately, it was not to be.

"Oh, well . . . it's just that, I was supposed to have my aerodynamics class today . . ." Megumi said.

"Oh . . . that's today?" Keiichi's expression changed.

The aerodynamics class was extremely popular—and it was only open to the first thirty students in the door.

Moreover, it was the only class that wasn't held on Nekomi Tech's main campus, but at the Inokuradai School, six kilometers away on a winding local road. For this reason, at 11:30 a.m.

on every third Wednesday of the month, that road became a race track, swarming with students rushing to make the class.

"Oh, please, Kei-chan . . . would you please, please, *please* drop me off at school?"

Megumi broached the question knowing full well that Keiichi hated to be late and that Chihiro didn't appreciate tardiness, either.

Keiichi regarded his sister for a moment, then finally smiled. "Aerodynamics, huh?"

It had been Keiichi's favorite class. As Megumi's brother—no, as a fellow lover of all things mechanical—Keiichi was painfully aware of how Megumi felt.

"You've got it," he said.

"Really?"

"I'll have to drop you off super early, but that's okay, right?"

"Yes!"

A smile spread across Megumi's face. Overjoyed, she threw her arms around Keiichi.

"Thanks, big brother!"

"Okay, okay!"

Keiichi always felt both tickled and a little flustered when Megumi called him that.

Their father believed firmly in "honoring the individual," and in the Morisato household, each member went by his or her first name, rather than by a title. Whether or not terms like "mother," "father," and "big brother" really qualified as titles was another question—but as far back as Keiichi could remem-

ber, his father had always been "Keima" and his mother had always been "Takano."

But when it was just the two of them, whenever Megumi wanted to pour on the sweetness, she would call Keiichi "big brother" instead of "Kei-chan."

It had been a while since Megumi had last used the term, and Keiichi's face split into a grin at the expression of his sister's heartfelt gratitude.

"Warm up my bike, will you?"

He pulled the keys out of his pocket and tossed them over. This was going to be a high-speed ride, so it was essential to get the engine good and hot first.

Sparkling in the sun, the keys arced toward Megumi.

She caught them securely with two hands and winked at her brother.

"You got it!" She ran behind the building where his motorcycle was parked.

Keiichi hurried off toward his room.

"Keiichi?"

At the sudden sound of the BMW's engine, Belldandy stopped still, kettle in hand. She looked up toward the clock hung on a beam overhead. It was still early for Keiichi to be leaving.

She returned to the living room with the tea tray just as Keiichi burst hurriedly into the room, socks in hand and one arm through his jacket.

"Keiichi, are you leaving already?" Belldandy asked, somewhat surprised.

"I'm sorry! Megumi suddenly needs a ride to school . . ."

"Megumi?"

Completely absorbed in making tea, Belldandy hadn't even noticed Megumi's arrival. She glanced briefly in the direction of the yard where Megumi was probably waiting.

"Today's her aeromechanic's class . . . but she blew a tire on her bike."

"Oh, my!"

As he spoke, Keiichi pulled his socks on. Belldandy set the tea tray down on the low table and helped Keiichi get ready.

Belldandy went with Keiichi to the Institute, so she understood the circumstances well.

"That class is hard to get in to, isn't it?!" She held the shoulder of his jacket and guided his other arm into its sleeve. With Belldandy's skillful assistance, Keiichi was ready to go in no time.

The trail of steam rising up from the tea filled the room with the aroma of Earl Grey. Normally they used mugs, but today Belldandy had put out dainty tea cups adorned with wild strawberries.

It pained Keiichi that they hadn't finished the full course meal Belldandy had prepared.

"I'm sorry, Bell . . . after you went to so much trouble—"

Belldandy cut him off with a gentle smile. "It's all right, Keiichi! I can make more tea at dinner time . . . besides, if you like, I'll make you a full course breakfast again tomorrow morning!"

"Fantastic!" Keiichi's face lit up immediately. "How about ham and eggs this time?"

He hurried toward the door, helmet in hand.

"Yes. With medium-done sunny-side-up eggs, right?"

Belldandy followed after him.

It was beginning to warm up a bit, but their breath still made faint white clouds.

The engine of the BMW echoed across the temple grounds, settling into a satisfied purr that meant it was good and warm.

"I'm sorry, Belldandy—I know this inconveniences you, too . . ." Megumi said apologetically from the sidecar of the BMW when she saw Belldandy.

"Not at all! You just worry about enjoying your class!" Belldandy smiled affectionately at Megumi over Keiichi's shoulder as he straddled the BMW.

She turned her smile toward Keiichi. "Keiichi, shall I call Chihiro?"

"Hmm . . . I think I should probably make it on time . . . but just in case, if you don't mind . . ."

"I'd be glad to. Your lunch?"

"I have it."

"Good."

They exchanged smiles at the perfectly coordinated exchange. Keiichi lowered his visor and opened up the throttle.

"Okay, see you later!"

"See you later! Take care, now, Keiichi and Megumi!"

The growl of the BMW's engine faded quickly into the distance, leaving a smiling Belldandy standing and waving.

The scenery streaked by.

Once they'd turned the corner, the hilltop shrine was no longer visible. The mountains glistened like jewels in the morning sun.

"Sorry about this, Kei-chan . . . on a work morning and everything . . ." Megumi shouted through her helmet and the roar of the engine.

"Don't worry about it. That class is special. I took it too, so I should know," Keiichi shouted back without turning his head.

"It is, isn't it! It's really fun, flying paper airplanes and stuff."

In addition to the conversation-hampering speed they were traveling, the oncoming wind stabbed into their bodies. But becoming one with the wind was part of the pleasure of riding a motorcycle. Keiichi drove even faster.

The BMW glided smoothly down the road. Just after the next curve, they would be within sight of Nekomi Tech's main campus.

Good. Looks like we'll both make it on time.

Somewhat relieved that things were going so smoothly, Keiichi was just about to lean into the curve when something crossed his field of vision.

"?!"

Automatically, he squeezed the brakes.

" . . . Kei-chan?"

Megumi looked up, surprised by the unexpected deceleration. She didn't see anything out of the ordinary ahead of them.

But Keiichi saw it clearly—an eight-legged bug with long ears. And not just one bug. They came from all directions, leaping straight into the middle of the road.

"Ack!"

They were approaching a blind corner as Keiichi swerved sharply in an attempt to dodge the swarm. Somehow, he managed to avoid them—but the next instant, Keiichi found himself staring straight into an oncoming truck, its horn blaring.

"!!"

The truck driver slammed on the truck's emergency brake. Its tires locked, and it began to skid at an angle. Without a moment's hesitation, Keiichi opened up the accelerator all the way, barely squeezing past the truck's rear end.

"Kei-chan!"

The sound of the screeching tires assailed Megumi like a monster's wail.

Ririririririri!!

The telephone in the hallway asserted itself for the second time that morning.

Urd had gone back to bed, hoping to catch just a few more winks, but the insistent ringing was like an alarm clock, forcing her to get up.

". . . Skuld."

There was nothing as aggravating as being interrupted just as you were drifting back to sleep. It had to be Skuld—the timing was too obnoxious to be anyone else. She'd probably thought of a way to get back at Urd for getting the best of her earlier.

Urd chuckled. "That's what *you* think, sucker!"

Slowly, she raised the ringing phone to her ear and was about to let loose a peal of triumphant laughter when . . .

"Hello? Hello?"

The unexpected voice caused Urd to gulp her laughter back.

". . . er . . . Peorth?"

Urd had anticipated that when things got serious, she'd be called upon to lend her expertise, but she definitely hadn't expected to be summoned so soon.

"So, you already need . . ." she began calmly.

But Peorth interrupted, her voice fraught with a surprising level of tension.

"Hello, Urd? It's Urd, isn't it?"

Something was wrong. Urds' normal blasé expression changed quickly to one of rapt attention.

"Peorth? What's wrong? New trouble with the system?"

"Trouble doesn't begin to describe it!" Peorth's voice trembled. "But I've no time to explain the details right now. Urd, I need you and Belldandy to create a maximum-level barrier shield at Tarikihongan Temple . . . *immédiatement*! We're going to evacuate as many beings from Heaven as we can!"

This statement was so absurd that it almost completely dispelled Urd's tension.

"Hold . . . hold it right there! That many gods descending to the Earth all at once?! If that's supposed to be a joke, it's not funny!"

"I know. That's why I'm telling you to make the highest level barrier shield possible. There's very little time. Please, Urd!"

"Peorth . . ."

But the only response was the mechanical echo of the dial tone.

"What the heck . . . ?!"

Urd frowned, completely baffled. Suddenly, she became aware of a dazzling glow of light behind her—a phenomenon that preceded the opening of a gate.

"Oh no . . . not already!!"

There was no time to mull things over. All she knew was that if they didn't create a barrier shield, the Earth was in for some major problems.

Frantically, she darted outside. In the middle of the light-flooded garden, Belldandy stood with her arms raised as she chanted the Barrier Shield spell.

"Belldandy!"

"I sensed the vibrations of a gate opening . . . but . . . this . . ."

The vibrations were unbelievably powerful. Hurriedly, Urd joined Belldandy's chanting. Between them, the overpowering brightness of the light grew visibly stronger with each passing moment.

"Peorth says . . . she's bringing everyone from Heaven down here!"

"All of the gods? But can the barrier shield sustain that many?"

The earth beneath them began to tremble. The gate would open in just a few more seconds.

". . . we'll never make it!!"

"Don't give up, Urd!"

High above, a stream of bright red light appeared like a geyser in the sky. The earth emitted a violent rumble.

"Maximum Defense Barrier Shield!"

Belldandy and Urd's voices rose in harmony.

Just as the barrier shield formed, a blinding light flooded their vision. A multitude of gods and goddesses began to stream down through the open gate.

"Oh good . . . we made it!"

"Barely! Sheesh, that was intense!"

Having somehow accomplished their formidable task, Belldandy and Urd breathed a sigh of relief. Then they looked around at the state of the temple and sighed again, this time out of worry. Even in Heaven, they'd never seen so many deities in one place at one time.

There was no telling how long the barrier shield would hold out. Wordlessly, they exchanged glances. Just then, they heard a familiar voice.

"Belldandy!"

"Skuld!"

A ball of intensity, Skuld came running into Belldandy's gentle embrace. The little goddess' face was streaked with tears.

"Belldandy . . . Belldandy . . ." She was sobbing too hard to speak.

"There, there . . . it's all right now!"

Hugging Skuld tightly, Belldandy looked over at Urd. Skuld's trembling body communicated the severity of the situation.

"Skuld . . . what's the matter? What happened?" Urd asked, repressing the impulse to simply comfort her little sister. They had to find out what was going on.

"It's the end of Yggdrasil." Behind them, a different voice answered on behalf of the weeping Skuld. Automatically, Urd and Belldandy turned.

"Peorth . . ."

The Peorth that stood before them was a goddess transformed. Normally brimming with poise and confidence, she looked as terrified as a lost kitten. She hugged herself, her arms crossed and her shoulders hunched.

"It happened so suddenly . . . we were barely able to make it here." Peorth managed somehow to squeeze the words out through trembling blue lips.

Out of nowhere, gray clouds gathered in the formerly blue sky and the wind grew tinged with moisture.

"Peorth . . . let's go inside . . . Skuld and Urd, you too . . ." Belldandy urged the three goddesses softly, glancing sideways at the yard full of gods and goddesses.

The low table with its lace tablecloth seemed to give off a faint light. Despite the spectacle outside, the tea room was the same as ever. Peorth sat down immediately, at home in the familiar surroundings. Belldandy and Urd sat on either side of her.

Skuld continued to sob, her face buried in Belldandy's lap.

"A little while ago, we had an outbreak of bugs. I called on

Skuld's help, so you know that much already," Peorth began slowly.

The paper *shoji* screens rattled in the wind.

"But that was just a plain old system error, wasn't it?"

"At first I thought so, too, Urd. But a few hours ago, we started to see an abnormal singularity value."

"Singularity value . . . ?"

"*Oui* . . . I'd never seen numbers like these. As if that weren't strange enough . . . they escalated rapidly for a moment and then suddenly . . . disappeared."

"'Disappeared' . . . ?" Belldandy repeated worriedly. Her heart was seized with an indescribable fear. For the first time, she regretted how accurate her presentiments always were.

". . . after that, it all happened so fast . . ." Skuld's small, tremulous voice joined the tense conversation. "Yggdrasil went completely out of control . . . here and there, it began to crumble . . . all of Heaven was in a panic . . ."

Once more, tears overflowed from her eyes. She squeezed them tightly shut but couldn't block out the horrific images. She struggled to breathe.

"We had no choice but to evacuate," Peorth finished.

In the midst of the mob of panicked deities, Peorth's leadership was commendable.

But their troubles were just beginning.

If Yggdrasil continued to rage out of control, the heavenly realm would be destroyed. If Heaven ceased to be, it would have disastrous effects on the Demon Realm and, ultimately, on

Earth. That prospect was incomparably worse than anything they had seen so far.

R-r-r-r-ringgggg!

The four goddess' silence was interrupted by the telephone. All four of them lifted their heads at once.

"Could it be . . . from Heaven?" Peorth murmured, but Belldandy shook her head.

"I think . . . it's probably Keiichi."

No doubt Keiichi had successfully delivered Megumi to school and made it to work, and was calling to check in with Belldandy so that she wouldn't worry.

"*Bien sur* . . . The Yggdrasil contact line wouldn't be functioning . . . silly me."

Peorth covered her face with her hands but the tears seeped out between her fingers. Urd put an arm around her comfortingly.

"I'll get it, Urd." Shifting Skuld gently, Belldandy stood up and hurried to answer the phone.

She reached for the ringing receiver.

"Hello, Morisato residence . . . pardon me . . . ?"

Thunk.

There was an unexpected sound in the hallway.

Urd was the first to react. She ran out of the room and the other two hurried after her.

"Belldandy . . ."

At the end of the dark corridor, Belldandy stood stock still. The dropped telephone receiver dangled from its cord, brushing against the floor.

"Belldandy . . . ?"

Urd approached her sister and laid a hand on her motionless back. No reaction.

"Belldandy!"

Urd pulled Belldandy's shoulders, forcing her to turn. Slowly, Belldandy raised her head. Her face was pale and expressionless. Then her trembling lips moved faintly.

". . . Keiichi is . . ."

After squeezing out the short utterance, Belldandy crumbled like a marionette with her strings cut, slumping listlessly on the hallway floor.

T A S O G A R E — T W I L I G H T

"Big Sister . . ." Skuld called out to her sister in a pained voice, but Belldandy didn't seem to hear. After being carried into the tea room, Belldandy had done nothing but stare at a fixed point, her expression frozen.

Urd fixed her downcast younger sister with a worried gaze, unable to find words.

The silence seemed to last an eternity. The only sound was the unnervingly loud clock ticking away the passage of time.

". . . they said . . . he died almost instantly," Belldandy murmured so softly, she was almost drowned out by the clock.

". . . what?"

For a moment, they couldn't grasp what she had just said.

"Who did?" Skuld asked immediately, without the slightest hesitation.

Belldandy's lavender eyes slowly looked out at the three

goddesses. Haltingly, she began to speak.

She'd answered the phone completely convinced that it was Keiichi calling . . . but the voice at the other end of the line was a stranger's. The caller had impassively recounted to her what had happened.

Twenty or thirty minutes ago, two siblings had been brought into the emergency room: Keiichi Morisato and Megumi Morisato. The younger sister, Megumi, had sustained only minor injuries and would be discharged in a week . . . but it had been too late to save the older brother, Keiichi.

". . . he must have given his life to protect her . . . *sa petite soeur . . .*" Peorth whispered.

They didn't know the details of what had caused the accident or how serious it had been. But it was easy to imagine that Keiichi had sacrificed himself to protect Megumi.

At this, Belldandy closed her tear-filled eyes.

Keiichi, that's why I love you . . .

A trickle of tears streamed out from between her eyelids.

The atmosphere in the room was so oppressive, it was suffocating.

Then Urd tossed her hair and let out a deliberately loud sigh.

"Belldandy, I'm sorry but . . . would you mind waiting until later to be grief-stricken?"

How could Urd say something so insensitive and cold? Skuld was about to blow up in Belldandy's defense but the moment she raised her head, her eyes met Peorth's.

Of course Keiichi's death was a terrible tragedy. But their

top priority right now was to get Yggdrasil under control. The destruction of Heaven was at hand and the clock was ticking—there was no time right now to be preoccupied with the death of a human being.

Peorth more than understood Urd's stance, and she silenced Skuld with a glance. The little goddess was left nodding wordlessly.

"Let's start at the beginning."

The mournful wind sounded like a funeral dirge.

"*Oui.*"

Urd and Peorth went back over what they remembered, examining the situation.

"The outbreak of bugs began . . ."

". . . two days ago, Earth time."

That was when Skuld had received the phone call.

"We tried everything . . . but rather than improving, the situation was getting worse . . . then the singularity disappeared . . ."

"And that was when Yggdrasil began to fall apart, right?"

Then, just after the successful evacuation of Heaven, they had learned of Keiichi's death. One thing after another.

"Gone . . . the singularity . . . and Keiichi . . ." Urd muttered to herself, lost in thought, and then gasped at what she had just said.

Everything stemmed from the disappearance of the singularity. And the two things that were gone were the singularity and Keiichi.

"Urd?"

". . . wait."

Urd brushed aside Peorth's inquiry and concentrated on her thoughts. She was beginning to connect the dots.

"Listen . . . what if . . . what if the accident—Keiichi's death— was what caused Yggdrasil to go berserk?"

Peorth had been on pins and needles, but now she laughed inadvertently at the pure absurdity of Urd's suggestion.

"Urd . . . you had such a strange look on your face, I was waiting to hear what you'd come up with . . . why on earth would you say something so ridiculous! Why would the death of a single human being cause Yggdrasil to run amuck, putting the entire heavens in peril? *Incroyable!*"

Belldandy reacted slightly at the word "death." She grasped what was going on with her mind, but her heart still hadn't caught up.

Meanwhile, Urd remained intently focused on piecing together the clues, unperturbed by Peorth's skepticism. Her intuition told her that she was on the right track. In her mind, she reviewed various events that Keiichi had encountered.

"Skuld!"

"Huh?!"

Skuld had sidled up to Belldandy, watching her shell-shocked older sister with deep concern. She gave a startled yelp when Urd suddenly called her name.

"Remember when you first came here, hunting down bugs?"

"Yes . . . I remember . . ."

It had been about three years ago.

Skuld's days had been filled with loneliness after being separated from her beloved older sister, Belldandy. When Urd, with her administrator's license, abandoned her post to join Belldandy on Earth, Skuld was left in Heaven to wrestle with the system all alone. One day, a huge infestation of bugs occurred, spilling down into the mortal world, and Skuld came after them in hot pursuit. That was how she had first arrived at Tarikihongan Temple.

"Energy in the form of a micro-black hole exposed a singularity . . ."

A "singularity" was a product of irregularities in the Yggdrasil system. Normally, such issues could be contained fairly easily in Heaven, but for some reason this time the problem had spread to the terrestrial realm.

"There was a huge infestation of bugs on Earth. It was a real mess!" Skuld still had vivid memories of the disaster.

On the other hand, although rounding up the bugs had been a huge undertaking, the incident had given Skuld the opportunity to remain on Earth. From her perspective, the benefits and drawbacks pretty much canceled each other out. Well, no—she supposed the benefits won out by a small margin.

"Right, right. And what was it that was attracting the bugs? Where did the singularity turn out to be?" Urd prompted, leaning forward in anticipation as she grew more and more sure of herself.

"Er . . ." Skuld shot Belldandy a hesitant glance before answering. "Inside . . . Keiichi's body."

"*Impossible!*" Peorth exclaimed incredulously.

Her disbelief was only natural. It was unheard of for a singularity—a glitch in the system that governed the Heavens—to appear in the body of a human being.

But Urd had a counterargument that trumped that anomaly. In order to connect Keiichi to Yggdrasil, she postulated, Keiichi would have to possess energy equal to that of Yggdrasil—or Keiichi himself would have to be a presence equivalent to that of Yggdrasil.

The mere existence of a singularity within Keiichi's body shouldn't have been enough to create an attraction between him and Yggdrasil.

There was an even more radical, more absurd possibility: Keiichi himself *was* the singularity.

Belldandy and the other deities inhabited a realm with more dimensions than the human sphere. Just as a thee-dimensional being is invisible to a two-dimensional one, goddesses were normally invisible to mortals like Keiichi.

For that reason, the goddesses continually regenerated their atomic structures in order to sustain a form visible to human beings. Under normal circumstances, the small amount of energy discharged by that process dissipated naturally, causing no problems.

But Keiichi's case was a little bit different.

Three years ago, even though a singularity had formed inside Keiichi's body, Keiichi himself couldn't have *become* a singularity. But things changed after Belldandy was joined on Earth by Urd and eventually Skuld. Keiichi had spent a great deal of time with the three sisters, who were not only divine beings, they were a special trio: the Goddesses of Time. On top of that, there had been frequent visits by Peorth, another Goddess First Class. And there had even been a time when Keiichi had become the temporary physical host of an angel belonging to Lind, a Goddess First Class, Special Duty Limited.

Above all, he loved—and was deeply beloved by—Belldandy, a Goddess First Class.

Wasn't it possible that the constant presence of these minute levels of energy—which would normally dissipate naturally—had affected Keiichi?

And if that unusual environment and accumulated energy had caused Keiichi to become a singularity . . . that was reason enough for a mere human being to become a presence that could influence Yggdrasil.

Yggdrasil was more than just a system that regulated Heaven. It supported the goddesses in many different ways. For one thing, it supplied the energy used by divine beings on Earth for their spells and regeneration. It was truly the lifeline of all beings divine.

The goddesses were directly connected to Yggdrasil, and Keiichi had continual contact with the goddesses.

If enough Heavenly Energy had built up gradually in Keiichi's body, creating an attraction to Yggdrasil, at some point, Keiichi, too, might have become connected to the system . . .

Urd's hypothesis sounded outlandish, but in fact it was surprisingly on target.

Even the tiniest of particles can add up to a mountain in great enough numbers.

The amount of Heavenly Energy Keiichi had absorbed was a quantity far beyond what would normally accumulate in the natural world, and ultimately, it had been great enough to transform Keiichi himself into a singularity.

This was why Keiichi had been able to see the bugs, whose forms would normally be invisible without the continual regeneration of their molecular structure.

"Keiichi and Yggdrasil were pulled together—they developed a relationship of mutual traction."

"Yggdrasil and a human being drawn together? What an absurd notion! On the other hand, it would explain Yggdrasil's bizarre behavior . . ." Peorth was skeptical at first, but faced with the logic of Urd's arguments, she had to admit they made sense. "When the values kept changing no matter how often we recalculated—it was because Yggdrasil was synchronizing with the fluctuating value of the singularity."

Skuld had been listening wordlessly to the explanation, but now the incomprehensible situation suddenly became clear to her.

"If I'd just kept better neutrino measurements . . . we might have been able to do something before it came to this!" The realization came with a flood of remorse. She bit her lip in frustration.

Softly, Belldandy patted Skuld's head. "Skuld . . . it's not your fault. It's nobody's fault." How could anyone have foreseen a situation brought about by so many coincidences? "Even the Almighty didn't know this would happen."

The painful tragedy had been unavoidable. Belldandy still strugged to contain the turmoil in her heart.

"*Aaaaiiieeeeee!*"

The four goddesses looked at each other, startled by what sounded like sudden howls of pain.

"What was that?"

The bloodcurdling screams were coming from outside. Not just a single voice—the cries were erupting from every corner of the temple grounds, as if by a chain reaction.

Something terrible was happening. Belldandy and the other goddesses ran outside.

The sight that met their eyes was unbelievable.

"Wh-what . . ."

Inside the barrier shield, the multitude of gods and goddesses had diminished. There were clearly far fewer of them than there had been before.

"What on Earth . . ."

Then they saw it. A god standing right in front of Urd began to flicker.

"Oh my . . ."

He melted away into thin air.

"Eek!"

Skuld buried her face in Belldandy's bosom.

The spectacle before them was so shocking that even the stalwart Urd wanted to avert her eyes.

"The energy . . . Yggdrasil's energy . . ."

The energy was being cut off to the lower-level deities first. With screams of agony, they vanished away, one after another.

The disaster they had feared most was already becoming a reality.

Trembling, Belldandy refused to look away. As she watched, the light returned to her lavender eyes.

"Urd . . ."

Despite the sadness that overwhelmed her, Belldandy summoned her resolve, raising her head. Until the moment that Yggdrasil was no more and Belldandy herself disappeared, as a Goddess First Class, she would do everything in her power to find a solution.

"Urd," Belldandy continued, "could we create some sort of temporary singularity? Perhaps we could stall Yggdrasil's collapse a little bit . . ."

"Impossible, Belldandy . . . with our energy cut off and Heaven on the brink of collapse, we don't have long before the four of us vanish, too." Peorth pronounced despairingly. It was Ragnarök, the twilight of the gods.

But Skuld, too, was unwilling to give up. "She's right! If we can make a temporary singularity . . ." Her black eyes widened.

"Not you too, Skuld!" Peorth admonished. "Even if it were possible, how do you intend to get access? And even if access were possible, how will you get Yggdrasil to respond when it isn't functioning properly?"

"If we don't try, we'll never know! I don't want to just stand here and watch everything end! Right, Belldandy?"

"Skuld . . ."

Belldandy racked her brains, hoping to encourage her little sister, but no further ideas came to her.

What can we do?

The more she tried to think about a temporary singularity, the more Keiichi's face popped up in the back of her mind.

Keiichi . . .

Just then, Belldandy felt a gentle arm embrace her trembling shoulders.

"Urd . . ."

Urd's indigo eyes gazed kindly at Belldandy. Finally, Urd broke her heavy silence.

"There's only one way, Belldandy."

"Huh?"

"A way to bring back Yggdrasil and Keiichi . . ."

Ominous black clouds had gathered overhead, shrouding the temple in a darkness like the dead of night. Now and again, flashes of blue light contorted in the sky like giant snakes. A fierce wind howled through the trees, shaking them violently.

Yggdrasil's destruction was beginning to exert its effects on the terrestrial realm, too.

"Urd . . . is that really true . . . ?"

Belldandy's long, chestnut hair streamed in the wind.

Silenced by Urd's miraculous pronouncement, both Peorth and Skuld stared at her with intense anticipation.

Urd spoke softly.

"We have to reset Yggdrasil."

"Restore Yggdrasil?"

"Right. To a system restore point."

A tremendous flash of lightning and a clap of thunder shook Tarikihongan Temple.

Goddesses appeared before people in trouble in order to grant them wishes. But what if a wish caused unforeseen problems— dramatically upsetting the fate of other living beings, even causing their deaths?

Of course, wishes were subjected to a stringent screening process before they were accepted, in order to prevent such mistakes . . . still, it was impossible to ensure that the system would be 100 percent error-free. As a protective measure, a special emergency program was set up to deal with these potential problems: the system restore function.

When a contract was made, the emblem on a goddess' forehead sent data to Yggdrasil. Only when that data was received and approved did the contract become valid. Whenever a contract was established, a restore point was also created.

But goddesses always avoided selecting clients who harbored harmful wishes. For that reason, there had never once been the need to perform a system restore.

*   *   *

"That's the first I've heard of such a function!" Peorth frowned. A program that was unfamiliar to her, a Goddess First Class?

"Ha-ha-ha! I just happened to stumble upon it myself! I guess there's something to be said for having an Administrator Limited License!" Urd countered lightly with a wink.

But that's not the only reason, is it?

Peorth responded internally, but she stopped short of voicing the thought aloud.

Urd was more than just a Goddess of Time. She was half-goddess half-demon, the daughter of the Great Demon Leader who ruled the Infernal Realm. Urd remained a Goddess Second Class only to be able to protect her younger sisters. But Peorth was plagued by the sense that Urd's true powers far outstripped her own, even though Peorth was a Goddess First Class

"I hate to admit it . . ." Peorth smiled self-deridingly and turned away, ". . . but I'm afraid you're our only hope." Still facing the other way, Peorth voiced her consent. All four goddesses were united.

"Now that everyone's on board . . . Belldandy, the system restore point?"

"The dorm at Nekomi Institute of Technology," Belldandy replied softly, remembering the first time she met Keiichi with nostalgia.

I want a goddess like you to be with me always.

The words were as fresh in her mind as if it were only yesterday. At first, the desire to be together always had been purely Keiichi's . . . when had it been that Belldandy had come to feel the same way?

But it was precisely those feelings that had caused the predicament they now faced.

"If we can go back to that time . . . this time, I'll be absolutely sure not to cause Keiichi to become a singularity. I'll protect Yggdrasil!"

Belldandy folded her hands as if in prayer as she renewed her resolve.

But Urd muttered softly, ". . . that might be difficult . . ."

". . . ?"

"Your memory will be reset as well. Everything goes back to zero. Yggdrasil, the Earth . . . everything."

"!!"

As if in response to Belldandy's surprise and confusion, the howling of the wind rose in pitch.

Click.

The hand moved on the Zero-Timer Clock that measured Yggdrasil's energy and computed the end of the natural world. Less than ten minutes left.

"Are you sure that thing works?" Peorth glanced dubiously at the far-from-high-tech contraption, which was fashioned from a large alarm clock fastened to a small rice cooker, with all sorts of wires and tubes running around it.

"Hmph! That's a rude thing to say in front the high-performance, elegantly and functionally designed Mr. Paku-Paku Bug Man!"

Mr. Paku-Paku Bug Man was a debugging device Skuld had devised when she'd first come to Tarikihongan Temple. The ingenious contraption automatically trapped bugs at the flip of a switch.

"If we put Mr. Paku-Paku Bug Man in reverse and input a bug injected with an anti-viral vaccine, we should be able to launch the Yggdrasil system restore program."

"Inject a vaccine? But are there bugs here on Earth?" Peorth was genuinely surprised.

Skuld expression clouded visibly. "It's detecting the presence of countless bugs. Their point of origin is this telephone."

When Skuld had called Tarikihongan Temple to gripe, she had created a connection between Heaven and Earth, providing the bugs with a route to travel. She was responsible for sparking this calamity—and even though it had been an accident, she was filled with remorse.

"In the middle of debugging . . . it was thoughtless of me to call Belldandy . . . it's all my fault . . ." she wiped the tears that threatened to spill down her cheeks.

"No, Skuld." Belldandy took Skuld's wet little hand.

"Belldandy . . ."

"It was inevitable. I can see that now."

Belldandy wasn't just biting back her sadness. With dignity and poise, she turned her focus toward their new future. "After all, we've been given another chance to start over . . ."

Even if they lost their memories, there was still a chance that things might work out—Belldandy could feel it, deep in her heart. "We mustn't lose hope!" she told Skuld.

Skuld nodded vehemently, as if to shake off her tears. She'd meant to comfort Belldandy, but in the end, Belldandy wound up comforting her.

Right . . . I have to be strong! For Belldandy . . . for everyone!

In order to make up for her careless behavior, she had to make this plan work, no matter what it took.

Even Peorth extended her support. "You have my help, too, though I don't know how much magic I'll be able to use."

Skuld's determination was renewed. "All right! Here goes!" Focusing all of her energies, she began to type at the keyboard. "First we have to access Yggdrasil, right? It'll take some time to figure out an entry value from this dimension . . ."

With their normal access line severed, they would have to secure an alternative route.

"Then we'll leave those calculations up to the two of you . . ." Encouraged by Skuld's renewed determination, Urd signaled to Belldandy. "The two of us will track down a bug, right? Let's get started."

"Right!"

Urd and Belldandy left the tea room to search for a bug to inject with the anti-viral vaccine. The dark, chilly corridor felt like the entrance to an abyss of blackness.

"Where should we start looking?"

Urd strode boldly into the hallway, as if to dispel that

atmosphere. They couldn't use much power and there was very little time—honing the focus of their search was critical.

"Let's begin in Keiichi's room."

"Okay."

Strapping on their bug-detection goggles, the two goddesses bounded forth.

When they opened the sliding doors to "Keiichi's Shop," everything was just as it had been before.

Several jackets hung on pegs on the walls, and a pile of freshly laundered and folded shirts still sat in a pile in front of the closet. The desk was strewn with unfinished homework and scattered reference books and documents. Several photos of a smiling Belldandy sat atop the bookshelf.

Belldandy hesitated slightly as she entered the room—normally, she never set foot in it when Keiichi wasn't home.

"Keiichi's . . . room."

Keiichi's scent still lingered here and there. It seemed unimaginable that this room's inhabitant was really gone. Gently, Belldandy reached for one of the photos—a picture of Keiichi and her goofing off together at the beach.

If I lose my memory . . . will I make Keiichi into a singularity and bring about the destruction of Heaven all over again?

For a moment, fear seized Belldandy's heart. In the photo, Keiichi was smiling happily.

If I can prevent that from happening by never seeing Keiichi again, I . . .

She straightened up resolutely and silently shook her head.

I believe . . . I believe in the future.

"Let's move on."

Urd's voice jolted Belldandy back to the present.

She replaced the photograph and took a deep breath.

"Yes," she said firmly.

"Skuld . . . the next coordinate is? 3R."

There were less than five minutes remaining on the clock.

Skuld's fingers rattled the keyboard without slowing, but they still hadn't managed to arrive at the target value. They'd managed somehow, however, to connect to another dimension, but accessing Yggdrasil from there remained a formidable task, and time was ticking mercilessly by.

Just then, the sliding doors to the tea room flew open.

". . . Skuld! Peorth! We got one!"

Belldandy and Urd burst into the room, their shoulders heaving. Urd held the bug aloft by its long ears, its eight legs thrashing wildly in the air.

"Where was it?"

"In the motorcycle shed. Boy, talk about a wily little bugger . . ."

It was definitely a spooky-looking thing, with its vacant eyes and almost ultrasonic squeals.

"How's this part going?" Belldandy peered at their work with concern.

"We're very close to achieving access . . ." It was the very last step that was proving elusive. Peorth was beginning to show signs of fatigue as she worked to detect coordinates while simultaneously protecting Skuld, who was still a Goddess Second Class.

"Peorth, I'll provide backup, too." Immediately, Belldandy's voice joined the spell Peorth was chanting.

A golden beam of light streamed in and bathed the goddesses in its aura.

"Is this . . . ?"

The wind had grown continually more violent and the sky darker. Outside the main building, the only deities left were Gods and Goddesses First Class.

"May this power aid the Goddesses of Time . . ."

Even as they could feel their powers waning, the remaining divine beings knelt and prayed heavenward. Their energy began to merge. Belldandy focused harder on the spell she was chanting.

Click. The cruel hand of the clock ticked off another moment. Only two minutes remained before Yggdrasil would come to a complete stop.

"Skuld, I've injected the vaccine."

"Wait, Urd! Just a little bit more . . ."

The roiling wind made the old house groan and creak. The prayer energy faded out, and the four goddesses knew that they were the last deities left at Tarikihongan Temple.

"Oh!"

Just then, the small hands typing at the keyboard began to fade. Belldandy and Peorth poured all of the energy they could summon into Skuld, but they seemed to have reached the point of no return.

Softly, Peorth closed her eyes and released all of her remaining energy in a single blast.

"Last coordinate . . . Ω7A . . . the rest . . . is up to you . . ."

Her pale skin became transparent, then melted away into a vapor.

"Peorth!"

Click. One minute left on the clock.

The sound of typing continued. Now only three goddesses were left in the room.

Then, Skuld felt Belldandy's hand on her shoulder waver and grow faint.

"Belldandy!"

Even as she felt Belldandy slip away, Skuld didn't turn. She typed away faster than ever.

Twenty seconds.

The room began to sway, and pockets of non-space began to appear here and there. Slowly, an eerie light began to fill the room.

Ten seconds.

". . . Sk . . . uld—"

Still gripping the bug, Urd used every last drop of strength in her body to maintain herself, but she couldn't hold out much longer. Her feet were already beginning to disappear.

. . . 4.

"Got it. 185937.299 . . . we're connected. Urd, input the bug."

Mr. Paku-Paku Bug Man was on.

. . . 2.

"ENTER!"

. . . 0.

There was a flash of blinding light. The room was enveloped in a pure white darkness.

Ririririririri . . .

The phone.

Keiichi picked it up just as it was about to ring a second time.

"Hello . . . I'm afraid Aoyama was suddenly called in to work . . . yes . . . he said he'll have to reschedule . . . he said to convey his regrets . . ."

Keiichi passed on the message with impeccable phone manners and hung up by pressing the switch hook with his finger. Then he slammed the receiver down with disproportionate force.

"Hmph! Buy an answering machine, why don't you?"

The cramped room was a typical crusty man-lair, with its perennially unmade futon practically rooted to the floor. On the fourteen-inch TV, a cute teenage songstress smiled sweetly as she belted out a hit pop song.

Much to Keiichi's chagrin, the upperclassmen in his dorm had ordered him to stay home and man the phone on a Saturday night. The worst part was, he could hardly complain since he had nowhere to go anyway.

It's not like I could get a date, anyway, so I guess it doesn't matter.

A freshman had no business disobeying his upperclassmen. Still, it made Keiichi more than a little bit disgruntled to be treated like a slave.

"What a bummer."

Keiichi stretched and slumped back against the wall. One of his hands brushed against the chilly surface of his wall-mounted mirror.

Sighing deeply, he reached for a cigarette. He wasn't much of a smoker, but at least it gave his hands something to do. Just as he'd put one in his mouth, the timer he'd set began to beep.

"Oh, right . . . I'm supposed to call Aoyama . . ."

He pulled the phone over and dialed the number. It was an old rotary phone, and the dial made a soft whirring sound between numbers.

Before the phone had barely begun to ring, Keiichi heard someone pick up at the other end.

"Hello . . ." he started to say, but a woman's voice cut him off.

"Hello, this is the Goddess Technical Help Line."

"Oops . . . I must have dialed the wrong number . . ." Keiichi had been expecting a male voice.

"I'll be there in just a moment to grant your request," the voice said. The line went dead before Keiichi had a chance to apologize for his mistake.

". . . hey!"

And just how did she intend to do that, when he hadn't given his name or address? Unless she had some way of tracing the call . . .

"Weird . . . Oh well, whatever . . ."

Keiichi was about to forget the whole thing and redial the phone when he heard a female voice above his head.

"Good evening!"

Startled, Keiichi looked up—straight into the face of an unfamiliar girl.

"!!!"

Even more unbelievable was the fact that the girl's upper body was protruding into the room from his mirror.

"What is your desire?"

It was the same voice he had just heard on the phone—that much was certain. But how had she managed to appear in his mirror? Keiichi turned pale with fright as the girl smiled sweetly and popped out of the mirror into the room.

"I am the Goddess Belldandy. I'm here to grant you a wish . . . but please keep in mind that you can only wish once."

"G-g-g-goddess?"

"May I ask your name?"

"U-uh . . . it's Keiichi . . . Morisato . . ."

KIZASHI — OMENS

A shower of wooden fragments rained down from overhead. The hole in the ceiling was about 30 cm in diameter, revealing the star-studded night sky above.

"E-er . . ." Keiichi finally managed to squeeze sound out of

his bone-dry mouth. But his brain was completely frozen as he stared up at the busted dormitory ceiling.

As if it wasn't bizarre enough that a goddess had popped out of his mirror, the event had already been eclipsed by several even more incredible surprises.

When asked to make a wish, Keiichi had blurted out "I want a goddess like you to be with me always." The fact that Belldandy was beautiful and seemed very sweet was a major factor, of course—but the biggest reason for Keiichi's wish was the fact that she seemed completely oblivious to how short he was—a quality that made him terribly self-conscious.

It had all begun the moment he had made his wish.

Belldandy's body had begun to give off a bluish-white light, as if a tremendous energy was welling up inside of her, and the emblem on her forehead began to glow. A beam of light shot out of the mark and blasted straight up through the ceiling and into the heavens as a swirling wind sent all of Keiichi's belongings flying, as if there was a poltergeist in the room.

This entire series of events had probably lasted no more than two or three minutes, but to the terrified Keiichi, it had seemed like much longer.

"Er-hrm . . ." Again, Keiichi attempted to speak. His room was destroyed, but it at least it was quiet again. Keiichi cowered in a corner, frozen stiff, gazing up at the lovely goddess before him with eyes brimming with fear.

"Accepted."

No longer illuminated, Belldandy's expression was calm as she conveyed the Almighty's message to Keiichi.

". . . huh?"

"Your wish has been accepted."

"Oh."

"So I can stay here forever."

". . . Oh."

"I'm pleased to have made your acquaintance, Keiichi Morisato."

"No, really, the pleasure is all mine . . ."

The goddess bowed politely and Keiichi returned the salutation with an even deeper bow. As he stared down at his feet, his brain slowly began to work again. The gravity of the situation began to dawn on him.

O-o-h no . . .

Up until now, Keiichi had simply allowed the sudden stream of events to carry him forward like a swift current . . . but having established a successful contract with a goddess was going to create some major problems.

This is a men's dorm . . . women are strictly forbidden. If the upperclassmen catch her in here . . .

Keiichi's brain locked up when he even just attempted to imagine what might happen.

The older guys in the dorm included Tamiya, the president of the Motor Club that Keiichi had joined, and Otaki, the vice-president. There were plenty of others, too, but those two were definitely the biggest headache. They really weren't bad guys . . .

but they got rabidly fired-up about every little thing and had a real talent for stirring up trouble. On top of that, Tamiya was the Dorm President. Keiichi strongly doubted they'd be able to settle this quietly.

"Um . . . I know I made that wish and everything and I really hate to ask this . . . but I'm afraid I need you to leave for just a little while, okay?"

"Oh my . . ."

It was hard to tell whether her reaction was one of surprise or consternation, and Keiichi felt his resolve waiver. But he had to be firm and stand his ground.

"I feel really bad about this . . . but there are no women allowed in the dorm . . . if they find you here, they'll kick me out."

"Oh!"

This time, her surprise was mixed with a slight affirmation. He was starting to convince her—somehow his frantic pleas seemed to be reaching her.

Now we're getting somewhere . . .

Encouraged, Keiichi was just about to make his final push, when Belldandy chirped, "That's all right! After all, I'm not a woman, I'm a goddess!"

Back to square one.

"Um, that's really not the issue . . ."

He wasn't getting through to her at all. Keiichi was about to launch into a renewed attempt to persuade her when his door burst violently open.

"Yo, Morisato! Didja take my calls?"

It was the moment Keiichi had been dreading.

"Tamiya . . . and Otaki . . ."

The hulking figures in the doorway had physiques that looked well-suited to some sort of combat sport—judo, or maybe wrestling.

"Um, this is . . ."

Keiichi gestured wildly, trying to explain the situation. But the coed party of two in his room was a situation that spoke for itself—no excuses.

"MO-RI-SA-TO!!!"

Keiichi was like a deer in the headlights. He couldn't speak.

"U-u-uh . . ."

Keiichi gulped as Tamiya and Otaki advanced toward him, cracking their knuckles.

"You know what happens when ya breaks da rules!"

He was beyond salvation. All Keiichi could do was nod.

There was a second of silence, and then Tamiya's voice reverberated through the dorm.

"Morisato, I hereby declares ya kicked out!"

"I figured."

The roar of shouts and stomps filled the air as Keiichi's dorm mates stampeded forth to carry out the decree.

"Yaaaaarrrr!"

"Kick them out!"

"Out you go!"

"Aiieee!" Keiichi and Belldandy were lifted aloft and in seconds, they'd been deposited outside.

"When ya finds a new place, we'll send over the rest of your crap!"

The door slammed shut.

As Keiichi sat in a stunned silence, a chilly gust nipped his cheek. It was early spring, and the nights were still cold and windy.

"I'm sorry." Belldandy looked up at him apologetically.

"Huh?"

Her chestnut strands danced in the wind.

"You were expelled from your dorm . . . because of me. When something threatens to separate us, it's hard to know what the system force will do . . ."

"'System force?'" Keiichi echoed the unfamiliar term.

"Yes."

Belldandy gazed up at the bright stars glittering in the night sky.

"The system force functions automatically to preserve wishes. You wished for me to be with you, always, so the force will interfere with anything that might split us up."

"Oh . . . I see."

Keiichi, too, stared at the stars. What far-off world was her home? Somehow, just thinking about it made him feel better.

Up until now, Keiichi had been utterly hopeless with girls. But now this lovely girl—no, not just a girl but a goddess— was going to be with him always! He had no right to sit here feeling sorry for himself—who cared about getting kicked out of the dorm! Suddenly, Keiichi found himself ready to embrace whatever lay ahead.

"First, we'd better find ourselves a place to sleep . . ."

Keiichi retied his shoelaces and stood up, filled with determination.

As the night wore on, the chill in the air would only get more severe. A few moments ago, stars had been visible, but thick clouds were beginning to cover the sky, threatening rain.

"Shall we?"

Shyly, Keiichi offered her his hand. He hadn't held hands with a girl since elementary school. His heart raced and his palms began to sweat, and he was about to pull his hand back and wipe it on his pants when he felt the gentle touch of her delicate hand.

"Yes, Keiichi Morisato!"

Belldandy clasped Keiichi's hand and slowly rose to her feet. She felt as light and immaterial as a feather.

Struggling to contain his giddiness, he smiled awkwardly back. "You can call me Keiichi." It made him embarrassed to have him call her by his full name.

"All right, Keiichi."

Bliss. When she pronounced his name in her clear, sweet voice, it made him both unbearably flustered and profoundly happy at the same time.

"Um . . . what would you like . . . me to call you?"

He wasn't sure of the proper way to address a goddess.

"Whatever works best for you, Keiichi."

"Huh?!"

This was a tough one. It was a foreign-sounding name, but

Keiichi didn't want to risk being overly familiar by omitting the customary Japanese suffixes. Still, the friendly "chan" didn't sound right, and the formal "sama" seemed overly ceremonious. He thought about it long and hard before finally making his request.

"Is it okay if I just call you 'Belldandy'?"

He was afraid his heart might explode.

"Yes," the sweet voice answered.

"You really don't mind?"

"I don't mind, Keiichi."

The goddess with the lavender eyes showered him in the warmth of her smile.

It's almost like she's my girlfriend . . . !

As Keiichi fitted the key into the ignition of his motorcycle behind the dorm, he was filled with more happiness than he'd ever experienced in his life.

A BMW Rennsport Oscar Liebmann Special with sidecar.

A bevel-driven 4-stroke OHC, water-cooled with twin air pipe. Displacement: 494cc. Maximum output: 48 horsepower. Four-speed shaft drive gears. It was a one-run special machine based on the BMW RS platform. Keiichi had put a lot of work into it in the time he'd owned it, and it had evolved into a truly one-of-a-kind ride.

Perfect—we can both ride together.

Now that he thought about it, perhaps this goddess was the reason he had been riding around alone with a sidecar all this time.

This is destiny. My luck is changing!

With a discreet jump for joy, Keiichi drew the bike up next to Belldandy and started the engine.

"Um, you can ride in the sidecar . . ."

The purr of the engine was like music.

After making sure that Belldandy was seated properly, Keiichi shifted into low gear.

"Here we go!"

Keiichi's spirits soared as he gave it the gas. But at that very moment, something dark moved in the road, just beyond his headlight.

"!!"

Immediately, Keiichi hit the brakes. His bike responded instantly. They had just barely begun moving, but still, it gave him quite a scare.

"What was that?"

Keiichi strained to see, his eyes still unaccustomed to the darkness.

Long, silky silver hair blowing in the wind. Golden-brown skin and a slinky, curvy silhouette. Piercing but kind indigo eyes like tanzanite peered back at Keiichi.

Keiichi's five senses told him loud and clear that whoever it was, she wasn't of this world. His spirits plummeted.

He shot a glance toward the sidecar.

There sat Belldandy, her cheeks lightly flushed and her bright eyes sparkling.

Perhaps they know each other?

The silver-haired woman strode toward Keiichi and Belldandy, her long, exotic-looking robes swaying as she moved. She, too, bore an emblem on her forehead, although it was different from Belldandy's.

She must be another goddess!!

Keiichi willed himself not to be surprised no matter what happened next. He flashed back to the moment when a beam of light had shot out of Belldandy.

But what Belldandy said next shattered Keiichi's resolve.

"Urd! When did you arrive here on Earth? Oh, Keiichi, let me introduce you! This is my older sister, Urd!"

O-o-older sister!?

For some reason, Keiichi felt his blood run cold.

Keiichi's fleeting happiness gave way to anxiety.

Having now encountered two goddesses in the space of less than an hour, he was no longer sure that this was his lucky day after all. Was this a harbinger of something really bad? Perhaps he didn't have much longer for this world? His mind was suddenly flooded with paranoid fears—a typical human reaction.

As Keiichi struggled desperately to contain his fright, Urd slowly turned her gaze toward him. It felt like she could see straight into his heart.

"Um . . . u-uh . . ."

This was awkward.

As Keiichi stood rooted to the spot, unable to function, Urd thrust a small piece of paper in his face.

"Follow this map."

"Huh?"

This was the last thing he had expected. It was a detailed map of a route that began at his dorm. The road was completely unfamiliar to him, even though he'd been attending N.I.T. for some time now.

". . . Tarikihongan Temple?"

The map's destination, marked by a large star, appeared to be a temple that stood deep in the mountains.

"Oh, Urd! I had no idea you had connections at temples in other realms! Isn't this wonderful, Keiichi? Now we have a place to stay!" Belldandy smiled radiantly.

True—it was the perfect lifeline, given that they'd been thrown out of the dorm and had nowhere to go. He was still unable to shake a feeling of total bewilderment . . . but this was Belldandy's older sister, after all. Surely it was all right.

"Uh-huh . . ."

Keiichi relaxed slightly and gave Belldandy an awkward smile.

Even the ominous rain clouds that had been gathering overhead had moved off toward the north, as if they couldn't bring themselves to overshadow the two goddesses.

Urd tossed her silver wind-blown tresses and gave a small sigh. Then she grasped her flying broom, straddling it nimbly. She hovered in the air, embodying Keiichi's preconceptions of what a sorceress looked like.

"Don't get lost, now!" she called, glancing at Keiichi one last time as she leaned forward in readiness for flight. In a blast of wind, she disappeared into the night sky in just a few heartbeats.

Keiichi stared in disbelief—it was like she had flown off at the speed of sound.

"T-t-that was unbelievably fast!"

Compared to the transport of the gods, his BMW felt like a pretty clunky ride.

"Urd's Stringfellow Broom is amazing. It's the fastest in Heaven!" Belldandy said with a note of pride.

For the first time, Keiichi felt a twinge of kinship with his new companion. It was nice to know that sisterly love was the same among goddesses and humans.

"Shall we?"

He opened up the accelerator.

"Yes!"

The BMW with the sidecar sped off cheerfully toward Tarikihongan Temple.

Keiichi parked his bike by the side of the road and gazed up at the stone steps that lead towards the gate.

"I guess this is the place . . ."

The temple was about halfway up a smallish mountain, and the city lights below sparkled like scattered glitter below. But the area around the temple was heavily wooded, making the darkness of night even denser.

But Belldandy inhaled deeply and scampered happily up the stone steps.

"This is a wonderful place. I feel no ill-will here at all!"

For some reason, the rustle of the trees in the wind was not at all sinister-sounding. In fact, it seemed somehow comforting.

The Great Hall, the house, and the scattered trees that grew here and there within the spacious complex all seemed to offer Belldandy and Keiichi their warm welcome.

"What a lovely temple!"

Belldandy gazed tenderly at the trees. They stood with their branches raised heavenward, eagerly awaiting the arrival of spring. Belldandy's eyes fell on a large, white-flowering plum. It was mostly finished blooming, but a few stray petals still clung to its branches, filling the air with a sweet, heady perfume.

"Keiichi, I'm just going to talk with this tree a little bit."

"Okay. I'll go look for your sister."

Keiichi headed toward the house—it was probably best to let Urd know they'd arrived. Keiichi didn't want to be overly solicitous, but he wanted to do his best to make a good impression. After all, she was Belldandy's older sister.

Just as he was about to open the door to the front entryway, he noticed something for the first time. The place seemed completely abandoned—not just the house, but the entire temple.

But it's such an elegant place, and so well tended . . .

The Great Hall cast something of an intimidating silhouette in the darkness. Keiichi stifled a shiver and reached for the door once again. Just as he was about to give it a good push, it slid open suddenly of its own accord.

". . . !"

Keiichi's startled gaze was met by an unfamiliar little girl.

Her thick black hair swung at hip length and she had big, dark round eyes like a puppy dog. But the emblem on her forehead told Keiichi that this was no ordinary little girl.

Don't tell me . . . this kid is another goddess!?

Determined not to be daunted by the child gazing sweetly up at him, Keiichi bowed and gave her his friendliest greeting.

"Why, good evening, young lady!"

Unfortunately, he seemed to have said the wrong thing.

"Hmph! How dare you treat me like a kid!" she spat, slamming the door shut again.

"Oh! Uh . . ."

Keiichi was at a loss—he had followed the directions he'd been given, only to be greeted like an intruder. As he stood pondering the situation, Belldandy came up behind him.

"What's the matter? Isn't Urd here?"

When Belldandy cocked her head like that, she was as pretty as a little bird. For a moment, Keiichi found himself lost in her beauty.

Hurriedly, he pulled himself together. "Oh, um, I haven't found her yet. But there was a smaller girl . . ."

As Keiichi struggled to explain, the front door flew open once more.

"What is it *now*?"

The sound of voices outside seemed to have compounded the girl's irritation.

"Uh . . ."

She seemed even more menacing than before, and Keiichi began to back away. But when the girl's gaze fell on Keiichi's companion, her expression quickly melted into a delighted smile.

"Belldandy! Oh, sister dearest!"

She shoved Keiichi out of the way and threw her arms around Belldandy.

"Oh, Big Sister, I'm so glad you're here! I was so frightened!"

From tiger cub to lamb in the blink of an eye!

"Skuld! You're here, too? What's going on?"

"Urd brought me here without telling me why. She didn't even give me a choice! But she said I could see you . . . so I . . ." Skuld's voice trailed off into tears, and Belldandy stroked her hair tenderly.

Belldandy's little sister. So there's three of them! No . . . they're goddesses, after all . . . maybe there are even more! In myths, gods and goddesses always have huge families . . . Keiichi mused to himself as he dispassionately observed the sisters' tearful reunion. He was surprised by how *un*-surprised he was by the appearance of yet another goddess.

"How long to you plan to stand out there carrying on in the entryway? Why don't you come inside?" Finally, the voice of the person they'd been looking for. Keiichi peered inside and saw Urd's impatient face staring out at them from a room at the end of the hallway.

All three of them removed their shoes.

*   *   *

A sliding paper door stood open at the end of the long hallway, and light seeped out of the room, faintly illuminating the dim corridor. Skuld went first, and Keiichi and Belldandy followed. It was a plain, medium-sized room: eight tatami mats. There was a small television by one wall. In the middle of the room stood a well-used low table, and against the wall opposite the TV, there was a low china hutch that stood about chest height.

The room had a mid-century feel to it that gave it a sort of nostalgic atmosphere.

"What a nice room!" Belldandy looked around. Then her eyes fell on the kitchen, which had an old-fashioned stove and tiled sink. "I'm going to make some tea!" she announced, hurrying off into the kitchen.

". . ."

Without Belldandy's unifying presence, the air in the tea room became so tense that even the ticking of the clock felt oppressive as the room's three remaining occupants lapsed into silence.

Keiichi glanced idly around the room, searching for something to spark a conversation. His gaze fell on several framed photographs atop the china hutch. Casually, he reached out to pick one up . . .

His fingers trembled.

". . .!!"

Standing next to a cheerful Belldandy, surrounded by a smiling Urd and Skuld, was none other than Keiichi himself.

Why?

Keiichi's heart pounded loudly in his ears.

What was he doing in a picture with Belldandy and her sisters—when he'd met them for the first time today? He hadn't the faintest memory of taking this picture.

He began to sweat profusely and his mouth became too dry to speak.

If he asked the goddesses sitting behind him, they might be able to provide an answer. But somehow, that prospect was even more terrifying. Keiichi struggled to contain his fright and act natural.

"Gee, it's been a pretty long day . . ." He said, half to himself, in a voice two octaves too high. "Ah-ha-ha-ha! I guess I'm getting tired!"

The best thing he could do right now was not think about it. With exaggerated casualness, he edged toward the door. Urd observed him coolly, then rose to her feet and grasped his arm.

". . . ?!"

"I'll show you to your room."

Was she being kind, or just making sure he didn't run away?

Still clutching his arm, Urd dragged Keiichi into the hallway. She opened a sliding paper shoji door next to a sign that read "K1's Garage." Inside, Keiichi was greeted by the sight of his desk and futon—and every last possession he owned. All of these things had been at the Nekomi Dorm just a short while ago.

Ah-ha-ha-ha-ha! This is too much!

Keiichi couldn't take it. His brain was overheating.

"Sleep well."

Keiichi collapsed on his futon before the paper door thudded shut.

"Aah, this is the life!"

Skuld drained her second cup with relish. The tea room was filled with the rich aroma of Earl Grey.

"Do you suppose Keiichi is all right?"

Having heard that Keiichi was tired and had turned in early, Belldandy cast a worried glance toward his room. But Skuld was in full-on puppy-dog mode, refusing to be separated from Belldandy for even a second.

"He's fine, Belldandy! I have more important things I want to talk to you about."

The sisters chatted and relaxed together for a while, enjoying their tea. After a spell, Belldandy looked up at Urd, who had been watching her younger sisters in silence.

"Urd . . ." Belldandy looked fixedly at her sister with her lavender eyes. "Are you ready to tell us what's going on?"

". . ."

Belldandy stood and picked up the photograph atop the china hutch. "It was no accident that you showed up and brought us to this place. This photograph and everything here is telling me that."

Urd stiffened. *Here it comes.*

This was what she'd intended—but, much to her own chagrin, a part of Urd was still ambivalent. She lowered her head, wrestling with her conflicted emotions. Her hands, folded on the low table, trembled slightly.

"Urd . . ."

Belldandy's pale fingers encircled Urd's tan ones. Her steady gaze and calm smile were filled with strength—she was ready to deal with whatever it was.

Skuld watched them anxiously, and Urd patted her lightly on the head. Then, summoning her resolve, she nodded. "Follow me."

The Great Hall cast a stately figure in the soft moonlight.

Its heavy double doors creaked softly as they welcomed the goddesses inside. No moonlight reached the interior, and the darkness was as black as ink.

"It sure is dark . . ." Skuld said in a frightened voice.

Belldandy intoned a quick spell. Between her outstretched hands, she conjured an orb of light the size of an orange and tossed it into the air. With a wave of her hand, the orb shattered into thousands of tiny fireflies.

The goddesses knelt at the entrance. The soft light of the fireflies illuminated the area at the base of the shining golden statue of the goddess Kanon.

"Urd, is that . . ." Belldandy furrowed her brow and stared.

"Yes. A Spiral Awakening Mandala," Urd replied softly, gazing out at the intricate magic circle that stretched across the floor.

It was forbidden even for gods and goddesses to look into the future.

But with the exception of certain prohibited events, it wasn't against the rules to look back into the past.

Goddesses First Class all had unique methods that allowed them to call up the past. Peorth, for example, used an animal: the Vanir bird. When it perched on someone's head, it summoned and replayed memories of the past.

But the Goddesses of Time—the three sisters, and they alone—had a special kind of magic. Memory differs from person to person, based on the events that have befallen that individual—but this magic allowed the sisters to synchronize their memories. In other words, they could call up every last feeling and perception from their past experiences and share that information between them.

"Based on my memory, we can revive your memories. Except that . . ."

An image of Ragnarök, the destruction of Heaven, flashed through Urd's mind.

That was the day Keiichi, who had become a singularity and had disappeared from the human realm, triggered Yggdrasil's destruction. On that terrible day, as a last resort, they had returned a bug treated with an antiviral vaccine. The attempt had succeeded—amazingly, Yggdrasil had been reset to a restore point, and peace and order had returned to Heaven.

"When the system is restored, our memories were reset as well. Accordingly, nobody in Heaven remembered . . . nobody except for me."

"But why?"

"Search me. I guess it was probably the work of my demon blood."

When Urd had discovered that she alone retained her memory, her surprise was outstripped by a feeling of unfathomable loneliness.

"Urd . . ."

Urd's robes fluttered as she strode into the center of the mandala.

"I've been waiting all this time for the day you would seal your contract with Keiichi, Belldandy."

At first, Urd's memories had been upsetting, but in time, that feeling had evolved into something special. "You said you believed there was hope, Belldandy. I knew beyond a doubt that it was my mission to help you realize that hope."

That was why Urd had descended to Earth by herself, restored the temple to its former state, and waited.

But remembering the past would bring her sisters not only joy, but also pain. It was this misgiving that still plagued Urd.

"Thank you, sis."

Belldandy pressed her cheek against Urd's back, embracing her gently.

"Do you know what I think?" she said. "I think you retained your memory because you needed to. I don't think it's a matter of demon blood or goddess blood . . . I think it's something much greater than that."

"Belldandy . . ."

Slowly, the concern in Urd's heart began to soften.

"So don't worry. Show me your memories, Urd . . . show me my past."

The warmth of Belldandy's body gave Urd strength.

"Right."

The two goddesses looked each other steadily in the eye.

"Skuld? What about you?" said Urd.

The youngest goddess had been observing the exchange in silence, her expression still fearful. She still didn't completely understand the situation. But even though she was young, she was still the Goddess of the Future. Deep in her heart, she knew that the right path was to follow her sisters. She puffed out her chest, indignant that Urd would speak to her in such a gentle tone.

"If Belldandy's doing it, I will too! Don't treat me like a child!"

"Well said! Here we go, then!"

The intricate pattern of the mandala contained the emblems of past, present, and future. The three goddesses assumed their positions, synchronized their breathing, and slowly raised their hands.

"Skuld, you follow me."

"Yes, Big Sister." The spell would put a heavy burden on the young Skuld. Belldandy winked at Urd.

"Revive, Light of Memory . . . Slumbering in a Far-off Abyss, the Wheels of Time . . ."

As Urd chanted, the emblems on the three sisters' foreheads began to glow. The spell flowed like a song.

"Burning flames, Illuminate the Deep Darkness . . . Powerful Wind, Show Us Thine Path . . . Sparkling Water, Flow through Thine Path . . ."

The three beams of light intersected and became one.

"The Goddesses of Past, Present, and Future Command Thee! Open, Doors of Memory . . . Spiral Awakening Mandala!"

The light gave off a dazzling burst of white, enveloping the three goddesses.

They were floating in a sea of light. Its glittering waves advanced and receded, receded and advanced. Each time the waves washed over them, memories blossomed like flowers.

Belldandy's eyes overflowed with tears.

". . . I . . ."

The light subsided rapidly and Belldandy slowly opened her eyes. She couldn't see straight through the tears that welled out of them. But they weren't tears of pain or sadness. Belldandy's heart was bursting with the joy that Keiichi was alive.

"Urd . . . I'm going to see Keiichi . . ."

With her memory restored, Belldandy wanted to see her beloved's face. She had to see for herself, once more, that he was alive and well.

Urd nodded silently, opening the doors wide with a magic spell. Belldandy flew out of the Grand Hall like the wind.

Good.

Urd had only a second to feel relieved before she was startled by the sound of something hitting the floor. She turned to see

Skuld collapsed in the middle of the mandala, her shoulders heaving as she struggled to catch her breath.

"Skuld . . . are you okay?"

Skuld's response was brusque.

"N-n-never better! T-that was a piece of cake!"

You did good, kid!

Urd smiled wryly at the sight of her little sister's posturing and thrust her right fist toward the little goddess.

"Huh?" Instinctively, Skuld assumed a fighting pose, anticipating a blow. But when Urd opened her fist, Skuld gave a gasp of surprise.

"Oh, Urd! Is this . . . ?"

"It's a reward for your hard work."

A tiny white egg shone in Urd's palm.

"Is it really okay?"

Just like Belldandy, Skuld had immediately thought of someone special when all of her memories came back. Her angel counterpart—no, the angel that *was* an actual part of her being.

Gingerly, Skuld reached for the egg. She took a deep breath and swallowed it in one gulp. Her body filled with heat and she fought for breath. But even the pain brought her joy.

We'll be together soon!

After a moment, tiny white wings sprouted from her back. In a burst of feathers, an angel with golden hair and blue eyes was born.

"Noble Scarlet!"

Skuld embraced her angle with profound love. Tears of joy streamed down her face.

Now everything is just as it was.

Urd gave a small sigh of relief as she quietly left the Great Hall.

The waning moon shone bluish white in the clear indigo sky.

Urd sat down at the base of the big white-flowering plum and exhaled deeply. It felt good—the sense of accomplishment in having carried out her mission, mingled with the fatigue that came with performing a high-level spell. An evening breeze played with Urd's sweet-scented hair.

Just then, out of nowhere, a shower of pink blossoms came floating down. They danced in Urd's palm—cherry blossom petals.

"A goddess's power is the power of love . . ."

One branch of a nearby cherry tree was blossoming. Urd gazed toward the house, where Belldandy was and smiled.

Spring was on its way.

☙ CHAPTER TWO ❧

H A R U B I — S P R I N G   D A Y
Ding . . . ding . . . ding.

From his bedroom, Keiichi could faintly hear the chime of the clock that hung in the tea room. He looked up from his homework.

Three in the afternoon . . . Belldandy would be serving tea.

"Might as well take a little break . . ."

He set down his mechanical pencil, stretched, and slowly rose to his feet.

Human beings have amazing powers of adaptation.

In no time at all, two weeks had gone by since the evening Keiichi had passed out from shock. There had been a million other little surprises since then, but somehow he had managed to grow accustomed to living with the three goddesses.

I guess everyone has his breaking point. Living in a spacious temple with goddesses . . . how could he complain, really?

Keiichi hummed as he opened the door to the tea room. On the low table, a steaming cup of tea and bowl of *chazuke*—rice with tea—already awaited him.

Today's teatime snack is Nambu Sembei crackers, Keiichi noted.

Belldandy always served a special treat at tea time, and it was never the same two days in a row. *She puts so much thought into every little thing*, he thought fondly.

As Keiichi savored this simple pleasure that had become a part of his everyday life, Belldandy poured fresh hot water into the teapot, raised her head, and smiled.

"Here you are!"

"Thank you."

Quickly, Keiichi picked up his tea cup.

"May I?"

"Go right ahead."

The room was quiet except for the sipping of tea.

Keiichi still felt awkward when it was just the two of them. He stole a glance at Belldandy. She was so beautiful, modest, and kind. He would have been grateful just to be blessed with her company, but on top of that, she cooked him elaborate meals every day and was a whiz at the housework and laundry, too. She was perfect in every way. Women like her were hard to find nowadays.

Still . . .

He should have been more than satisfied . . . and yet, Keiichi found himself wanting more. He was profoundly aware that he was already spoiled rotten. But Keiichi was a healthy male . . . and here they were, living under one roof. If only he could get closer to Belldandy, even just a little bit.

I don't expect her to be my lover . . . but maybe she'd be willing to be my girlfriend?

With that ardent wish in his heart, Keiichi looked down into his green tea. A leaf of tea was standing straight up and down, a very lucky omen.

Yes! It's a sign! I have a chance! His heart raced, but immediately he checked his euphoria.

I'm drinking tea with a goddess . . . Of course the tea leaf is standing straight up and down! He sighed, his spirits sinking.

Just then, Keiichi realized he was being observed. He raised his head, and his eyes met Belldandy's attentive gaze.

Oh, geez . . . she was watching me!

It was embarrassing enough to have someone watch Keiichi's internal emotional turmoil play out on his face, but he got the sense that Belldandy could see straight into his heart, and his entire body filled with embarrassment. Quickly, he drained his tea in a single gulp and held his cup out to Belldandy.

"Could I have a refill?"

The heat made his eyes tear—the tea had scalded his mouth. Still, he forced a smile and made the coolest face possible. Male pride—it was a sad thing.

Brrrrrinnng! Just then, the kitchen timer trilled.

"The muffins must be ready!"

Belldandy was her usual smiling self. It was impossible to

know whether or not she was aware of what was going on in Keiichi's mind.

"Keiichi, would you like some?"

"Absolutely!"

"Coming right up!"

Keiichi watched Belldandy disappear into the kitchen carrying his empty cup. Yes, he was truly a lucky guy.

And she promised to stay with me forever . . .

Remembering that his wish had been accepted, Keiichi gave himself a secret double thumbs-up.

No need to rush things . . .

The inside of his mouth still tingled.

When Belldandy opened the oven, a sweet fragrance filled the room. Plain, blueberry, sesame seed . . . she piled the steaming muffins into a basket.

"Mmmm, they smell good!"

She pulled the tub of margarine out of the refrigerator. She was about to reach for the marmalade, but then she stopped herself.

No—Keiichi likes strawberry jam better.

Belldandy closed the refrigerator door and extracted an unopened jar of jam from the back of a cabinet.

Oh, Keiichi . . .

She cradled the jar gently in both hands. Even these little memories felt like precious treasures. She wanted to see Keiichi's smiling face, wanted to do more things to make him happy.

Memories from the past filled her heart with satisfaction. If only she could just let herself go . . .

No.

She shook her head, as if to shake away that desire. She stared at the jam jar, then set it quietly on the tray. After recovering her memory, Belldandy had locked those feelings away as she'd gazed at Keiichi's sleeping face. She had to maintain distance from him in their interactions, in order to make sure she didn't repeat the same mistake.

I swore to protect him no matter what.

Softly, Belldandy closed her eyes and took a deep breath. She took the sweet feelings that had welled up inside of her and sealed them up inside, admonishing her heart to guard them well.

I am Belldandy, a Goddess First Class.

Belldandy's face regained its quiet composure.

She picked up the tray and gently opened the door.

"Here they are!"

"Oh, sister dearest! You baked muffins!" A squeal of anticipation greeted Belldandy's return. The youngest goddess, drawn by the smell, waited eagerly in Keiichi's usual spot.

"Why, Skuld!" Belldandy sat down next to her sister, who was clearly ready to dig in. "You know we don't need to eat!" Belldandy scolded.

"But Belldandy . . ." Skuld puffed out her cheeks and scowled.

Keiichi looked on from the sidelines, his position usurped by Skuld.

"What do you mean, you don't need to eat?" he cut in.

It was true—in the time that they'd lived together, Belldandy had never eaten with Keiichi. But Keiichi had assumed that she was simply following the old Japanese tradition of eating separately, after the man of the house had finished. He'd certainly never suspected that she might not be eating at all.

"You mean, all this time, you haven't eaten anything?"

"That's right."

Belldandy remembered the last time, when Keiichi had shown similar surprise at making the same discovery. She felt a twinge of déjà vu as she began to explain.

"In order for humans like you to be able to see us, we goddesses maintain our appearances by continually regenerating our molecular composition. The energy we need to do this—and the energy we need to survive—is supplied by Yggdrasil, the system that governs Heaven. That's why we don't need to eat."

". . . Oh."

"Of course, we're capable of the act of eating, and we can enjoy food. But it's disrespectful to the food for us to eat it even though we don't need it for energy. That's why, as much as possible, I make it a practice not to eat."

". . . Oh."

"But when our energy levels are dramatically reduced, such as after using a high-level spell, it is possible for us to replenish that energy using alternative sources from this realm. I use sleep, Urd uses Japanese sake, and Skuld uses ice cream."

"Oh!"

Finally, it all fell into place. At that moment, Keiichi felt a wave of guilt that Belldandy had been cooking exclusively for him . . . and a surge of deep gratitude. These muffins, too, had been baked for him and him alone!

"I know that. But Sis . . ." Skuld had been listening quietly, but now she began to protest again. "It's not fair!"

"Skuld . . ."

"Only Keiichi gets to enjoy your home cooking! It's not fair! I want to eat the things you make, too! Come on, Big Sister, pleeeeease?" Skuld wheedled, clasping her hands together.

She reminded Keiichi of his own little sister. Apparently, sibling relationships were the same for both goddesses and humans.

". . . I would enjoy them more if we could eat them together," he offered.

"Keiichi . . ." Skuld stared at Keiichi in surprise at the unexpected gesture. For a brief moment, her face registered gratitude, but then immediately switched back to her normal triumphant expression.

"Well, I guess if it makes Keiichi happy, I could help him eat his muffins . . ."

Belldandy couldn't help smiling—Skuld had completely changed the tack of her argument.

"You win, Skuld!" Carefully, Belldandy set a small plate, a knife, and a fork in front of Keiichi. "Run and get your own plate, then!"

"Yes, ma'am! Mmmm, I think I'm going to have mine à la mode!"

Belldandy's muffins would be perfect with Skuld's favorite ice creams, which she kept stocked in the freezer. Skuld scampered off into the kitchen. Belldandy and Keiichi exchanged wry smiles at the little goddess' free-spiritedness.

"I'm sorry, Keiichi."

"No problem! I have a little sister, too, so I'm used to it!"

For a brief moment, it felt like their hearts were beating in perfect unison.

"Belldandy . . ."

Just as Keiichi's heart was about to venture forth one step further, a voice more cheerful than the tropical sun interrupted him.

"I'm ready!" A chipper Skuld skipped back into the room and plopped herself down right between Keiichi and Belldandy. Talk about lethal timing.

No big deal. We've got plenty of time. Patience, Keiichi, patience . . . Keiichi sent encouraging messages to his own parched heart. The steam from the muffins seemed to sting his eyes.

"These look delicious! Thanks, Belldandy!" Skuld squealed.

Divided between their two plates, the muffins gave off a tantalizing smell.

Skuld's plate was piled high with ice cream. She dug in immediately. The cold ice cream melted together with hot muffin in her mouth.

"Thanks, Belldandy! May I?" Keiichi said.

"Please! Oh! I guess black tea would be better with muffins, wouldn't it?"

"Good thinking. You really like black tea, don't you, Belldandy?"

"I do. I'll go make some. Go ahead and start eating."

"Right!"

In no time at all, Skuld was already on her second muffin. Hurriedly, Keiichi reached for one, too, and was just about to sink his teeth into the warm treat when . . .

"Anybody home?" a voice shouted from the front entryway. Lethal timing, yet again.

"Uh . . ."

Skuld's mouth was bulging with muffin. Keiichi didn't suppose she'd be able (let alone willing) to get up and answer the door. And Belldandy had gone back into the kitchen to make tea, so he could hardly expect her to handle another chore.

Keiichi sighed, returned his muffin to its plate with a heavy heart, and reluctantly headed toward the door.

"Yes? Who is it?"

Keiichi couldn't repress a note of irritation in his voice. But the visitor standing in the front entryway greeted him with bright-eyed enthusiasm.

"Yo!"

Speak of the devil! The little sister Keiichi had mentioned just moments ago was standing right in front of him!

"Megumi!" Keiichi ran toward her. "What're you doing here?"

"What am I doing here? Is that all you can say?"

Megumi lowered the large bag she was carrying over her shoulder.

"I didn't know you'd moved, so I went to the Nekomi dorm

. . . they told me I'd find you here. This place is a real trek from the dorm, you know!"

"Oh, sorry . . . things have been kinda crazy lately . . ."

Keiichi had been so busy adapting to his new life with the goddesses that he hadn't thought to notify anyone of his change of address.

"I had to drag this bag all the way up the hill . . ."

Megumi wasn't finished complaining. But the rest of her tirade was cut short when her gaze fell on the girl with light chestnut-colored hair in the hallway behind Keiichi.

"?!"

"Keiichi? Do we have a visitor?" Belldandy asked.

"Yes!" Keiichi said.

"K-kei-chan . . ." Megumi fell silent for a moment. She stared at her brother with eyes wide with surprise.

Uh-oh.

How on earth could he explain all this to Megumi? Of course he couldn't tell her the truth. He frowned, panicked. As he stood there racking his brains, Megumi slapped her brother on the back.

"Way to go, Kei-chan!"

"Huh?"

Megumi let out a hearty, gleeful laugh.

She'd always worried about her wishy-washy, late-bloomer of an older brother, and she was truly overjoyed by this new development. Ever since Keiichi had left home, she hadn't heard any cheerful news from him. When she'd heard he was living in a temple, Megumi had even wondered if perhaps he'd gone and joined the Buddhist priesthood. But here he was living with a girl who was a total knockout—even by fellow-girl standards.

"Man, this is great! Your springtime has finally come, Kei-chan!"

Just as she was getting going, Megumi was cut short again. This time, by a young girl with black hair holding a dish of muffin and ice cream in one hand.

"If you don't hurry up, I'm going to eat your share, too, Keiichi!"

Once again, Megumi stared at her brother in astonishment.

Had Keiichi's late springtime already matured into summer? A love triangle? No, the girl was too young. Their child, then? No, she was too big for that. Megumi's smile faded—her brain was completely overloaded.

It was Belldandy who, smiling sweetly, reached out to the foundering Megumi.

"Why don't you come on in?"

Somehow, Belldandy's gentle voice and mellow warmth managed to assuage Megumi's confusion.

"Um, thanks . . ."

Megumi removed her shoes and allowed herself to be ushered inside.

"Wow, what a surprise! I never expected you to be living with foreigners, Kei-chan!"

At first, Megumi had looked dubious at the explanation

Keiichi had cooked up about rooming at a temple with foreign sisters who had come to Japan to learn about Japanese culture. But somehow, he'd managed to convince her.

Whew!

Keiichi breathed a sigh of relief. In the end, the two pairs of siblings had wound up sitting around the low table together, getting properly acquainted. There was never a dull moment when you lived with goddesses!

"So, what *are* you doing here all of a sudden, Megumi?"

After all, it was Megumi's sudden visit that had spawned this whole crisis.

Megumi thumped a fist into the palm of her hand as if suddenly remembering something. "Oh, *right!*" she said casually, as if the whole thing had nothing to do with her. She rummaged around in her bag and withdrew a manila envelope. "I was supposed to bring this to you."

". . . ?"

Inside the envelope was a carefully folded letter that bore a concise message. "Please take care of your sister while she's in town for her college entrance exam." It was from Keiichi's mother, Takano, who had never been one to mince words.

"Oh, and there's ¥40,000."

A bundle of cash was enclosed, meant to cover Megumi's room and board.

"So, you have an exam?"

With his own exams behind him, entrance exams seemed like a distant phenomenon to Keiichi. Especially when it came to his younger sister, who had always done better than he had done in school anyway.

"When is it?"

"Next week."

"What school?"

"Morning, everyone!" Without warning, the tea room door slid forcefully open, cutting off Keiichi and Megumi's dialogue. The newcomer made a dramatic entrance, tossing her silver hair and yawning languidly.

"Wh-who . . . ?!"

Another compatriot of the foreign sisters? Megumi gawked at this new presence. Her rumpled cotton robe was fastened dangerously low over her buxom chest, and her exposed brown flesh was irresistibly supple and sexy.

Keiichi and the others were already used to her, but this first encounter was a bit overwhelming for Megumi—even though they were both girls, she wasn't sure where to look.

But Urd settled herself down in the circle around the low table and began to talk to Megumi like an old friend.

"Hey, Meg! Long time no see! You've been such a stranger these days, I was afraid you were sick or something!"

"Huh?"

"Oh, right . . . you've been busy with the Nekomi School Festival, right?"

Urd's eyes were sleepy and she looked barely awake. Her internal timeline was completely scrambled.

". . . How did it go? Did the softball club's booth do well?

Wait, you had an intramural match, right?"

"Urd . . ."

Belldandy tried to shush her, but Urd's brain was still in REM sleep mode. She rattled on and on about things that had happened, to her, in the past.

Meanwhile, Megumi looked as if she'd seen a ghost. Not only did this person know her name—even thought they'd never met before—she knew Megumi was applying to Nekomi Tech, and she spoke as if she knew Megumi was going to be accepted.

"H-h-how do you know my name? And that I'm applying to N.I.T. . . . I haven't even told Kei-chan yet! And . . . am I going to get in?"

That was the million-dollar question. Megumi swallowed her fear and leaned forward in anticipation.

This was a disaster. If someone didn't stop Urd, there was no telling what she might say. Frantically, Belldandy tried to bring her sister back to reality.

"Sis!"

She grabbed Urd's arm and sent beams of energy toward her sister.

A sensation like a gust of wind surged forth from Urd's chest and spread throughout her body, waking her from her dream-like state.

"Uh . . . huh? *A-ha-ha-ha!*"

She hadn't meant any harm, but there was no taking back the things she'd said. When Urd saw her sisters' expressions, she felt even worse.

"Um, so, good morning again . . ."

Surprisingly, it was Megumi who dispelled the heavy tension.

"That was amazing! You got everything right!" she exclaimed, regarding Urd with something that bordered on awe. "Um, Urd? Are you a . . . fortune teller?" The question was out of her mouth before she could edit it.

"Huh?!"

"Yeah! She's the Sleep-Addled Fortune Teller!" Skuld grappled wildly to bring the situation under control. "Um, you see . . . sometimes, when she's sleeping, Urd can see into the future . . . I mean, she can foretell the future. So, I guess she saw a dream about your future. Right, Urd?"

This was really stretching it, and for a moment, a tense silence filled the room. But surprisingly enough, Megumi shrieked with glee.

"Oh my god! That's sooooo cool!"

Mission accomplished. She'd swallowed it hook, line, and sinker.

"So, wait . . . do you know what's going to be on the exam, too?" Megumi went straight for the money. College applicants have one-track minds.

"Oh, well, that's asking a bit much . . . but I'm a whiz at chemistry, so I can help you prep."

The breadth and depth of a goddess' knowledge was incomparable to that of a human being. Urd gave Megumi a proud wink.

"Oh yeah? Well, I'm a whiz at math and physics—and any other technical topic you can name!" Even though Skuld was young, she had skills to rival those of a graduate student.

"That's great! I've got one more week, so I'll give it everything I've got!"

"All right!"

Before Keiichi knew it, the three girls were fast friends. Ironically, he was the one who felt like the outsider. *Not that I mind*, he told himself.

Keiichi spent the week on edge, terrified that Megumi would discover the truth about the goddesses . . . but for the rest of the household, the time flew by.

The plum tree had completely shed its blossoms and was already getting ready to sprout new growth, and buds were beginning to swell on the cherry tree. It was a beautiful, clear Japanese spring day.

Belldandy's knife tapped out a rhythmical ditty on the cutting board. Before long, the tantalizing fragrance of miso soup began to emanate from the kitchen.

"Good morning, Belldandy!" Keiichi made his appearance a half-hour earlier than usual.

"Good morning! You're up early today!" Ladle in hand, Belldandy turned to greet him.

Keiichi's heart raced. "Yes—well, Megumi has her test today, you know?"

Had he managed to sound casual? Keiichi felt his palms

begin to dampen with sweat.

"Breakfast is almost ready. Just a little bit longer, okay?"

"Mm-hmm."

Keiichi leaned against the paper screen door that divided the kitchen from the tea room and watched Belldandy. He recalled what Megumi had whispered in his ear the night before.

"Kei-chan, have you ever gone on a date with Belldandy?"

The sudden question cut straight to the point.

Keiichi was so frustrated by his inability to get anywhere with Belldandy, he was unable to answer.

"Just as I thought! You like her, don't you? You've got to be a man and make the first move!"

He knew she was right.

But after the first day they'd met, Belldandy had never again gone for a ride with Keiichi in the sidecar of his motorcycle. Aside from taking a bicycle to go out alone for groceries, she never set foot outside of the temple grounds. Keiichi had tried inviting her to go places a number of times, and she always smiled and said, "I'd love to, one of these days"—but that day never seemed to come. Keiichi was afraid that if he was too pushy, Belldandy would grow weary of his advances, and it was harder and harder for him to make further overtures.

"Then this is your chance! You can use me as a decoy—invite Belldandy out tomorrow!"

"What? How?"

"Pack some lunches and come with me to campus . . . as my guardians, or moral support or whatever. Just make up some excuse. When the exam's over, the two of you can go somewhere on your own. How's that?"

It was a fantastic idea.

All night, Keiichi had tossed and turned, his mind racing. It was no wonder he was early for breakfast—he hadn't slept a wink all night.

Keiichi clenched his fists.

If I don't hurry, everyone will get up. Come on, Keiichi! Be a man!

"B-belldandy?"

"Yes?"

Belldandy turned toward him with her exquisite lavender eyes. Keiichi thought his heart would leap out of his throat.

"Um . . . I tell you about school a lot, right?"

"Yes. I always enjoy hearing about it."

Keiichi felt the inside of his mouth dry up. "Then . . . would you go there with me today?"

"Excuse me?"

"Megumi . . . has her exam, right? I figure, she'll probably feel more confident if she has some company. You know . . . to cheer her on. What do you say?"

Still holding her cooking chopsticks, Belldandy's hand froze. He saw her lavender eyes fill with concern before she averted them. She was clearly perplexed . . . he'd blown it!

". . . I'm sorry, Belldandy! I knew I shouldn't have sprung it on you like that. I'll just go by myself . . ." Keiichi was furiously backpedaling when salvation came from an unanticipated source.

Washoe County Library

Library name: NV
User ID: 21235008983501

Item ID: 31235031757409
Title: Death note. 8, episodes 29-32 [DVD videor
ecording]
Date due: 4/13/2010,23:59

Item ID: 31235033533949
Title: First end
Date due: 4/13/2010,23:59

Thank you
www.washoe.lib.nv.us

"That's a good idea. You should go."

"Urd!"

How long had she been standing there behind him? Urd stood with her arms folded, watching Belldandy, in her usual disheveled cotton robe. "Don't be so uptight. It's just one day. It'll be fine."

"Sis . . ."

"It's good for you to get out and get some fresh air every now and then."

"But . . ."

Keiichi stood caught between the debating sisters, unable to move. Like a confused child caught between two arguing parents, he stood helplessly looking back and forth, observing their reactions.

"Look at poor Keiichi!" Urd said.

"Keiichi . . ."

Despite herself, Belldandy felt her heart go out to him.

Perhaps just a little . . . perhaps just a little won't hurt.

"It'll be fine," Urd reassured her, as if reading her thoughts.

Belldandy looked up, surprised.

"Making other people happy is what makes goddesses happy, right?" Urd said.

Those words convinced the wavering Belldandy.

Yes. If it makes Keiichi happy . . .

Belldandy smiled brightly, slowly nodding her head.

"Yes. Let's go together, Keiichi."

"REALLY?" His face lit up.

"Yes. I'll pack lunches . . . we'll all go together!"

"Uh . . . all of us?" Keiichi's smile froze.

"Yes. Urd, Skuld . . . and you and I."

"Oh . . ."

For a moment, Keiichi's heart sank. But still, Belldandy was going to go out with him! He had to be happy about that first step. Besides, there was still hope. If things went well, there was always a possibility that they might end up alone together somehow.

"Okay! We'll all go together!" A big smile spread across Keiichi's face. "I'll go wake up Megumi!"

His step was light as he left the kitchen, and he did a little dance for joy.

Talk about an open book! Urd rolled her eyes. Keiichi was so easy to read.

"I'd better hurry up and pack the lunches!" As she bustled about making her preparations, Belldandy had a little spring to her step, too.

It's too bad they can't just open up to each other.

Urd sighed as she watched them both.

Modern buildings lined the spacious campus.

In the spring, the rows of blossoming cherry trees formed a beautiful canopy overhead, and in the neighboring woods now and again a mother raccoon-dog emerged with her babies. The Nekomi Institute of Technology was situated in an ideal location: not too urban, and not too rural. It was a free-spirited school, filled with the energy of students enthusiastically going about their studies and club activities. But on exam day, the atmosphere was fraught with tension.

"Wow, what a great campus!"

Even with the exam looming, Megumi was cool and relaxed, surveying her surroundings as if she was there just to sightsee.

"Hey . . . are you okay?" Even though he was just along for the ride, Keiichi was much more affected by the strain.

"No problem! I really hit the books with Urd and Skuld. Watch and learn, Kei-chan!" She smiled mischievously, tapping her forehead.

"Oh, really?"

Keiichi's little sister always got the best of him.

"So, when your test is over, meet us at the fountain. You have the map I gave you."

"Got it. The whale fountain in the courtyard."

"Knock 'em dead, Megumi!"

"I will. See ya later!" She skipped off. It was hard to believe she was about to take an exam.

"Good luck, Megumi!" Belldandy said as she and the others waved at her receding form.

The rest was up to her, Keiichi told himself as he gazed toward the building where the exam was to be held. He knew she would be fine and yet he couldn't help but worry—call it brotherly love. But for now, all he could do now was wait.

"So, what do you want to do until the test is over? Want to have a look around campus?"

It was hard for Keiichi to tear away, but he made himself do it.

"Hooray! I always wanted to have a good look around this place!" Skuld cheered immediately.

Unlike Belldandy and Urd, Skuld had never frequented the campus since a child her age would have stood out among the students. She'd watched with envy as her older sisters had departed to attend the school festival or sit in on lectures, and had always harbored a keen curiosity toward the Institute.

"All right! I'll give you a tour!" Encouraged by Skuld's enthusiasm, Keiichi led the three goddesses through the quiet campus.

The breeze was still cool as it riffled through Belldandy's hair, but the sun was warm and pleasant.

She walked a few paces behind Keiichi and the others, smiling to herself at the familiar surroundings.

It's just like before . . .

The happy memories came flooding back, one after another. *Oh! That's the lecture hall where I sat in on lectures with Keiichi . . . and that's the bench where we ate lunch together . . .*

It made her heart throb to remember the look on Keiichi's face whenever he opened the lunches she'd packed for him. Even after dozens of lunches—hundreds, even—he always gave her the same bashful smile as he had the very first time.

I wonder if I'll get to see that look on his face again today . . .

Her heart swelled with anticipation as she looked down at the picnic basket she was carrying. It was nothing fancy, since she hadn't had much time to prepare, but she'd put plenty of love into it. She was looking forward to lunchtime by the fountain in the courtyard.

But the scene that greeted them was a far cry from her expectations.

The fountain featured a modern sculpture of a well-built male figure, like a Greek god, lifting a whale aloft over his head. It was the school's symbol, and for generations it had been a popular spot for students to converge and hang out. But today, a blue tarp covered the fountain, and the water was shut off. The courtyard was roped off and deserted. From the part of the whale sculpture sticking out from under the tarp, they could see that the whale's tail was missing. The whale itself was badly damaged, almost as if it had been struck by lightning.

"Oh, the poor thing!" Belldandy murmured. Her heart ached for the injured whale sculpture.

Keiichi, too, was taken by surprise.

"Shoot! I'd planned on passing the time here . . ."

The detailed date itinerary in Keiichi's mind began with sitting down for a leisurely chat by the fountain. But with the area roped off and the atmosphere gloomy, it hardly seemed fit for a meeting place now, let alone an enjoyable conversation.

"I guess I should have told Megumi to meet us somewhere else . . ."

Keiichi was despondent—there went his careful plans! Skuld chose that moment to kick him while he was down.

"Keiichiiii . . . We're not going to wait here, are we? I want to sit down . . . I'm tired!"

"You're tired? You haven't even done anything!"

"I have a delicate constitution—unlike *you*, Urd!"

"Why, you little . . ."

Keiichi had seen this pattern before: Skuld's whining got on Urd's nerves, and before you knew it, the explosions were flying. He had to prevent that from happening while they were on campus, no matter what it took.

Quickly, Keiichi stepped between the squabbling sisters. "Let's go to the cafeteria, then. We can sit down and have a nice rest and some tea."

"Is there ice cream?"

"Yes."

"I'll go, then."

Somehow, he'd deterred them.

As usual, Keiichi found himself accommodating the headstrong youngest goddess. He was about to start walking when Belldandy broke in.

"But will Megumi be all right?"

She had a point—Megumi might worry.

"I'll wait here," Belldandy offered. "The rest of you can go have a rest."

But Keiichi's response was upbeat. "As long as we get back here a little bit early, it should be fine. After all, Megumi isn't the type to be upset about something like this."

In fact, even if she showed up and discovered a real whale spouting in the fountain, Megumi would probably take it in stride.

"Let's all go together, Belldandy." Keiichi reached for her hand, and for the first time, it felt like the most natural thing in the world. But a split second before Keiichi's fingers reached hers, he found himself yanked away by the opposite arm.

"Come on, Keiichi, *hurry up*!"

. . .Too bad. He'd been so close!

Urd watched as Skuld pulled Keiichi on ahead and then whispered to Belldandy.

"Did the fountain ever break in the past?"

"No. This is the first time."

"That's what I thought, too." Urd's expression clouded.

"Sis . . . ?"

"Huh? Oh, sorry . . ." Urd fell silent.

The chilly wind riffled their hair. Belldandy let the matter go and headed off after Keiichi.

"This is it!"

The white, contemporary building stood at the top of a wide stone stairway. In contrast to the tightly clustered classrooms, the building had a spacious feel, with large windows on all sides. "So this is the cafeteria!" Skuld exclaimed.

Beyond the potted plants that lined the windows, they could see students inside, laughing, talking, and enjoying their lunches. Skuld raced up the stairs.

"She sure has a lot of energy!" Keiichi chuckled.

Skuld swung open the glass doors, calling back impatiently to Keiichi and the others, who were still just starting to climb the stairs. "Come *on!* Hurry *up!*"

The cafeteria was filled with the mingled smells of different foods and a cacophony like a thousand CDs being played at once. The trilling laughter of college girls peppered the air, punctuated by the intense debates of graduate students.

"Belldandy, do you want black tea?"

"Yes, please."

"Urd?"

"I don't want anything."

". . . And ice cream for Skuld, right?"

"Yes!"

"I'll go buy the food tickets. Why don't the three of you find a table?"

Keiichi stuck his hands in his pockets and disappeared into the throng. Urd watched him out of the corner of her eye and tossed her silver hair.

"Where should we sit?"

They glanced around the crowded cafeteria. Luckily, there was an empty table for four right over by the window.

"Perfect. Let's sit there." Urd sauntered off. She was wearing straight-leg jeans with a white top and a black leather jacket. Belldandy followed in her pale blue dress and white cardigan.

"Wait for me!" Skuld scrambled to catch up. She wore beige culottes, cowboy boots and a red stadium jacket.

Their goddess clothing was too conspicuous to wear in public, so they'd changed into regular clothes. Still, the three dazzling beauties had a dramatic presence. They were bound to draw attention, whether they liked it or not.

"Hey, who's *that*?"

"What a hottie!"

Forks and chopsticks hovered in midair as all eyes turned to follow the three goddesses. Urd stopped suddenly amid the gawking college boys.

"Hey, you there!" she said.

"Y-yes?" The student leapt to his feet and stood at attention at Urd's sudden beckoning.

"Do you know what happened to the whale fountain?" Urd regarded him steadily with her tanzanite eyes.

"Um, uh . . . There's a rumor that it got suddenly struck by lightning . . ."

Like a deer in the headlights, the boy's body was rigid and rivulets of sweat began to stream down his forehead. Immediately, the boy's companions began to chime in, trying to improve on the stammered, unconvincing answer.

"No, I heard there was this flash of blue-white light . . ."

"And aren't there rumors of a ghost haunting the fountain?"

". . . a ghost?" Urd's ears perked up.

"Uh, yeah! A lady ghost, with long hair. They say she rides on the whale sometimes . . ."

"Eek! Belldandy!"

"It's all right, Skuld."

Skuld recoiled violently. She hated stories of the occult.

"I see . . . Thanks." Urd winked casually at the flushed, drooling boys and began to walk again.

"Sis . . . ?"

Behind her hair, Urd's expression was stern. Belldandy tried to catch her eye, but just then, Keiichi appeared bearing a tray laden with tea and ice cream.

"No tables?"

"There's one over by the window—we were just headed over there now," Belldandy told him.

Pandemonium erupted behind them among the crowd of boys to whom Urd had spoken. The boys who hadn't received any attention from the foxy goddess were giving hell to the ones who had.

They'd caused enough commotion already. Belldandy's long skirt swayed as she steered Keiichi toward the table.

"What a nice spot!" Belldandy's eyes sparkled happily behind the steam of her hot tea. All around them, students continued to steal glances at the breathtaking trio.

After all, they are goddesses, Keiichi reminded himself.

In the searing spotlight of everyone's attention, Keiichi found himself slightly puffed up with pride—after all, he was the only guy in the entire world who had a personal entourage of live-in goddesses. He struggled to repress a satisfied grin.

The glass doors of the cafeteria swung open once more and a pair of Ferragamo heels clicked against the floor.

"It's quiet in here today."

Clad in a sophisticated Gucci dress, an elegant co-ed strode gracefully into the dining hall, her shiny black locks swinging gently as she walked. A crowd of devoted lackeys followed close at her heels.

"Ah, well. Bring my French Roast to my usual table, please."

The barista-type she spoke to separated from the other hangers-on, bowed crisply, and disappeared into the kitchen without so much as glancing toward the ticket machines. His mistress was not a paying customer at the student cafeteria.

"Come along, now."

Her Hermes scarf fluttered as she walked.

She made it an ironclad rule to always walk slowly in crowded places, making sure to give everyone a good eyeful. Boys gaped at her with longing, and cries of adulation filled the room. Oh, it was absolute bliss!

That's right, boys . . . worship me!

The scent of Chanel N° 5 drifted in her wake. But no matter how gracefully she sauntered, the admiring gazes remained absent today.

"How strange!"

In fact, the entire student population seemed completely oblivious to her presence.

"What's going on?"

This had never happened before.

Fighting to conceal her consternation, she maintained her poise as she continued toward her seat. Just then, she heard something that made her question her hearing.

"Do you think they're foreign exchange students?"

"The girl with the black hair is a real cutie!"

"Are you serious? You're a pedophile, you know that? Didn't you see the one with the totally hot bod?"

"The one with the chestnut hair was like an angel!"

Her expression darkened as she took in the chorus of admiring exclamations . . . about somebody else.

I'm the queen of this school! Me! Exchange students? Don't make me laugh! No greenhorns better try to steal my thunder!

The clicking of her heels grew faster as she broke her own rule. The bracelets on her wrists tinkled musically.

I'll show them who's queen!

Just then, she realized for the first time that the focus of the students' stares was the very table toward which she was headed. She scowled.

Just a minute . . . that's my table!

Her indignation reached its peak.

How dare they!

Not only had they stolen her attention . . . they'd usurped her table as well! This was adding insult to injury! Her hair bounced as she approached the table by the window and came clicking to a stop. She folded her arms and struck a pose before speaking—a queen had to look gorgeous at any given moment.

"*Pardon* me!"

Keiichi was the first to look up.

"Oh, no. Not Sayoko Mishima!" he groaned despite himself when he saw the fierce eyes glaring down at him.

*   *   *

Sayoko Mishima was a second-year electronics student at the Nekomi Institute of Technology.

Known as the "campus queen," whenever Sayoko took a stroll, anywhere from thirty to fifty boys would try to hit on her. Even Keiichi had been in awe of her at the beginning of his freshman year, and had invited her out on a museum tour. Not surprisingly, he had been swiftly and brutally rejected.

"Um, uh . . ." he stammered.

But Sayoko seemed oblivious to Keiichi's presence. She stared at the three girls sitting with him. There was a brown-skinned knockout with a body like a swimsuit model, and a prim beauty with light chestnut hair and a smile brimming with kindness and love. The little girl with black hair was too young to be an issue—it was the other two who required Sayoko's attention. She peered at Urd and Belldandy, her gaze fierce.

"And who might you be?"

Urd slumped morosely in her seat. Just what they needed—an encounter with the biggest troublemaker of all.

In the past, Belldandy had attended school with Keiichi. She'd been so popular that Sayoko had feared Belldandy would dethrone her as campus queen, and she'd caused one crisis after the next: pursuing the goddesses ruthlessly to try to expose their true identities and ultimately falling under the influence of Mara, their demon rival, causing a tremendous quasi-space disturbance.

Here we go again, Urd sighed internally.

As Sayoko bore down on them like a raging harpy, it was clear that she hadn't changed one bit. Once again, she was all fired up to fight over the perceived threat to her monarchy.

"I understand you're foreign exchange students."

Urd was about to cook up a random story and make their escape, but Belldandy responded before she had a chance to speak.

"No. We're not foreign students."

For a moment, Urd and Skuld pondered the implications of Belldandy's response. Then they both gasped in surprise.

"*What?*"

"Big Sister!"

Urd grasped Belldandy's shoulders almost violently.

Belldandy's answer could only mean one thing: she had made up her mind not to attend school with Keiichi. Of course, by cutting back on the amount of time she spent with Keiichi, it would be possible to reduce the effect of her presence—but still, this seemed like an extreme measure.

"Wait a minute, Belldandy! Are you sure? Are you really sure?" Desperately, Urd tried to persuade Belldandy to rethink her decision.

But Belldandy continued, her voice soft. "We're only here today to accompany Keiichi's little sister during her entrance exam. We've been having a look around campus while we wait for the test to end . . . right, Keiichi?"

"Um, yeah. Just for today," Keiichi said.

"Oh! Is that so?" Sayoko's aggressive demeanor subsided, deflated like a punctured balloon. If they weren't students at N.I.T., they weren't a threat after all. There was absolutely no need to wage war. "Dear me! I seem to have completely misunderstood!"

Quickly, she shifted gears and graced them with a confident smile. "In that case, I'll make a special exception and grant you the use of my table today. Enjoy, and have a pleasant day." Relieved, Sayoko let out a peal of slightly shrill laughter and made her exit, her pack of yes-men trailing behind her.

Like the sea after a storm, the tense atmosphere evaporated and a chorus of sighs and disappointed exclamations rippled through the cafeteria. Those who had been praying fervently that the mysterious beauties were new students had had their hopes cruelly dashed to pieces.

"I'm really sorry about that, Belldandy," Keiichi apologized.

"Not at all. I'm glad we resolved the misunderstanding," Belldandy replied.

Urd watched the two of them in silence. Skuld, too, was unable to disguise her concern.

"Keiichi, we should be going now. The exam is probably almost over," Belldandy said.

"Yes, you're right."

They left the cafeteria and headed for the courtyard with the fountain.

It was darker now, and no longer sunny. The sky had been perfectly clear earlier, but out of nowhere a bank of dark clouds had gathered.

"I hope Belldandy's really okay . . ." Skuld said softly to Urd.

"..."

A northern wind blew through the overcast sky.

BANRYOKU — VERDANT HORIZONS

The rainy season made its curtain call, and at long last, the hot sun blazed down with vigor. Snails cowered timidly in the shelter of the bloomed-out hydrangeas, while cicadas finally emerged from their subterranean refuge to regale the world with their resounding summer melodies.

"Thanks, Belldandy!" Megumi exclaimed happily. It was morning at Tarikihongan Temple, and a traditional Japanese breakfast adorned the low table in the tea room.

Fresh steamed rice, broiled fish, parboiled spinach, fermented soybeans, and miso soup. It was hard to know where to start.

"You again?" Keiichi grumbled at his sister. "You've been here every morning lately!"

"What's wrong with that? I pitch in for groceries, don't I? Besides, I just can't get enough of Belldandy's cooking!" Keiichi was clearly disgruntled, but Megumi didn't let it bother her.

"Thank you, Megumi!" Belldandy smiled. "Here, have some minced dried *kisu* fish. I seasoned it with vinegar, soy sauce, and sweet sake."

"Ooh, that looks delicious!"

Megumi took an enthusiastic mouthful. The satisfying texture of the dried fish was combined with the ocean-like fragrance of the seaweed. The tanginess of the vinegar was not only refreshing, it gave Megumi the feeling that her whole body was being cooled.

"Boy, this type of food really whets the appetite when it's hot out!" she exclaimed.

"You eat like a pig no matter what the weather's like!" Keiichi shot back.

"Kei-chan . . ." Megumi scowled. Her brother's barb had finally penetrated.

"Here's some for you, Keiichi." Belldandy placed a dish of minced kisu in front of Keiichi, unperturbed by the squabbling siblings. "Vinegar dissolves the lactic acid in your system, so it's very good for you when you're tired . . . and it helps alleviate irritation, too."

"Belldandy, you're amazing! You're like a nutritionist or something!" Megumi marveled.

"I'm just repeating what I heard on a cooking show I saw." Belldandy smiled bashfully at Megumi's praise. "It's hot today, so I made cold tea. I'll go get it now!"

Belldandy disappeared into the kitchen with her tray in hand. Keiichi sighed deeply as he watched her leave. His chopsticks still in his mouth, his gaze wandered aimlessly in space.

"It's been half a year already . . ." he lamented sadly.

Megumi watched her brother out of the corner of her eye, her mouth stuffed with minced kisu. She decided to get straight down to business.

"Kei-chan, have you ever kissed Belldandy?"

"What?!" Keiichi dropped his chopsticks. "Of-of course I

have!" he squeaked, his voice a whole octave too high.

It was such an obvious lie that Megumi couldn't bring herself to call him on it. *Kei-chan's such a terrible liar! Of course, that's one of his best qualities* . . . Megumi smiled wryly to herself. She reached into the pocket of her shorts and pulled out a large bundle of tickets.

"What're those?"

"Tickets for the drawing they're having down at the market. I'm friendly with a lot of the shopkeepers down there, so they gave me a ton of these things. You can have them, Kei-chan."

"A drawing?"

"Yeah. The grand prize is dinner and one night's stay at the Hotel Koenig. The first prize is a day-trip with all-you-can-eat meals included . . . or something like that. Anyway, with this many tickets, you're bound to win something. If you're lucky enough to win the dinner, you can use it to invite Belldandy out on a date."

"Megumi . . ."

The Hotel Koenig was the fanciest hotel in Nekomi City. Its restaurant was very exclusive, with a world-class chef and a formal dress code. Normally, Keiichi would never have an opportunity to set foot in such a restaurant. If he could take Belldandy out to a place like that . . . it could be his big chance.

"Thank you, Megumi!" Keiichi was moved to tears.

"Hey, you haven't won yet . . ." Megumi tried to keep things in perspective. But Keiichi was already in a dream world, imagining a romantic soiree amid elegant surroundings at the Hotel Koenig.

"Right! I think I'll go right now!"

"Huh?!"

In a mad sprint, Keiichi raced out of the house.

"Kei-chan, wait!"

Alone in the tea room, Megumi rolled her eyes and sighed. Keiichi's tendency to dive into things head-first was just like their father's—it was almost scary how Keiichi grew more and more like the old man every year. A real chip off the old block.

"Geez, Keiichi! You didn't even finish eating!" Megumi looked down at the table. Keiichi had barely touched his breakfast. "Now that's a violation of the Morisato family rules!" Since childhood, they'd been strictly trained to clean their plates at every meal. It was one of their Big Three family rules.

"Then again, I might as well look on the bright side . . ." Megumi grinned and plunged her chopsticks into Keiichi's broiled fish. Actually, she'd been hankering for a second helping. "Thanks again!" she sang, pulling all of the dishes toward her and digging in.

The electric fan nodded its head this way and that. When Megumi had polished off half of Keiichi's breakfast, Belldandy reappeared carrying a glass pitcher of chilled tea.

"Here it is!"

Keiichi was gone. Belldandy looked around the room in confusion.

Megumi continued to eat. "Oh . . . Kei-chan ran off to take care of something . . ."

"Oh . . ."

Megumi felt rude for not providing a proper explanation, but she didn't want to spoil the surprise. She busied herself wolfing down her food to give herself an excuse not to speak.

The wind bell on the veranda danced in the breeze.

"Belldandy, can I have another serving of rice?"

Ting-a-ling, ting-a-ling! The bell sang sweetly.

A breeze blew over the freshly watered grounds, cooling the air. The sun was high in the sky, casting small shadows here and there.

"It looks like it's going to be a hot summer."

Belldandy squinted up at the dazzling sun overhead.

When Megumi had eaten to her heart's content, Belldandy had seen her off at the front gate. She was about to head back to the house, but stopped still in her tracks.

Perhaps I'll wait for Keiichi to get back, she thought suddenly. Maybe, just maybe, it would make him happy. As she imagined Keiichi's surprise, Belldandy leaned back against the trunk of the cherry tree, which was now covered in green leaves, and sat down at its base.

White clouds floated leisurely across the blue sky. The little birds flying in and out of the trees frolicked innocently, unaffected by the heat.

"What a lovely feeling . . ."

The breeze caressed the ponytail at the nape of Belldandy's neck. Before she knew it, she succumbed to nature's gentle overtures, breaking into song.

"Oh, how beautiful!"

Skuld was in the middle of washing dishes—these days, she often volunteered to help out around the house. When she heard the sweet strains of Belldandy and Holy Bell's voices, she ran out of the house with soap suds still clinging to her hands.

She and Noble Scarlet lingered at a short distance from the cherry tree, enraptured by the lovely harmonies. The breeze carried the melody, wafting it away into the sky. How long before they would be able to sing like this, too? The small goddess and her angel lost themselves in the soothing music, dreaming of that day to come. Then Holy Bell folded her wings, and the last crystalline note faded away.

"Oh, Belldandy! That was wonderful!"

A deluge of tears ran down Skuld's cheeks and she applauded wildly as she ran toward her sister.

"Thank you, Skuld."

Belldandy and Holy Bell looked up and smiled at Skuld and Noble Scarlet, whose eyes glittered with admiration.

"Belldandy, will you teach us to do that, too?" Skuld pleaded.

"Of course. We'll have a nice long practice session together sometime."

"Hooray! Now that you're not going to school with Keiichi, there's plenty of time!"

"Yes . . ." For a brief moment, Belldandy's expression stiffened.

"You know what? I'm actually really happy that you aren't going to the university anymore. Now we can be together all the time!"

"Yes . . . that's right." Belldandy's heart ached.

"Okay, well, I'll go finish cleaning up."

Skuld scampered cheerfully back toward the house. As Belldandy watched her leave, the smile quickly faded from her face.

Alone, she leaned back against the cherry tree and shut her eyes tightly.

What is this agitation I feel?

The wind rustled through the trees.

Belldandy, too, enjoyed spending time with her sisters. And more than anything, she was confident that her decision not to attend school was the best possible strategy.

Still, her heart wavered.

Just as Belldandy's internal turmoil grew almost suffocating, she heard Keiichi's footsteps come tearing up the stone steps to the temple and charging toward her at top speed.

"BELLDANDY!" He shouted at the top of his lungs, his voice raspy and out of breath.

"Welcome home! Is everything all right?"

In his haste, Keiichi had run out of the house carrying nothing but the tickets. His shoulders heaved from running as fast as he could. Gently, Belldandy laid a hand on his back and peered into his face.

"You didn't take your bike, so I figured you hadn't gone far . . ."

". . . on!"

"Pardon?"

"I won!"

As he gasped for breath, a dazzling grin spread across Keiichi's face.

"You won?"

"I won the drawing! I won the super-ultra grand prize of all!" He thrust a pamphlet at Belldandy.

"You have to go with me, Belldandy, okay?" he shouted, grinning from ear to ear. Then he whooped like a wild animal and ran off toward the house.

"Megumi! I did it!" Keiichi whooped again as he opened the door.

Belldandy watched him in quiet bewilderment, then looked down at the pamphlet Keiichi had handed her.

This is a drawing prize?

In their previous lives, Belldandy had enlisted the help of spirits and had won the grand prize at a drawing—dinner for two and one night's stay at the Hotel Koenig—out of the desire to make Keiichi happy.

But this time, she hadn't even known he was going to the drawing. And it simply didn't seem possible that Keiichi could have won the grand prize on the strength of his own good fortune—after all, he was a terribly unlucky person. Even when his fortune was at its highest tide, it wasn't strong enough to win a fourth place prize, let alone a grand prize!

A gust of wind blew.

"Urd, you're here, aren't you?"

Belldandy tossed her chestnut hair lightly. In contrast to her quiet voice, the pulsing energy in the air grew stronger and a sharp aura shone brightly.

"Why the frown, Belldandy?" A tiny Urd, just 20 centimeters tall, popped out from the shadow of the tree.

Powerful goddesses could alter the process of their molecular regeneration to create multiple miniature doubles—true doppelganger magic.

"If you're angry all the time, your heart will get wrinkles, you know."

Belldandy looked up. The full-sized, original Urd was sitting above her on a branch of the cherry tree. She executed an elegant dismount and reabsorbed the mini-Urd on the ground.

"You followed Keiichi and used magic to help him, didn't you?"

"It was no big thing. I didn't use a high level spell or anything."

"But you tampered with the drawing, didn't you? You won him the super-ultra grand prize, a two-night, three-day trip to a south sea island!"

"A lot more fun and exciting than dinner and a night's stay at the Hotel Koenig, don't you think?"

"Urd!"

A gust of wind whooshed by. A passing cloud obscured the sun, and the sky grew slightly dimmer.

"Belldandy . . ." Urd's fluttering silver hair glinted like the strands of a spider's web. After a moment, Urd broke the silence. "You want to see Keiichi's smile, don't you?"

Belldandy shot Urd a look of utter surprise.

"Excuse me?"

"I'm asking you if you want to see Keiichi's smile."

"Of course I do!" Belldandy felt slightly indignant at being asked such an obvious question. "I always want Keiichi to be happy!"

That was all she had ever wanted in the past, and all she wanted now, too. That was why she'd exercised the utmost caution ever since their lives together had been restored. In that respect, Belldandy's confidence was unshakable.

Urd softened slightly when she saw Belldandy's reaction.

"Listen, Belldandy . . . I know how hard you're trying to make sure you don't turn Keiichi into a singularity and cause the destruction of Yggdrasil. But if that's all you think about, don't you think it might be kind of rough on Keiichi?"

Belldandy was taken aback. "Rough on Keiichi . . .?"

The idea had never occurred to her. For a moment, her thoughts froze.

"What do you mean? Urd, have I been hard on Keiichi?" Her voice quavered.

"I'm sorry. I shouldn't have put it that way . . ." Gently, Urd put an arm around Belldandy. Her tanzanite eyes glinted.

"How did Keiichi look just now?" she asked.

Belldandy remembered Keiichi's exuberant grin and the joy

he'd radiated from his entire body when he'd come charging toward her.

"It's been a while since you've seen him smile like that, hasn't it?"

". . . !"

How long had it been since Belldandy had seen a look of such unrestrained happiness on Keiichi's face? Now that she thought about it, it had been an awfully long time.

"Keiichi wants to get closer to you. He wants to go on dates with you, take trips with you. Think of how drawn you both were to each other—you understand, don't you?"

". . ."

Belldandy looked steadily into Urd's eyes and nodded silently.

"But the way you are with him now—the perfectly disciplined goddess—Keiichi can't find an opening."

If in trying to maintain distance between herself and Keiichi, Belldandy had caused him needless concern and stress . . . she was having the opposite effect of a goddess' true purpose: bringing people happiness.

"Duty is important, of course." Urd patted the frowning Belldandy's back as if comforting a child. "But it's not everything, right?" Urd winked, tossed her silver hair, and headed back toward the house, humming as she walked.

"Sis . . ."

Belldandy felt her hardened heart begin to soften. As if to encourage her, the sun reappeared from behind the clouds. The

wind carried the heat of the warm earth, suggesting tidings of
a south sea island.

"Keiichi . . ."

Belldandy answered the wind with a bright smile, clasping
the pamphlet tenderly to her heart.

"Let's see . . . I'll need my toothbrush, towel, and swimming
trunks . . ."

Back in his room, Keiichi was bustling about busily, grabbing
items as they occurred to him. This was like a dream come true.
He could hardly contain his giddiness.

"Hey, wasn't there an article in the last issue of *Brutus* . . ."

Keiichi had bought the magazine to read a feature article about
audio equipment, but he remembered noticing an article about
a tropical island resort. He tore through his pile of magazines
and finally located the one he was looking for in the back of
his bookshelf.

"Let's see . . . page 136 . . ."

After checking the table of contents, Keiichi riffled through
the pages until he came to the two-page spread. Cerulean-blue
waters sparkled against a glittering white coral sand beach. The
photographs were so vivid, Keiichi could almost hear the roar
of the waves.

"Wow . . . a South Sea island!"

Keiichi's imagination began to run wild. Belldandy in a
bathing suit . . . the two of them running hand-in-hand down
a sandy beach . . .

The feature article had been shot in Cancun, Mexico.

"That reminds me . . . I forgot to read the details of the pamphlet."

Keiichi had seen the words "South Sea island" and completely lost his head. He'd handed the pamphlet over to Belldandy without really even looking at it.

Of course, the most likely destination was Okinawa. Or it could be Guam or Saipan. If they'd really gone all out, it could be Hawaii—but Keiichi didn't want to set his hopes too high.

In any case, they were going to a sizzling beach paradise for both body and spirit. The thought of it almost made him drool.

"Maybe I should bring extra underwear . . ." Keiichi's imagination raced in unsavory directions. He was reaching into his underwear drawer just as the door to his room flew open.

"Yikes!" Quickly, he slammed the drawer shut. "OUCH!" Unfortunately, he'd neglected to remove his hand first.

Skuld stood in the doorway, gazing coolly at Keiichi's frantic, suspicious behavior.

"What're you doing?"

"Huh? N-nothing! *Ha-ha-ha-ha!*"

Skuld was wearing a pair of sunglasses on her head, and now she pulled them down over her eyes and advanced toward Keiichi until she was right up in his face.

"Just as I suspected!"

"What?"

"Nothing."

She glanced momentarily at Keiichi's mounding suitcase and crossed her arms.

"So? What should I pack?"

"Huh?"

"We're going on a trip, right? I've never packed for a trip before. Tell me what I'll need."

Keiichi's spirits came plummeting back down to earth.

"Oh, right. I forgot about you two." Belldandy's sisters had completely slipped his mind. "Uh, I guess you're coming too . . . ?"

Keiichi thought back to when he'd invited Belldandy to come to Nekomi Tech with him. That was only a short motorcycle ride from the temple, but even then, it hadn't been just the two of them. Judging from that experience, there was a good chance Belldandy would again suggest that they all go together . . . in fact, he was sure she would. Since they were goddesses, issues like the cost of airfare and lodging probably weren't major obstacles. But the issue of Keiichi's feelings was a different matter.

Then again, we'll still be getting away from it all . . . I'm sure there'll be a chance to be alone together . . . sometime. Keiichi struggled to reassure himself even as he felt his fantasies of romantic evenings with Belldandy slipping away. But to top it all off, one final surprise awaited him.

"By the way," Skuld said, "where's Yakushima Island?"

"Huh?"

Yakushima was a tiny island often touted as the Galapagos of Japan, and it was registered as a Natural World Heritage Site.

"Skuld, you're interested in Yakushima? That's pretty unusual!" Keiichi regarded her with surprise. Yakushima was a tourist destination of sorts, but primarily for travelers with relatively obscure tastes.

"What do you mean? We're going there, aren't we?"

Skuld pulled the pair of tickets out of her pocket.

". . .Yakushima?"

Keiichi stared for the first time at the tickets that came with the pamphlet he'd received.

Sure enough, they were printed with the words "Yakushima Island: two nights, three days." Yakushima was located at the bottom of Kagoshima Prefecture, quite a distance south of the Tokyo area. He supposed that technically, that qualified it as a "South Sea island," but it was definitely a misleading description.

"Yakushima . . ."

So they weren't even going as far as Okinawa. Had Urd's magic been too weak, or was the market's budget too tight? Either way, Keiichi would need to readjust his fantasies somewhat.

"Oh. Yakushima . . . Island . . ." he repeated woodenly, the wind gone from his sails.

"Wow, what a beautiful day!"

The constant rain of the last few days had vanished, and it was a gloriously clear morning. The stickiness caused by the lingering humidity was slightly unpleasant, but all of the plants were unfurling fresh green leaves, quenched by the blessings of the rain. Skuld scampered about happily, deftly leaping over the many rain puddles.

"That's the great thing about goddesses . . . they're the best lucky weather charm," Keiichi mused.

The morning sun promised a hot day. Keiichi took a deep breath of fresh air and gave a mighty stretch.

At first, he'd been sorely disappointed that they were all going together to Yakushima Island. But a week had gone by since he'd won the drawing, and with each passing day, his spirits had lifted, until his excitement over the trip far outweighed his misgivings.

Yesterday, he'd been as charged up as a small child. Unable to contain his excitement, he'd had difficulty falling asleep. He'd gone to bed early but had spent most of the night tossing and turning.

"Better make sure I haven't forgotten anything, one more time."

How many times had he already checked? Keiichi returned to his bedroom once more.

"For crying out loud," Urd said, sitting on top of the shoe cabinet in the front entryway, "it's not like we're moving to a new house!" She was dressed simply in jeans and a tank top and carried only a waist pack.

"We can always come right back whenever we need to," she muttered, to nobody in particular. She watched as the other members of the Morisato household scurried about, tending to a hundred different things.

Belldandy, too, was completely absorbed in making sure that the doors were all locked and the appliances turned off. She pointed at each item as she struck them from a mental checklist, then collected her lunch basket and her small duffel bag.

"Please look after our home while we're gone!"

In response, a number of small creaks resounded from unidentified locations in the house. These were the multitudinous Shinto gods of ancient Japanese tradition . . . not only did inanimate objects have their own gods, each room in the house, from the bathrooms to the kitchen, had a specific deity to protect it.

"See you soon!" Belldandy gave a little bow to the house spirits and quietly shut the door.

"Sheesh! Between the two of you, it'll be dark before we get going!" In the middle of a yawn, the telephone Urd was leaning her elbow against began to ring.

"See! This is what happens when you take forever getting ready!" she chided.

Phone calls at times like this were never a good thing. It was probably best not to even answer. For a moment, Urd sat on her hands, but when the phone continued to ring insistently, she felt compelled to pick it up.

"Hello?"

"Hey, MO-RI-SA-TO!"

It was Tamiya, the president of the motor club.

"You was supposed to be here hours ago!" he roared angrily.

I knew I shouldn't have answered!

A goddess' intuition was seldom wrong. She held the receiver away from her ear and listened reluctantly to the heated bellows of Tamiya and Otaki.

"So tell him to get his scrawny butt down here immed-yutly!"

"Huh? Now?"

"The whole motor club's gotta take part!"

Apparently, it was the day of the big motor club training sleepover. Keiichi had been so excited about his first trip with Belldandy that he hadn't noticed that he'd double booked himself. At this point, for better or for worse, he'd forgotten completely about the motor club trip.

There's no way I'm letting you doofuses mess this up! For Belldandy's sake, Urd was determined to make sure nothing interfered with this trip. Her eyes gleamed.

"I can't."

"Whut?"

"Keiichi's joined the priesthood for the summer."

"Huhhh?"

It was a pretty audacious lie.

"So invite him again sometime next semester, okay?" Urd made her voice extra honey-sweet right before hanging up on them.

She decided for the moment not to tell Keiichi that later he could expect the motor club members to come after him with electric clippers, eager to give the new priest a buzz cut.

"Good, good. That takes care of that!" Urd was pleased with her work.

Finally, Belldandy appeared with her luggage in hand. "Who was that on the phone?"

She looked like a honeymooner, in her white summer dress and a wide-brimmed hat.

She looks perfect! Urd let out a sentimental sigh. In the background, Keiichi was still running around like a chicken with his head cut off. *Their first trip together—this really is a special occasion.*

Urd hopped down from the shoe cabinet and clasped her hands together apologetically.

"I'm sorry, Belldandy! I can't go after all!"

"What?"

"It seems the system's acting up again . . . they need my help, what with my administrator's license and all. Oh . . . and they want Skuld to come, too."

It was the most plausible excuse she could come up with.

"So that call just now was from Heaven?"

"Yes . . . uh, it was from . . . Peorth."

"Oh!" Belldandy gazed at the telephone, her face full of worry. "Shall I go with you?"

Urd had anticipated this. She had to convince Belldandy, or the whole thing would go up in flames.

"Don't be silly!" Urd tossed her silver hair languidly and let out a peal of confident laughter. "It's the same old debugging routine as always. Besides, you don't have an administrator's license. You'd have nothing to do if you did come!"

"I suppose that's true . . ."

"Don't worry. If anything happens, we'll contact you right away."

Finally, Belldandy nodded. Urd, too, gave a satisfied nod. She opened the front door and called out to Skuld, who was still playing in the garden.

"Skuld! Time to go!"

"Okay!" Skuld shouted cheerfully. She came running, blissfully unaware that she was about to be sent back to Heaven. "Are we leaving now?"

"Yes."

Without warning, Urd cast a spell.

"Huh?" Skuld's body floated up into the air. "H-hey! Why . . . ?" Angered by the surprise attack, she flailed her limbs wildly, but she was unable to escape the spell. "What do you think you're doing, Urd?"

"We're going back to Heaven."

"Why?!"

They moved quickly down the corridor and before Skuld knew it, they'd arrived in the bathroom.

"I'll explain everything when we get there. You go on ahead, now."

With that, Urd tossed Skuld into a water gate.

"BELLDANDYYYY!"

Skuld's desperate cry was extinguished by the rippling water of the bath.

"Poor Skuld . . . sis, are you sure about this?"

"Yes. Work is work!"

Urd didn't relish the prospect of dealing with her outraged little sister back in Heaven, but if it meant things would go well for Belldandy and Keiichi, it would be more than worth it.

"Okay, I'd better be going, too."

Urd returned to the tea room and stuck one foot into the television.

"Sis . . . thank you."

"Don't worry . . . as soon as things settle down, we'll come straight home. Your job is to have fun with Keiichi. Got that?"

". . . yes."

Urd slid lithely into the television. "Later!" she called.

The television glowed faintly for a moment as the gate opened, then returned to normal. Belldandy gazed at the screen after Urd disappeared. Then she heard Keiichi calling her from the front entryway.

"Belldandyyyy! Are you ready to go?"

My job is to have fun!

Internally, Belldandy shifted gears. "Yes! I'll be right there!"

Softly, she closed the tea room door.

Yakushima was located approximately 60 km south of Satamisaki, at the southernmost tip of Kyushu Island.

With a circumference of 126.7 km and an area of 504.55 km2, it wasn't large by any means. But the round island of granite jutting out of the ocean boasted more than 50 peaks over 1000 meters tall, earning it the nickname "the floating Alps."

"I can see it, Belldandy!"

From above, the island was an imperfect circle, like a cookie shaped by a first-time baker.

There were no direct flights from Tokyo, so they'd transferred at Kagoshima Airport. Keiichi and Belldandy leaned together, gazing out the window of the small aircraft.

"It's lovely, isn't it?"

"Yeah . . ."

Keiichi had been so eager to take a trip alone with Belldandy, but now that it was really happening he was so nervous he thought his heart might jump out of his mouth. The conversation wasn't exactly flowing, but even so, it was a taste of pure happiness as far as Keiichi was concerned.

I'm alone with Belldandy . . . alone with Belldandy!

His could feel his temperature mount.

The hot sun blazed down on Yakushima, as if egging Keiichi on.

"We're finally here!"

The sun had been in the eastern sky when they'd left the temple, but now it was listing decidedly to the west.

"Let's explore the town a bit and then go back to the inn and take it easy," Keiichi suggested. They walked toward the bus station, leafing through Keiichi's guide book. "We want to be fresh for the Jomon Cedar trek tomorrow."

Belldandy cocked her head quizzically.

"What's the Jomon Cedar trek?"

"The Jomon Cedar is a cedar tree that's thought to be somewhere between two thousand and seven thousand years old.

It's deep in the mountains, so it's a ten-hour hike to get there and back. It's supposed to be pretty strenuous, but I figured we should see it since we came all this way."

"Oh!"

Keiichi grew slightly nervous when he saw Belldandy's wide-eyed surprise.

The Jomon Cedar trek was almost synonymous with traveling to Yakushima—but he could understand it if Belldandy wasn't thrilled about taking a ten-hour hike.

"Of course, if you don't really want to go, I can cancel it," he added worriedly.

But Belldandy was peering into the guidebook, her eyes brimming with anticipation.

"Is that the Jomon Cedar?"

At 25.3 meters tall, with a chest-height circumference of 16.4 meters, it was clear even from the photograph that the Jomon Ceder towered over its companions.

"How wonderful! I can't wait to meet it!"

"Really? Oh, good!" Keiichi breathed a sigh of relief at Belldandy's enthusiastic reaction.

"In heaven, we have a great tree called Yggdrasil," she told him.

"Yggdrasil?"

"Yes. It's a very important tree; it presides over the system . . . this ancient cedar is almost like the Yggdrasil of Earth!"

Belldandy's chestnut strands glistened in the southern sun.

"The Yggdrasil of Earth, huh? That has a mystical ring to it. I'm excited to meet it, too!"

Though Belldandy's company still made him somewhat bashful, Keiichi swelled with new anticipation of tomorrow's adventure.

The bus for downtown pulled up in front of them, only slightly behind schedule.

After a leisurely bath in an outdoor hot spring overlooking the mountains followed by a mouthwatering dinner cooked over a traditional fire pit, Keiichi and Belldandy had completely luxuriated in the comforts of the traditional inn. They decided to turn in early in order to be rested for tomorrow's activities.

When Keiichi opened the door to their bedroom, his breathing stopped.

Oh my gosh.

Two futons lay crisply side by side.

His heart beat wildly. Just when he'd finally gotten comfortable being around Belldandy, he was consumed by nervousness all over again.

"Right, well, I'm off to bed."

He could barely bring himself to look at her. Feigning normalcy with every atom of his being, Keiichi crawled into bed, hyper-aware once again that they were all alone together. He wanted to say something smooth, but the only words he could manage sounded like the troupe leader of a group of boy scouts.

"Tomorrow we rise at 4:30 and depart at 5:00. We need to arrive at the Arakawa Trail Head at 6:30."

Talk about unromantic. No sooner had the words left Keiichi's mouth than he was filled with self-loathing. But Belldandy's response was enthusiastic.

"Right! It should be a beautiful day tomorrow!"

She sat by the window, gazing out at the full moon that shone above the ocean.

"Goodnight, Belldandy!"

"Goodnight, Keiichi!"

With the lights out, the room was bathed in soft moonlight.

The susurrations of the ocean were a rhythmic lullaby. Keiichi was convinced that he would be too nervous to sleep, but before he knew it he was out like a light. After all, he hadn't slept a wink the night before and they had traveled quite a distance that day.

Belldandy gazed at Keiichi tenderly, watching his chest rise and fall. She crept toward him and sat down at his side.

As softly as possible, she laid her hand over his.

"Keiichi . . ."

The warmth of his touch filled her with happiness. Like the ocean waves, the sensation was infinite and sustaining.

The full moon watched over them protectively as the night passed quietly by.

"It's like a demented whack-a-mole game!" Skuld cried out in frustration.

No matter how many calculations and corrections she made, the bugs continued to proliferate. Her shout reverberated against the domed ceiling and bounced back with more vehemence than ever.

"*Sacré bleu!* I heard you all the way down at the other end of the passageway!"

Peorth's heels clicked as she strode gracefully into the room, exuding the perfume of roses. Though it was probably unintentional, everything Peorth said always managed to sound caustic.

"It's just that . . . I've never dealt with bugs like these!" Skuld turned around, her face radiating displeasure.

"I understand, *chérie*." Peorth smiled coolly. "I'm at quite a loss myself," she said, thrusting a small stack of data pads toward Skuld.

"What's . . . this?"

"New data. Apparently, the numbers were slightly off again . . . they were just issued from the control room."

"!!"

Just when she'd finished fine-tuning her calculations—now she had to start all over again! Skuld slumped her shoulders despondently.

"*Merci.*"

Peorth gave the almost-sobbing Skuld a gentle pat on the back and made her way over to Urd, who was glaring intently at her monitor.

"How's it looking?" she asked.

"Not good," Urd responded without looking away from the endless stream of numbers.

"Just as I feared." Peorth peered into the screen, her hand pressed against the black strands of hair that brushed her cheek.

"I see I made the right call in soliciting your help."

"So we would have been called back anyway . . ."

Initially, Urd had lied in order to give Belldandy and Keiichi a chance to be alone together. But they'd arrived in Heaven only to discover Yggdrasil in the middle of a system meltdown. Peorth and the other goddesses had welcomed the extra help with open arms, putting them to work immediately on repair operations.

"Then I was telling the truth, after all. I suppose it's just as well!" Urd muttered.

"?"

Urd had been spared the trouble of placating Skuld, but now Yggdrasil refused to be appeased. Urd, too, was having quite a hard time of it. The errors persisted stubbornly no matter what she tried.

Just then, an unusual aberration occurred in the energy flow.

"What was that?" Urd had a bad feeling.

"Oh! There it is again!" Peorth frowned. "That's the second time now. Up until now, I'd never seen anything like it. I've no idea what it could be . . ."

Peorth's tone was unconcerned, but Urd found herself flashing back to the past. She could still hear the excruciating cries of the gods and goddesses. As her memories of that fateful evening came flooding back, her body trembled and she let out a deep breath.

"Would you mind backing me up a bit?"

"*Pardonnez-moi?*"

". . . I think we really ought to wipe the system completely clean."

Peorth was slightly surprised by the unusual gravity of Urd's voice.

"What's come over you, Urd? You're not ill, are you?"

"You never know . . ." Urd quipped in her normal lighthearted tone. She felt a slight pang of envy toward Peorth for having no memory of that prior existence.

On the glowing, ever-changing panels, numbers and equations streamed by like music.

Better check the neutrino value, too . . . As Urd interlocked the system, she remembered what Skuld had said that day.

"Skuld, take a break from debugging and come give us a hand," she called over to her sister. Peorth, too, took a seat between the two sisters and quickly got down to work.

"Um . . . what are we doing?" Skuld ventured timidly, intimidated by the serious looks on the older goddesses' faces as they began to process the huge quantities of data on the control panels.

"We're wiping down the Yggdrasil system," Peorth told her, her fingers moving rapidly.

"Wiping it down? Which part?" Skuld asked, summoning her courage.

Urd and Peorth turned toward her. "All of it," they answered in perfect unison.

Skuld's faint hopes were completely dashed. How much time and effort would it take to accomplish such an undertaking?

"~~~~~~!!!"

Once again, Skuld's voiceless lament echoed through the skies of Heaven.

"Only three thousand more meters, everyone! Hang in there!"

The group of hikers gave a few scattered grunts of assent in response to their guide's cheerful encouragement.

More than five hours had passed since they had set out from the Arakawa Trail Head at 6:25 that morning. The first eight kilometers had been relatively flat and easy, almost like strolling along the rails of a trolley car. But that last four kilometers or so had been much harder, and although they were encouraged along the way by such sights as a tremendous tree stump called the Wilson Stump and the second largest cedar on the island, the steep wooden steps and uphill slopes seemed to go on forever, and the group was showing signs of exhaustion.

"Just a little bit further, Keiichi!" Belldandy turned her head to look at him without slackening her energetic pace. The group was almost at the Jomon Cedar.

"Yeah . . ."

The motto of the Motor Club was "strength and endurance," and the upperclassmen put Keiichi through a rigorous exercise regimen on a daily basis. He wasn't out of shape or weak by any means . . . but on the final, steep lag of the mountain trail, Keiichi found himself painfully out of breath.

Down in the plains, the temperature had been on the hot side, but up at 1300 meters the forest air was quite cool. Keiichi's face was sticky with sweat, but at least it wasn't streaming down his face. Just then . . .

"Oh! The Jomon Cedar!"

The excited cry came from up ahead. At last, they had arrived!

"All right, let's go!"

"Right!"

Keiichi and Belldandy quickened their pace.

"Wow!"

It was unlike any tree Keiichi had ever seen before. The other nearby trees looked like shrubs by comparison. The massive trunk reared in their path like a wall, and the branches stretched upward like pathways to the sky. It loomed majestically in the sunlight, like a terrestrial god.

". . . Wow!" Keiichi marveled again, dumbfounded.

He was completely overwhelmed by its magnificence. What sort of things had this tree witnessed in the thousands of years it had stood on this spot? As the aura of antiquity swept through Keiichi's body, he felt his exhaustion drain away.

"Isn't it incredible, Belldandy?"

Keiichi turned toward her, hoping to savor the profound moment together.

But when he looked over, Belldandy's expression was full of pain.

"Wh-what's wrong?"

Her reaction was so different from his own that Keiichi was

unable to hide his bewilderment. Belldandy clasped her hands, her eyes closed, as she quietly read the tree's energy.

The wind caressed her flushed cheeks. After a few moments, Belldandy murmured softly, "Keiichi . . . this tree is ailing!"

"Huh?" Keiichi was taken aback. "Ailing . . .?"

He looked up at the Jomon Cedar once more.

The tree's grandeur still filled him with awe, but this time he looked it over more carefully. He began to notice what Belldandy meant—on closer inspection, the great branches and needles seemed somehow enervated. And even though the treetop received plenty of sunlight, its greenery was dappled with patches of brown.

". . . You're right . . ." he said.

"Its vibrations are very weak," she told him.

". . . I wonder what's wrong with it?"

As the other travelers busied themselves happily taking pictures, Belldandy and Keiichi stared at the Jomon Cedar in silence.

"You made it!" a voice said suddenly.

They turned. The teenaged boy who was their trail guide stood grinning at them. He was a conscientious leader and, throughout the trek, had been alert and attentive to the group's energy levels.

"Are the two of you doing okay?" he asked. "*You* look like you're just fine!" he added, looking at Belldandy.

Belldandy had exclaimed enthusiastically over the scenery the entire way, without ever losing her breath or sweating a drop.

"I've never seen anyone like you," the guide said with admiration. "This is a rough climb, even for a boy!"

"Thank you."

It was only natural, since she *was* a goddess. Even climbing Mt. Everest would probably be a walk in the park for Belldandy.

"We'll leave again in about an hour." The boy glanced at his watch. "It's not a lot of time, but have yourselves a good rest and try to eat a little something if you can."

It had taken five hours to get this far, so of course it would be a long five-hour hike on the way back as well. By the time they reached the Arakawa Trail Head, it would be after sunset.

"Got it!" Keiichi smiled.

Satisfied by this response, the guide led the rest of the group over to a nearby rest spot.

"Belldandy, do you know what's wrong?" Keiichi and Belldandy were left alone by the tree. The sunlight streamed down over its massive roots.

"No . . . I can't tell without touching it directly."

The tree was surrounded by an observation platform, to protect from visitors getting too close. Even though Belldandy was a goddess, they couldn't break the rules when other people might see.

"Such an important cedar . . ." Keiichi murmured.

Perhaps the tree wasn't in immediate peril, but it was clear that something needed to be done, the sooner the better. Besides, Keiichi could tell that Belldandy wanted badly to help.

"Okay . . ." he said.

He told her his plan.

The only sounds at the rest spot were the singing of the birds, the rush of the wind, and the cheerful voices and laughter of the hikers. As they munched happily on the packed lunches provided by the inn, the satisfaction of seeing the Jomon Cedar soon made them forget how tired they were.

"Mind if I join you?"

Keiichi sat down next to the guide.

"Sure, go ahead!" The boy smiled. His white teeth shone against his bronzed skin. "Where's the girl you were with?"

"Oh . . . she said that breathing the air up here is more energizing for her than eating lunch. She's over by the Jomon Cedar . . ."

"Really! Wow . . . she's really something, isn't she!"

"Yeah . . ."

The rest spot was only a little ways away from the cedar. The rest of the group had just begun eating their lunches, so they'd be here for a while still. If Keiichi could just keep the guide distracted, Belldandy would have plenty of time to touch the tree and work her magic. That was Keiichi's plan.

Keiichi unwrapped the aluminum foil around his rice balls. The guide had polished off his rice balls in nothing flat.

As Keiichi looked at him, he had a sudden thought. *I wonder if he's noticed?*

Since the boy lived in the area and saw the cedar often, he

might have some important information. Keiichi broached the subject as casually as possible.

"I really don't know much about plants . . . but it seemed like the Jomon Cedar wasn't looking very well."

"Yeah?"

"I was just wondering if it was okay . . ."

At first, the boy looked startled, but his expression quickly relaxed again. "I'm impressed," he said. "This is the first time a visitor has ever noticed."

Slowly, he began to explain. "It started in early spring of this year . . . At first the tree just looked kind of tired, but before long, parts of it began to turn brown . . . All of us guides were pretty worried, so we called in all sorts of experts and tried lots of different things, but we still don't really know what's wrong."

"You don't know . . ."

"Yeah." For the first time, the boy's cheeriness faded and his expression grew pained. "Of course, that tree's been here far longer that human civilization has. Maybe it's arrogant of us to think we can help . . ."

Just then, a powerful gust of wind shook the nearby trees.

"Don't worry," Keiichi assured him. "I'm sure it'll recover."

He sensed that Belldandy was behind that wind.

After all, he added internally, *we've got a goddess on our side!*

*   *   *

Belldandy stood alone in front of the cedar and slowly raised her arms. White feathers sprouted from her back, and a blue-eyed angel emerged, stretching her wings.

"Holy Bell . . ." The sun glistened through the angel's golden hair as it streamed in the wind.

"I want to give energy to this cedar."

The two joined hands and softly began to sing. Their magic became sound, and then song. The holy voices of goddess and angel merged into a band of light, gently encircling the Jomon Cedar. The warm energy of that light spread out around them, revitalizing the nearby trees and flooding the forest with strength. But the Jomon Cedar alone remained unchanged.

"I wonder what's wrong . . . I can still sense a strong will to live . . ."

When Belldandy had touched the cedar's trunk earlier, she'd sensed powerful vibrations. She couldn't understand why her magic wasn't working.

"Jomon Cedar . . . please, respond to me."

Again, Belldandy pressed her hand against the tree's trunk. Suddenly, she felt a pulse of rigid energy run through her arm.

?!

"W-what did you say?"

She'd been unable to decipher the tree's intent, and she sought wildly to hear its voice once more. But the tree never spoke to her a second time.

Holy Bell looked on with concern as Belldandy hung her head in sorrow.

"Let's sing . . . just once more."

Once again, they clasped their hands together as if in prayer and focused their energies.

"Please accept our help . . . if only a little bit!"

Belldandy's body gave off a golden glow. The sweet music reverberated through the ancient forest and faded into the distance.

KYOUEN — BANQUET

"What're we gonna do, Den-chan?"

"I dunno, Dai-chan."

The mornings and evenings had grown chilly, and the change of seasons was visible in the dress of the students bustling around campus at the Nekomi Institute of Technology. They wore sweaters, boots, and jackets—the particularly fashionable ones sported fur garments. But Tamiya and Otaki were the exception to the rule.

As always, Motor Club President Tamiya wore jeans and an athletic jacket, and Vice President Otaki wore a black leather jacket stocked with dozens of tools. The two friends wore the same outfits like uniforms year in and year out. It would seem that they were oblivious to the passage of the seasons . . . except for their anguished dialogue.

"We got troubles, Den-chan!"

"Yeah. Big troubles, Dai-chan!"

As they hunched over extra-large portions of ramen and curry rice in the school cafeteria, their conversation seemed to be going nowhere.

With the joys of summer vacation behind them, the next big event on the horizon was the school festival. It was an exciting time, offering opportunities to mingle with students from other schools and to display the fruits of their labors. But it was more than that. For student clubs who aspired to bigger and better endeavors, it was a time when funds were absolutely necessary. For this reason, it was the most critical time of year for clubs seeking to replenish their coffers.

Unfortunately . . .

". . . Dis ain't good."

Tamiya drained the very last drop of soup from his ramen bowl, let out a deep sigh, and slumped back in his chair.

For the eternally strapped-for-cash Motor Club, the Nekomi Festival was a critical lifeline. That lifeline was in danger of being severed.

"Hey, I hear the ghost with the long hair appeared in the teacher's room last night!" a voice said at a nearby table.

"For real? They say she appeared out behind the north buildings just the night before last!"

"Whoa, that's a lot of sightings!"

"Back in the beginning, she used to only appear out by the fountain . . ."

The rumors had begun to circulate in early spring. At first, it seemed like just a school ghost story . . .

"They say she's the spirit of some woman who killed herself a long time ago . . ."

"How long ago?"

But lately, it was the talk of the school.

Ever since summer vacation, the ghost's appearances had increased dramatically, as had the number of students who had seen her. Some were so traumatized that they stopped coming to classes, and the administration could no longer ignore the issue.

"That's totally lame!"

A group of girls walking by complained loudly.

"I know! Too bad—I was looking forward to the chance to show off my boyfriend at school . . ."

"Wait, so it's definitely being canceled?"

"No, not yet. They're supposed to announce their decision next week. But the way things are going, it doesn't look good."

"Great. If they cancel the Nekomi Festival—how boring will *that* be!"

Tamiya's eyes gleamed.

He'd heard vague rumors that the administration and the Festival Committee were considering canceling the festival due to the unpredictable situation, but he'd never expected that things would move this quickly—and in an ominous direction, no less.

"What'll we do, Den-chan?"

"Dis is bad, Dai-chan."

"The Motor Club's gotta protect the Nekomi Festival, no matter what!"

"Right!"

Their arms folded, they fell silent again for a spell.

"Hey, Den-chan . . . If the thing causin' all this trouble was gone, there'd be no problem, right?" Draining his glass of water, Otaki stated the obvious is a low voice.

". . . Yeah . . . Right. If duh thing was gone, there'd be no problem." Tamiya made a tight fist.

"So all we gotta do is get rid of that troublemaker!"

Their faces spread into confident grins.

". . . Dai-chan . . ."

"Yeah, Den-chan."

They nodded decisively. Their chairs rattled loudly and almost fell over as they leapt to their feet and charged out of the cafeteria.

Soft rows of cirrocumulus clouds drifted in the bright blue sky, and between dying leaves, persimmons began to blush a deep sunset orange. Fall made its presence felt quickly at Tarikihongan Temple.

"Welcome home!"

In the tea room, Belldandy looked up from her sewing. A plastic bag with a square box inside was plopped down unceremoniously on the low table.

"What a *pain!* This is the last time I ever do this!"

Urd sighed loudly and sank down to the floor in a dramatic expression of exhaustion. Her face was discontentment itself. Belldandy let out a soft cluck as she shifted her posture and called down the hallway.

"Skuld! Urd's home!"

A moment later, the sliding door skidded open.

"You sure took long enough!" the youngest goddess came bounding into the room, brusque and impatient, her black hair swinging behind her. "I assume you bought the ice cream I requested?"

Irked by Skuld's extra-imperious tone, Urd grew grouchier than ever. "Whatever . . ." she muttered sullenly.

Normally, this type of provocation would elicit Skuld's heavy artillery, but today she looked down at Urd with surprising composure.

"Oh, is that so? Are you sure that's your answer?"

Skuld had good reason to lord it over her sister.

They'd been almost finished with their work in Heaven, when Peorth had inadvertently said something that gave away Urd's deception. Skuld's outraged cries had reverberated throughout Yggdrasil, and her indignation had erupted like a raging volcano.

It was understandable . . . she'd been carted off to Heaven on the morning of a trip, made to assist with debugging and even a complete wipe of the system. Her anger knew no bounds. At first, Urd had ignored her seething sister. But there was still work left to do and they needed Skuld's help. Left with no other choice, Urd had caved . . .

"A promise is a promise!" Skuld chided.

In order to win Skuld over, Urd had promised to grant her sister any one favor she asked for when they got back to Earth. It was a promise she would live to regret. They'd only been back at the temple for four or five days when Skuld issued her edict.

"Urd, the new issue of *Dobon* comes out today. I want you to go and buy it for me—on foot—and pick up the ice cream flavors on this list, too." Just the memory of Skuld's gloating voice made Urd furious.

"I hope you haven't forgotten the jamocha almond fudge, chocolate mint, cookies 'n' cream, or rum raisin . . ." Skuld peered into the box.

Urd cast a glance in her direction and tossed her hair in annoyance. "I bought every flavor they had, so they should be in there."

"What?" Skuld froze in disbelief. "All thirty-two flavors?"

No wonder the box was so huge!

"Yippeeeee!" Skuld whooped, grinning from ear to ear. She hugged the box to her chest, plastic bag and all, and did a little dance for joy. Aroused by the commotion, Skuld's angel popped out of her back.

"Noble Scarlet! It's the new issue of *Flower Girls*! Let's go read it together and eat ice cream!"

Angels shared their masters' tastes. Noble Scarlet's eyes sparkled as she nodded her assent.

"Urd, I'm willing to call it even now!" Skuld bounded happily out of the room, her tiny angel in tow. She probably wouldn't re-emerge from her bedroom until evening.

"Sheesh!"

As peace and quiet returned to the tea room, Urd and

Belldandy exchanged glances. While only a few days had gone by in Heaven, more than a month had passed on Earth. Nobody was happier and more relieved than Belldandy to be finally reunited with her sisters.

"Sis . . . thank you for working so hard. You had quite a lot to contend with, didn't you?"

"Oh, it was no big thing."

Belldandy smiled—she'd missed Urd's unshakable bravado. From the back of a shelf, she pulled out a large bottle.

"I brought you back a present. I hope you like it."

She and Keiichi had chosen it together while trolling the souvenir shops in Yakushima.

"Potato shochu! I've never had this before . . ."

Made from sweet potatoes from the town of Satsuma and the pristine spring water that earned Yakushima the nickname "water island," potato shochu was a specialty sake that enjoyed a strong following. After savoring the aroma that filled the air when she broke the seal, Urd filled her ceramic cup to the brim.

"Now this is what being back on Earth is all about!"

She drained the cup in a single draught. A satisfied grin spread across her face as she relished the fullness of its flavor.

"Oh, good. I'm glad you like it."

Urd poured herself another glass and immediately knocked it back.

"So? How did it go with you guys?" Urd peered into Belldandy's face, anticipating a juicy story to go with her tasty drink. But rather than the flushed bashfulness Urd had hoped for, Belldandy's expression was colored by a dark shadow.

"Belldandy?"

"I . . ." When she saw the kindness in Urd's indigo eyes, the pent-up worry in Belldandy's heart came bubbling to the surface. "Sis . . . I . . . I don't know what to think . . ."

Belldandy had nicknamed the Jomon Cedar "the Yggdrasil of Earth" in her mind, and had looked forward to meeting it even more than spending time alone with Keiichi. But the oldest cedar on Earth had refused to respond to her, and no matter how she'd tried, it had thwarted her efforts to give it strength. Concerned that there might be something wrong with her powers, after returning to Tarikihongan Temple, Belldandy had sought answers from the mountains behind the temple and the ocean in the distance. When she found trees whose life-force was failing them, she and Holy Bell had sung them their healing music, as they had for the Jomon Cedar. The mountains and sea responded to her as they always had, and without exception, the ailing trees regained their vigor.

"Maybe that cedar just happened to be really obstinate," Urd suggested. Proud beings were often difficult to deal with.

"I hope that's all it was . . ."

"Well, all of the others responded to you just fine, right?"

"Yes . . ."

"Then everything's fine. There's nothing to worry about."

It was strange—no matter how hard Belldandy had tried to

tell herself that same thing, a part of her had remained dubious. But her older sister's simple reassurance brought Belldandy tremendous relief.

"Thank you, sis."

Her concern wasn't completely alleviated, but Urd's presence gave her as much reassurance as if she'd had an army of allies.

"So . . . did you kiss Keiichi?"

"Sis!"

Belldandy's smile returned. As the two sisters laughed together, the engine of a BMW broke the stillness outside. Keiichi was home.

"Oooh, it's your darling lover-boy! Better go meet him at the door!"

"Yes!" Belldandy nodded vigorously. Her chestnut hair fluttered behind her as she left the room. Urd watched her go and let out a soft sigh.

Could this have anything to do with the aberrations in the system?

She drained her sake cup once more and gazed at the bottle of shochu, now one-third empty.

"Welcome back! You're home late, aren't you?"

Keiichi had told her that his class would be over in the early afternoon, but it was well after three already. Belldandy had been a little bit worried when she hadn't heard from him, but she was relieved that he was home now, safe and sound.

"Have you eaten lunch already?" she asked. "If not . . ."

Keiichi remained motionless on his bike, his back to Belldandy, though he'd shut off the engine. Something was wrong.

"Keiichi . . . ?"

Slowly, Keiichi turned toward her, wearing an expression so miserable, it looked like a mask from traditional Japanese Noh theater.

"Belldandy . . ." Deep creases wrinkled his brow, and his mouth was a thin, straight line.

"What's the matter?"

"Belldandy . . ."

This was serious.

"Whatever it is, let's go inside, okay, Keiichi?"

Gently, she ushered him toward the house and opened the front door.

"Hey, welcome back." In the tea room, Urd was still communing with her bottle of sake. The liquid inside was already half gone.

"Why the long face?"

Wordlessly, Keiichi slumped his shoulders and sank listlessly to the floor, his helmet still cradled under his arm.

"I'm screwed."

"Is that so?"

"Yeah . . . on the way home, the seniors stopped me to talk."

The seniors. That meant Tamiya and Otaki. The mere mention of their involvement hinted at some sort of ridiculous trouble.

"What did they want this time?"

Keiichi looked from sister to sister. Slowly, he began to recount what had happened at school.

*   *   *

"Yo, Morisato-kun! You headin' home now?"

"Oh, hi, guys . . ." When Keiichi saw the two upperclassmen waiting for him in the parking lot by his bike, their arms crossed, he had a premonition that something unpleasant was about to unfold. ". . . What is it?"

The fact that they'd stuck the relatively respectful suffix of "-kun" to the back of Keiichi's name was a sure giveaway that they wanted something from him. It was also safe to assume that it was probably something monumentally troublesome.

"As a matter of fact, we gots a job for you."

Here it comes—!

Alarm bells went off in Keiichi's mind. If only he could run away somehow and not hear the rest of what they had to say to him. His heart filled with the desperate feeling of sinking inexorably into a pit of quicksand.

"What . . . is it?"

With those simple words, Keiichi opened Pandora's box.

"Keiichi Morisato, we officially appoints you . . . Chief of Special Forces!"

"?"

This was definitely not what he had expected, and he tilted his head to one side in confusion. Based on past experience, he'd imagined something more along the lines of cleaning out the Motor Club clubhouse from top to bottom, or hunting down and scrounging junked motorcycle parts . . .

"Special Forces? What's that?" Keiichi asked, bewildered by this unexpected development.

This was the very question Tamiya and Otaki had been waiting for.

"It's for the MMG Survival Game!"

"Survival game?"

"Yup. M for Motor Club, M for Million Yen, and G for Ghost Hunt. MMG Survival Game for short. Pretty cool, huh?"

Not another harebrained scheme . . .

Keiichi sighed deeply as he watched the upperclassmen bluster proudly. There could only be one explanation as to why they'd come up with something this ridiculous.

"Don't tell me . . . does this have something to do with saving the school festival?"

Keiichi, too, had heard wind that the Nekomi festival was in peril. He also knew that it was because of the ghost sightings.

"Bull's-eye, Morisato-kun! We gots a brilliant plan to save the Nekomi Festival, and to guarantee a bright future for the Motor Club!"

I knew it.

Any plan this pair had cooked up was bound to be a disaster. Desperately, Keiichi searched for counterarguments.

"But guys, that's impossible! MMG? A better name might be the 3U-Survival game, for Unsavory, Unrealistic, and Unsafe!"

"Whoa! That's pretty clever!" Oddly enough, this seemed to impress them.

"Anyways, Morisato-kun, here's why we's appointing you

Chief of Special Forces . . ."

But his protests had fallen on deaf ears.

"You're gonna be our sniper."

A whirlwind of thoughts spun wildly through Keiichi's brain.

Knowing them, they want me to shoot down the ghost and win the million yen in prize money. They expect me to take down a phantom?! What do they think this is, Ghostbusters?

Keiichi leaned forward. Before he could organize his thoughts, a stream of protests flew out of his mouth. "That's impossible! Out of the question! I'm no ghost expert—I'm just an ordinary college kid! There's no way I can snipe the ghost of some suicide victim!"

Tamiya interrupted his pleas with a violent roar. "Fool! Not the ghost! We wants you to shoot down the contestants!"

". . . *Huh?!*"

With a self-satisfied grin, Otaki explained the scheme.

The winner of the survival game would receive a million yen. The competition would begin at a specific time, and both individuals and teams could register to participate. The rules would be based on those of an ordinary survival game: participants who were shot by an opponent were "dead" and had to leave the game. At the beginning of the game, the participants would have ten minutes to disperse before combat began. Combat would proceed without a time limit, and the first contestant to subjugate the phantom would be declared the winner.

"Then why do you want me to shoot the participants?"

"Keep listening!"

There was no fee to enter the game. That way, anyone could feel free to take part. This was where Catch #1 came into play: the Motor Club would raise funds by selling a map of all of the places where the ghost had been sighted on campus, as well as a manual on ghost-hunting written by Remi Zweiganir, the old Nekomi matriarch. This brilliant strategy hinged on the desire of the contestants to seek whatever edge they could over their opponents.

"Who's Remi Zweiganir . . . ?" Keiichi wanted to know.

"All for the remarkable low price of 3000 yen!"

They brandished a detailed map. Keiichi wondered who on earth had drawn it.

"That brings us to the duties of da Special Forces Chief!"

Tamiya brought his face right up to Keiichi's.

"What?"

"Don't make us spell it out, Morisato-kun!"

Yes . . . this was Catch #2. Of course they didn't have a million yen in prize money to award the winner. If a non-Motor Club member actually won the game, there'd be hell to pay. But if Keiichi shot down all the other contestants, there was nothing to worry about, and the Motor Club could simply profit hand-over-fist from the proceeds of the map and ghost-hunting manual.

"Of course, da best scenario is if you actually defeats the ghost and saves the Nekomi Festival . . ."

"B-b-but . . ."

"Yeah . . . knowing good old Morisato-kun . . . he might actually pull it off!"

"But guys . . ." Keiichi pleaded.

Tamiya's eyes flashed mercilessly.

"Morisato, we ain't forgotten how you bailed on da Motor Club training camp this summer!"

". . . !"

This was Keiichi's weak point—he'd been so excited about the trip to Yakushima he'd completely forgotten about the overnight. Ever since summer vacation, the Motor Club members had used it against him on numerous occasions.

". . . Fine . . . you win . . ." Keiichi's voice was as weak as a mosquito's hum.

"We's counting on you, Special Forces Chief!"

Enthusiastic slaps rained down on Keiichi's back.

"That basically sums it up . . ."

Belldandy had served Keiichi a fresh cup of tea on the low table. As usual, the tea leaves were standing straight up and down—but there was no way he could interpret that as a sign of good fortune at a time like this.

"I see . . ." Belldandy looked at Keiichi sympathetically as he slumped his shoulders in defeat.

All he could do was to give it his best shot, knowing full well that failure was inevitable.

But Urd responded to Keiichi's misfortune with surprising enthusiasm. "Sounds like fun!" she said.

"Huh? You mean you like this sort of thing, Urd?" Keiichi raised his head, surprised.

"Why not? Could be a great opportunity."

"An opportunity?"

"Exactly." Urd tipped the last of the shochu into her cup and chugged it. "Here we've been home for just a few days, and already things are getting interesting!"

In high spirits, she rose to her feet and swaggered out of the room. Immediately, they heard muffled shouts and scuffling from other end of the hallway. Apparently, Urd had gone to settle her score with Skuld. After a brief melee, there was a shout of "Headlock!" followed by silence.

". . . I guess they settled it . . ."

"Yes . . ."

From the soundof it, Urd had paid Skuld back in full for her irritating behavior earlier. Belldandy grimaced, and Keiichi cleared his throat to broach the difficult subject he'd been avoiding.

"Belldandy . . . ? Actually . . . there's one more thing . . . the upperclassmen insisted on . . ." At first, Keiichi had been firmly resistant . . . but due to certain ulterior motives of his own, he'd found himself unable to refuse.

Sweat erupted from Keiichi's pores. He hung his head, too overcome by both reluctance and excitement to look up. Clasping his hands in supplication, he shouted out the request.

"Would you mind dressing up in a nurse's outfit?"

*　　*　　*

In the darkness of the brush, insects offered up their lilting melodies. There was no moon, but the crystal-clear night sky glittered with stars. The darkness imbued the campus with a completely different atmosphere, and the familiar buildings loomed eerily, like abandoned relics.

But in the student parking lot adjoining those buildings, a lively party atmosphere reigned. Decked out in whimsical costumes, the combatants were in high spirits as they waited for the game to start.

Tonight was the big night of the Motor club Million yen Ghost hunt—the MMG Survival Game, and a whopping six hundred participants had turned out.

"Business is good, boys, business is good!" Tamiya said. The organizers were over the moon. Tamiya was sporting an old-fashioned headband and cotton jacket, in addition to his ubiquitous track jacket, and Otaki wore his treasured chrome-plated suit of knight's armor.

"Don't let us down, now, Morisato-kun!"

"Uhh . . ."

Keiichi sighed glumly.

Armed with a variety of BB guns, including electric, CFC gas, air tank, and air-cocking types, the combatants had dressed up in themes ranging from the traditional—SWAT team and police, WWII, Vietnam, and contemporary military uniforms—to the bizarre—western wear, civil war, samurai, barbarian, sci-fi, movies, animation, video games, comics (both Japanese and American), and the occult.

These were the fanatic lunatics Keiichi would have to contend with.

"Um, Tamiya? Where are Imai and the other guys from the Motor Club?" he asked.

Keiichi had been named Special Forces Chief, but there was no sign of the other club members.

"Right . . . some of them's running the game or working as referees, some's selling refreshments and stuff. Everyone's shorthanded."

Selling refreshments?! Talk about the entrepreneurial spirit. So it's just me and these two?

As if he could read Keiichi's thoughts, Tamiya immediately doused Keiichi's last hopes.

"'Course, the two of us has gotta be standing by out here."

"What? You mean you're not going to join the battle?"

"Right. We'd love to if we could, but as organizers of dis here game, we gots to be on call to help with the wounded."

"B-b-but . . ."

"Duh glory of battle is all yours, Morisato-kun!"

"B-b-but . . ."

There was no arguing with an excuse that lame. The Special Forces was to be comprised of only Keiichi, Urd, and Skuld.

Keiichi sighed and slumped his shoulders.

A hand slapped him energetically on the back.

"Buck up, kiddo!" said Urd. "With the two of us on your side, you've got the courage of thousands, the strength of millions!" Urd wore a black jumpsuit à la Charlie's Angels, the zipper opened dangerously low in the front to reveal the tight cleavage of her generous chest. She looked unbearably wild and sexy.

"Yeah! We're an elite team of the best and the brightest! We don't need excess numbers!" Skuld was dressed in her ordinary clothes, but she'd brought along something that made Keiichi's eyes pop.

"W-what's . . . that?"

"I thought you'd never ask! It's the new and improved Banpei RX: The Return!"

"Banpei?"

With a round white face, a round red body, and a black conical hat, the Banpei RX seemed to be patterned after an old-fashioned Japanese foot soldier. Keiichi stared at the robot—he'd never seen anything like it.

"Wow. That's amazing."

"I know, right? He looks just the same as before, but on the inside he's more advanced than ever. Can you tell the difference, Keiichi?"

Skuld brimmed with confidence as she boasted, her nose stuck high in the air as Keiichi circled Banpei.

He stopped still in his tracks. "Huh? Um . . . but I've never seen this robot before . . ."

"What?"

"Was it at the temple?

For a moment, Skuld froze.

"Right! She left it up in Heaven. Guess she thought she'd

already shown it to you!" Urd answered smoothly.

"Oh!" Keiichi was easily convinced, and the two goddesses breathed a sigh of relief.

Urd elbowed Skuld, annoyed at her awkward behavior.

"That was dumb. He doesn't remember, so you can just tell him anything!" she whispered.

"Well, unlike you, I don't tell lies!"

"You're such a child."

"What did you say?!"

Just when it seemed that a battle gong was about to break out before the game even got started, Belldandy's voice cut in.

"Is everyone all right?"

Keiichi turned, and reality melted away.

Belldandy was a vision of loveliness in her early twentieth century nurse's costume. She wore a long, pale blue dress with puffed sleeves like little lanterns. Her snow-white long apron was adorned with adorable lacy ruffles at the neckline and sleeves, and a nurse's cap rested pertly atop her lustrous chestnut hair.

"B-b-belldandy . . . !"

Keiichi's temperature soared and his pulse raced. *Gee, it's good to be alive!* he thought.

For the first time, Keiichi felt grateful to Tamiya and Otaki for concocting this whole scheme. As he stared, mesmerized by her beauty, he suddenly felt motivated to do his very best.

Belldandy blushed at Keiichi's stunned expression.

"Do I look strange?" she asked.

"Uh, no! You look really good. Really cute."

Keiichi wanted to say something more eloquent, but only managed to produce the most banal of compliments. His heart pounding, his face turned an even deeper red than Belldandy's.

"Oh, good!"

She smiled at him, her lavender eyes dancing, and Keiichi thought he would lose his mind. In an effort to control his excitement, he hoisted his heavy equipment to his shoulder, trying to use its weight to hold on to his sanity.

"Well, I guess we'll just try to get as far as we can!" Keiichi feigned calm as best he could as he averted his eyes and changed the subject.

"What kind of nonsense is that! We came to win, and only to win!" Urd shouted.

"Duh!" Skuld agreed.

The two goddesses emitted a fiery aura, all but slapping the reluctant Keiichi on the buns. Just then, out of nowhere, they heard the trumpet of a conch shell. The hour was midnight. The battle was beginning.

The wild cries of six hundred combatants shook the air.

"Be careful, Keiichi!" Belldandy called, but her voice was drowned out by a shrill whistle.

There was a split second of silence, and then an earth-shaking rumble as the contestants charged forward from the starting line. Keiichi turned back momentarily to wave, but was instantly enveloped by the sea of warriors.

*   *   *

Inky darkness ruled the moonless night. In the far-off heavens, the myriad stars glittered like diamonds, but their light was too faint to illuminate the Earth. Beneath this exquisite autumn night sky, a ferocious battle had been raging for almost an hour now.

The campus became a Hamburger Hill, its frontline stretching larger and larger until it threatened to encompass the entire school.

"Does it look like we can break through their forces?"

"Hard to say. They've got tremendous firepower."

Messages flew through the air on miniature wireless radios.

The battle raged white-hot at the Inokuradai Building, where there had been a rash of ghost sightings since summer.

"A Team, have you succeeded in penetrating the building?"

"D Team is mobilizing to back us up . . . please stand by for now."

The game was comprised of competing teams and individuals, but the players at the Inokuradai Building front line had joined forces. A number of individual teams had been completely obliterated when they'd tried to approach the building, and the teams that had observed the carnage had banded together in an improvised coalition. The truth was, they'd sensed that this was the only way they had any hope of contending with the ferocious foe awaiting them.

"This is C Team. We want to synchronize with the assault."

The fighters advanced cautiously, waiting for their opening. But after making their way up the city road, they found themselves unable to gain further ground.

"Holy cow! What the heck is that!?"

Before they even managed to get a good look at the enemy, the panicked exclamation from the radios of the invading team was followed immediately by the roar of artillery mixed with screams.

"From the three o'clock side of the building . . . Aaaaughh! We're under heavy fire!"

The message cut out in a cloud of static. The other combatants listened on pins and needles for further news.

"Hey . . . what was that sound!"

"Do you feel shaking? Are we having an earthquake?"

Just then, the mystery enemy reared its head. With an earth-shaking explosion, an enormous vehicle with six gun barrels in front emerged from the shadow of the building. For some reason, Banpei's innocuous face gazed out from the massive, vicious gun turret. The strange juxtaposition made the spectacle even more horrifying.

"I give you the 'Banpei Riot Control Attachment Precision Maneuver 8-Wheeled Armored Vehicle, Mark 3'! Bring it on, suckers!"

Skuld stuck her head out of the hatch and unleashed a peal of high-pitched laughter that would have made Urd proud.

"Hey! Nobody ever said oversized vehicles were allowed!" a combatant shouted, poking his head out of the bushes.

Banpei responded immediately to the voice. The tank was integrated with Banpei's eye monitor, rendering maneuvering and aiming unnecessary when the "vanquish enemies" setting was activated.

Slowly, the gun turret focused on its prey.

"Hey! That's breaking the rules!"

But this was a Motor Club game—there were no rules. The Maxwell-stone-powered chain gun unleashed a merciless stream of 8mm BBs at its target.

"AAAAAUGGH!!!"

"Retreat! Run for cover!!"

Though the combatants had taken up offensive positions on each side of the building, they scattered in a disorganized panic. Skuld was unperturbed by the sudden exodus. Tilting her head sweetly to one side, she pressed the blue button on her instrument panel.

"Banpei Pursuit Sensors: ON!" she giggled.

Vreeeeeeee.

Banpei's eyes glowed eerily.

Moments later . . .

Needless to say, the six kilometers of road between the main campus and the Inokuradai Building was soon littered with fallen soldiers.

No sooner had the players fled to the road, believing themselves to be safe, than they had been thoroughly obliterated by Banpei's Pursuit Sensors. The Battle of Inokuradai was over, and a full third of the game's participants had been annihilated.

"Man . . . dead already, and the game was just getting started!" A soldier in a military costume trod dolefully back down the road. Gear never felt heavier than after an untimely demise.

"Cheer up! Being a casualty has its merits, too!" a samurai called out to him.

"Oh, right!" A pleasant memory revisited the soldier. "The angel in white!"

This was no time to drag their feet!

"Belldandy!"

The fallen soldiers joined hands and scampered happily back.

"Wounded soldiers, line up here!"

The student parking lot was overflowing with people. It was not only the game's starting point, but also the only designated Safe Zone, which housed the game's field hospital tent. Establishing a hospital for a mere survival game seemed somewhat excessive, but in fact this was another of Tamiya and Otaki's schemes.

Belldandy had become something of a legend after her one-day visit to campus on exam day. The students who had seen her in the cafeteria spread stories, and those stories were further embellished in the imaginations of those who hadn't seen her. If Sayoko was Nekomi's queen, then Belldandy was Nekomi's diva. It followed that if Belldandy was willing to make a special appearance on campus—dressed in a nurse's outfit, no less—there was no way the boys were going to miss out on it. She was the hidden treasure of the MMG Survival Game.

"Here goes, Dai-chan!"

"Right, Den-chan!"

Otaki hearded the crowd into a line.

"Thank you for your patience! Nurse Belldandy will now begin her rounds!" he bellowed.

Belldandy emerged from the tent's entrance wearing her long, pale blue dress and white apron. Silently, she bowed, and a chorus of oohs and low cheers rippled through the crowd. She was like a solitary flower blooming on a battlefield.

"Wow . . . the legendary Belldandy!"

"I can't believe I'm seeing her with my own eyes!"

Even after Belldandy disappeared back into the tent, the aftershocks of her presence continued to cause tremors in the crowd of boys.

"The fee for medical care is 3000 yen!"

Otaki brandished a cash box and a bundle of numbered tickets. In no time at all, the box was overflowing with bills.

"Den-chan, our plan is a success!" Otaki whispered.

After taking a single hit, the participants were cut from the game. The fallen were bound to be frustrated by the fact that there was no way to get back into play. Under the motto of "physical and emotional TLC," Belldandy's field hospital was an added bonus for the game's participants—and for the non-participants as well (read: another money-making opportunity).

"Man, we're on fire!"

Otaki's face spread into a wide grin. He strained to contain it as he called out to the crowd, "3000 yen! 3000 yen for Nurse Belldandy's medical treatment!"

Keiichi was not privy to this scheme—he'd been led to believe that Belldandy's care would be free of charge.

"Way to go, Morisato!"

Before long, the line of wounded soldiers stretched beyond the limits of the parking lot.

Ka-pak!

A crisp pop shattered the stillness.

"Hit!"

Yet another soldier met his demise.

In contrast to the mayhem of the Inokuradai front line, the "modern whale sculpture front line" was fraught with silent tension. Almost two hours had passed since the game's start, and the combatants were pitted in a fierce deadlock. Two rows of four-story buildings framed the plaza with the fountain, making it the ideal spot for sniping. For that reason, numerous shooters had holed up inside the buildings, targeting the "sniper street" below. Anyone moving through the area had to exercise extreme caution.

The players had to be on a constant lookout for the ghost, and that vigil demanded absolute patience and concentration.

Those who didn't cut it were goners.

Two such snipers searched for the enemy with a night-vision-equipped video camera.

". . . Next target?"

"I'm on the lookout . . ."

Although it was still autumn, the night air was already sufficiently cold, a condition exacerbated by the fact that they had to remain absolutely still.

"Damn, it's chilly in here with all the windows open!"

All of the second floor and third floor windows were open wide, in order to make the snipers' positions harder to ascertain.

"Hey, don't just watch the ground. Pay attention to the rooftop, too!"

"I am! But . . . it isn't easy, you know."

They'd been staked out on the third floor of the North Building for some time now. As soon as the game had started, they'd headed straight for this spot. But . . .

"Do you really think the ghost is going to show up?" The first sniper asked his partner without looking away from the video camera.

Sniper Two was staring into a high-magnification scope designed for a real rifle.

"Oh, it'll show up," he said confidently. "I even consulted Izumi the Great."

"Izumi, the electronics major?"

"Yeah. I went all out. I had her run a statistical analysis on the department's computer."

"Wow . . . you really pulled out all the stops!"

"Yup."

"So how did it go?"

"Oh, she's *really* cute. Super smart, but she's not stuck-up or anything . . ."

"Not the girl, man! I've heard all that already! I mean the results!"

"Oh. According to our analysis, at 2:00 a.m. today, there's an 87 percent chance that the ghost'll appear on the roof of the South Building."

The buildings opposite them were approximately 40 meters away. Given that their top priority was sniping the ghost, it was clear that these two had unusual confidence in their shooting abilities.

"About five more minutes. When the ghost appears, I'll nail it with my 'sanctified BBs.' We'll collect the million yen prize and split it 70-30 . . . *augh!*"

He fell silent.

The sniper with the video camera froze and turned toward his partner.

"What's wrong?"

His face contorted in pain, the sniper's reply was succinct. ". . . Hit."

He keeled over. From the looks of it, he'd been shot at close range.

"W-w-what?"

The soldier with the night-vision-equipped video camera scanned furiously for the enemy. Seeing his partner taken out so quickly shook him to the core.

"Where? . . . *Damn it* . . . where *are* you?"

He scanned every nook and cranny, but there was no sign of the shooter. Just as he was beginning to panic, a single BB whizzed through the night sky and hit him.

Thwak!

It was a perfect hit, but at first the boy was too overwrought to notice. This time, a series of shots rained down on him.

Tak-tak-tak-tak-tak-tak-tak-tak-tak-tak-tak-tak-tak-tak!

The barrage of BBs was enough to bring him back to his senses.

"I'm . . . hit."

At this, the silver-haired sharpshooter finally released the trigger.

"Then get a move on!"

Hovering in the night sky on her broom Stringfellow, Urd removed the multi-shot cartridge from her 20-inch folding single-shot rifle. With perfect timing, Keiichi's voice came crackling over her wireless radio.

"Looks like that wraps it up for sniper-hunting, Urd."

From his position on the rooftop of the South Building, Keiichi exhaled deeply and sat upright. He was wearing a load-bearing vest and headgear that looked like a helmet with rabbit ears attached.

"Pretty bizarre-looking," he commented to himself as he removed the device and looked it over once more. Needless to say, it was one of Skuld's creations: the Static and Moving Object Sensor Machine with Amazing Visible and Invisible Light Wave Detector, or Super McMoneagle for short. With the Super McMoneagle on his head, Keiichi had issued directions to Urd from the rooftop, who in turn had crept up silently on her victims astride the Stringfellow broom, picking them off from the sky when they least expected it. Working together like a well-oiled machine, they had eliminated more than ninety pairs of snipers. Odd-looking or not, Keiichi had to admit that the Super McMoneagle got the job done.

"All right, Urd . . . let's move down to the ground."

Now all that remained was to round up the stragglers cowering below, still unaware that the snipers had been obliterated.

"Okay. This should be a snap!"

Deftly, Keiichi packed the apparatus away in his backpack and stashed it in the shadows where nobody would notice it. It was heavy, and he could always come back for it later. Then he removed his electric machine pistol from its holster and made a dash for the emergency stairs, much lighter on his feet without the excess weight.

Meanwhile, Urd exchanged her large-caliber rifle with optical sight for a gas blowback machine gun as she quietly began her descent.

Just then, violent surges of energy shook Urd's body.

This was no mere ghost or spirit. Its force was cold, massive, and overwhelming.

"Don't tell me . . ."

Urd spun around. The energy was coming from the roof of the South Building.

"Keiichi . . . !"

Flinging down her gas gun, Urd zoomed off on her broom at top speed.

"Belldandy?"

Belldandy was sweetly tending to a wounded soldier when suddenly her hands froze mid-task. Her smile disappeared and her body stiffed. The atmosphere in the tent grew tense.

"Are you okay?" The boy she was ministering to asked worriedly.

But his words fell on deaf ears. Belldandy was straining with all of her might to recapture the vibrations she'd detected for a brief moment.

That energy . . .

The residual impression of the vibration still lingered in her body. She could sense its urgency.

Belldandy stood up suddenly. "Please excuse me."

"Huh?"

"You'll have to take care of the rest!"

She handed her nurse's cap to Tamiya and raced out of the tent.

"Keiichiii!"

When Urd landed on the roof, she found Keiichi collapsed from fear, sitting flat on his butt. There, in the middle of the roof, shone a flare-shaped shimmer of pale white light. Was this the famous ghost? Urd's instincts violently rejected that explanation.

"Are you okay?"

Somehow, Keiichi managed to nod.

"I'll draw its attention—you just get out of here!" Urd instructed.

Still glued to the roof, Keiichi began to edge away from the apparition, while Urd to a step forward to protect him.

Looks like my fears were right on the mark.

Urd remembered the strange feeling she'd had when she'd

heard the ghost rumors on their first visit to the N.I.T. campus.

Time had an intrinsic ability to self-correct its axis, so that while certain processes might change, their ultimate outcomes seldom varied.

But this presence is different.

Ever since the system restore, there had been small differences in their lives. But this ghost story was another matter altogether. Nothing like it had existed in the past. And the rumors had begun circulating less than two weeks after the system restore, without any interference by the goddesses.

Perhaps this is behind Belldandy's experience in Yakushima . . . and the abnormal values in the Yggdrasil system, too.

Urd stared straight at the apparition and addressed it in Goddess-tongue.

"I am a Goddess of Time. Why do you disturb the Earth Realm? Identify yourself!"

Her words elicited a reaction. The apparition began to emit new pulses of energy from its cocoon-like shroud of light.

What's this . . . ?!

Urd shrank back momentarily. Immediately, the apparition expanded, glimmering more brightly. Then, so quickly it was barely visible, it swooped toward Keiichi.

Oh, no!

Tentacles of light reached toward Keiichi, encircling him. The moment they touched him, a dazzling shower of sparks rained down from the point of contact.

"AAUGHHH!" Keiichi cried out as the impact jolted his entire body.

"Keiichi!"

Writhing in agony, Keiichi was propelled backwards by the bluish-white explosion. The apparition, too, drew backwards, its power slightly weakened.

"Now! Lightning Bolt . . ."

Urd raised her hands, determined not to miss her opening, when she was interrupted by a violent crashing sound.

". . . !"

The cover and light bulb of the electric safety light that illuminated the roof exploded in a shower of tiny shards.

"Wait, Urd!" Belldandy emerged from the reflective hood of the light fixture just in time to stop Urd from casting her lightning bolt.

"Belldandy! Of all the places . . ."

It had required a great deal of strength for Belldandy to travel through an object so far removed from a mirror, and her shoulders heaved from the exertion. She landed in front of Keiichi, her legs shaky, and poured her energy into a barrier shield spell.

"I'll protect Keiichi!"

There was no telling how the apparition might react to Urd's spell, and there was a good chance that Keiichi would be hurt, too. Belldandy summoned Holy Bell, making her barrier shield spell stronger still in order to ward off the apparition.

But the apparition refused to be blocked. It charged into the barrier shield, expanding as it absorbed power from the wind. A wild, storm-like gale began to howl, creating a huge discrepancy in air pressure. If they didn't do something, the fabric of space itself would be torn!

"Urd! Keiichi . . ."

"I'll take care of him!"

First they had to ensure Keiichi's safety. Then they could deal with the rest of the situation.

"Barrier Shield Spell, maximum power!"

As Belldandy poured every last drop of her energy into her barrier shield, Urd began to chant.

"Oh, my Counterpart . . ."

In response to Urd's summons, World of Elegance, Urd's Heavenly companion, emerged in a burst of flames, her black and white feathers dancing.

"Teleport Spell . . . now!"

As Urd and her angel sang, the spell formed a band of light and sliced through the raging wind. At just the right moment, Belldandy weakened her Barrier Shield spell, steering the light toward Keiichi. In a tremendous surge of brightness, the band enveloped Keiichi, and he vanished from sight.

"Belldandy! The teleport was a success!"

Belldandy nodded. She released the barrier shield and shifted into combat mode. The wind died down and the air was fraught with tension. Just as Urd raised her hands to perform an attack spell—

"What's this?"

Suddenly, the white glimmer began to contort wildly, as if writhing in pain. It gave off a flash of blinding light and then melted away like a fog.

"It's gone . . ."

Once again, the rooftop was quiet. The same darkness reigned as if nothing had happened. The only evidence of the battle that had just transpired was the shattered light bulb.

"Belldandy!"

Urd caught her sister gently as her body crumpled.

Every drop of her energy spent, Belldandy had lapsed into a deep sleep. Gently, Urd brushed back the strands of chestnut hair that lay across her face.

"You should really be more careful, sis . . ."

Several angel feathers still hovered in the air. Urd looked silently up at the pitch-black, moonless night sky.

"There's trouble brewing . . ."

The momentary pulse of energy she had felt from the apparition . . . Demon energy. It was unmistakable. To Urd, there was nothing more despicable . . . or more familiar.

Urd's long silver hair danced in the crisp breeze. Her thoughts, too, were swept away by the wind. The twinkling stars foretold winter's arrival.

ꙮ CHAPTER THREE ꙮ

T S U K I H A N A — M O O N F L O W E R
"AAAAIIIIIEEEEEEEEEEE!!!"

A scream shrill enough to shatter glass . . . such words completely failed to describe the piercing shriek that echoed across the grounds of Tarikihongan Temple. The flock of sparrows roosting on the roof of the house rose up into the sky, voicing their irritation in a chorus of chirps.

"What the . . ."

"It came from the front gate."

The front door slid open with a bang and Keiichi and Belldandy came running out. By the side of the gate, Banpei the guard-robot had someone in a full nelson.

"Not again!"

After her satisfying victory in the MMG Survival Game, Skuld had assigned Banpei to guard the front gate of the temple, with his enormous Banpei Riot Control Attachment at the ready. It was a little bit like living in a fortress. Unfortunately, this created mayhem every time the mailman or a delivery person came by the temple.

"That Skuld . . ." Belldandy sighed.

"I asked her to put that stuff away . . ." Keiichi added.

As Keiichi and Belldandy stood making offhand remarks, Banpei's captive struggled desperately to escape, her short hair swinging wildly.

"Hurry up and help me, Keiichi!"

"Oh . . . Megumi!"

Today's victim was Keiichi's younger sister, Megumi.

"I'm sorry, Megumi . . . Skuld, you apologize, too!"

At Belldandy's bidding, Skuld sat in a polite kneel, but she wore a defiant pout on her face.

"Ah-ha-ha! It's okay! I was just a little surprised, that's all."

Smiling cheerfully, Megumi took a sip of the tea Belldandy had immediately served. Skuld glanced up at her briefly but quickly looked back down.

"You could at least call before coming over. Then we would have been prepared, you know!"

"Skuld . . ." Belldandy admonished her sister sternly for her complete lack of contrition. But Skuld only clamped her mouth tightly shut and ran out of the tea room. "Skuld!"

The little goddess tore down the hallway and slammed the door to her room.

"What was that about?" Megumi asked, startled by the outburst.

"Well . . . Urd had to go back all of a sudden . . ." Keiichi explained.

"Oh! To her home country?"

Keiichi had almost forgotten that the three sisters were supposed to be foreigners.

"Um, right. To her home country."

"Is something wrong?"

"Well, I don't really know the details, myself."

After the Survival Game, Urd had gone back to Heaven. She hadn't offered much of an explanation, except that she "needed to see about something."

Skuld had been overjoyed. She had the television and newspaper all to herself, and there was no one to pick on her or to interfere with her projects. But her euphoria had lasted only a few days. Before long, boredom set in, which then turned to loneliness, end eventually to irritability and moodiness.

"I guess sisters are sisters," Megumi said.

"Yes. Even though they fight, Urd and Skuld are actually very close," Belldandy said, "so much so that I envy them at times."

"You never realize how important siblings are until they're gone," Megumi agreed.

A delicate trickle of steam wafted up from the tea.

"I think I'll go check on her," Belldandy said.

Although she'd been stern with Skuld, Belldandy couldn't help worrying about her little sister. Quietly, she excused herself from the room.

For a moment, the tea room was silent. Then, now that she

had Keiichi alone, Megumi folded her arms deliberately across her chest.

"Well? What happened to you?"

"Huh?"

"I just heard yesterday that you haven't come to school ever since the big survival game debacle. It's been two weeks! What happened? Are you okay?"

"Oh! Uh, yeah."

Keiichi couldn't remember anything after the ghost had touched him on the school roof. The next thing he knew, he was in his futon in his own room back at the temple—with three goddesses chanting over him, no less. The first thing he saw when he opened his eyes was Belldandy, her eyes welling with tears. He still recalled vividly the mixture of sadness and happiness he saw in her face at that moment.

"I thought you'd never wake up!" Urd had joked.

In fact, the ghost's touch had inflicted a tremendous shock, and even with the three Goddesses of Time pouring all of their energies into him, it had taken three days and three nights for Keiichi to regain consciousness. Without their intervention, it would have taken him six months to recover. So actually, it wasn't really much of a laughing matter.

"I'm sorry. I didn't want you to worry," Keiichi told Megumi.

Since then, he'd stayed home from school to recover from the physical and emotional trauma of the encounter.

"I'd have worried less if you'd let me know what was going on!"

When Megumi had finally learned that Keiichi hadn't been at school, after two whole weeks, she'd come running to see him. It was a relief to find him looking the same as ever.

"Anyway, I'm glad you're okay. But next time . . ."

"Yeah. I'm really sorry, Megumi." Keiichi clasped his hands together apologetically, and Megumi finally smiled. Reassured, she reached immediately for the tea cookies.

"Then again, you were probably better off not coming to school anyway."

Megumi munched away, unable to resist Belldandy's home cooking. Now it was Keiichi's turn to lean forward anxiously.

"Why? What happened?"

Keiichi hadn't been in contact with anyone from school, so naturally he had no idea what had been going on there. The news Megumi brought was surprising in a sense, but in another sense it wasn't surprising at all.

First, in the middle of the game two weeks ago, there had been a sudden, very localized storm at a school building near the courtyard with the fountain, injuring quite a few students. The situation took a turn for the worse when the wounded had sought medical care at the field hospital and learned that Belldandy had disappeared and no first aid was available. The enraged students had turned their wrath on the game's organizers, demanding their money back and clamoring to see Belldandy, and before long a full-fledged riot had broken out.

"Are Tamiya and Otaki okay?"

"No."

Because they hadn't applied for permission to conduct a survival game on campus, Tamiya and Otaki had been taken to task for the extensive damage caused by their business venture, including the fallen trees by the Inokuradai Building (caused by Skuld's Banpei Riot Control Attachment), the broken safety light on the roof of the South Building (caused by Belldandy's teleport), and the school buildings with all of their windows broken (caused by the psychic vibrations from Urd and Belldandy's battle with the apparition). Both organizers had been indefinitely suspended from all club activities.

"Poor guys . . ."

"And because of the whole fiasco, the Nekomi Festival's been canceled, too."

"What? Seriously?"

This was an unexpected twist.

"How'll I show my face at school!" Keiichi moaned.

There was bound to be a strong backlash against the Motor Club for a while. As Keiichi scratched his head in consternation, Megumi scarfed down the last cookie in the basket.

"Well, there is a little silver lining," she told him. "The ghost is gone."

Some silver lining. Perhaps they'd gotten rid of the ghost, but there was no million yen prize to be had—zero payoff for all of their troubles!

"Oh, and it looks like you're the stand-in president for the Motor Club," Megumi added.

"What?"

"There was a notice posted on the clubhouse door."

Great. Now Keiichi would be the direct target of the students' backlash.

"Man . . . now I really don't want to go back to school." Keiichi slumped his shoulders.

Megumi thrust a camera toward him.

". . . your camera?" Keiichi said, confused.

Suddenly, Megumi's voice took on a sugary-sweet tone. "Say, Kei-chan . . ." she purred.

When Megumi was like this, Keiichi knew he had to be on his guard. He set aside his concerns about the Motor Club and focused on his immediate self-defense. Poor Keiichi. Was there no end to his troubles?

"Kei-chan, you like photography, don't you?"

"Well, yeah . . ."

"This is a really nice camera."

"Yes . . ."

"You could take some gorgeous pictures of Belldandy with it."

"Uh-huh . . ."

Megumi maintained a sweet smile as she circled in on her point. Finally, Keiichi lost his patience.

"What is it? Spit it out!"

"Would you buy it off of me?" Megumi said quickly, as if she'd been waiting for this very moment.

"Here I thought you came rushing out here because you were worried about me . . . now I see how it really is!" Keiichi sighed.

"That's not true! Of course my concern for your health was paramount! But . . . you seem to be fine and everything, so I figured . . ."

Oh, boy.

Still, Keiichi couldn't help getting swept up by Megumi's momentum. He picked up the camera and inspected it closely, remembering how Megumi had saved up her allowance to buy it. Her very first camera.

"I thought this thing was really important to you."

"Yeah . . . but I've got no choice. The softball club made plans to all go on a trip together at the end of the year . . . but the Nekomi Festival's been canceled, right? We were counting on it to raise the funds. The deadline to pay for everything is coming up soon, and there's no time to get a part-time job or anything."

She had him in a corner. Based on what she'd just told him, as a Motor Club member he could hardly say no when she put it in those terms.

Score another victory for Megumi.

Reluctantly, Keiichi pulled out his wallet.

"How much?" he asked simply.

"Exactly 30,000 yen, no more, no less!"

"That much?!"

"Well . . . it's the Christmas season, you know! We made the reservations six months ago, and even then we were lucky to get them! Somebody just happened to cancel. Otherwise, there's a one-year waiting list . . ."

"Okay, okay, I get it."

Keiichi let out a deep sigh and gritted his teeth. He removed three crisp 10,000 yen bills from his wallet all at once and grudgingly handed them to Megumi.

"Thanks, big brother!"

Megumi grasped the money tightly with both hands, her eyes sparkling. It was painful shelling out the cash, but as an older brother Keiichi couldn't help feeling satisfied by the happy smile on his sister's face. But Megumi didn't let him savor that feeling for long.

"So . . . any special plans for Christmas, Kei-chan?"

"I can't believe you would ask me that right after taking all my money."

The more pressing issue was how he was going to make ends meet after this. Only four lonely 1000 yen bills huddled forlornly in Keiichi's wallet.

"*Ah-ha-ha!* You have a point there!"

Quickly, Megumi slid the 10,000 yen bills into her own wallet and drained her now lukewarm tea.

"But there's still time before Christmas," she pointed out. "You could get a job or something. I bet Belldandy'd be thrilled if you got her a present."

"Belldandy . . ."

Keiichi hadn't celebrated Christmas since he was a small child. "We're not Christians, after all," his father had pronounced, and New Year's had always been the more important event at the Morisato household. Since starting college, Keiichi had been more aware of the holiday because of the other students. But since he never had a girlfriend, it was more a season of wistful envy than anything else.

But this Christmas would be different. Perhaps he was still a long way from actually being able to call Belldandy his girlfriend, but still—he was lucky enough to have a goddess with him always.

"Right . . . a present."

Now that Keiichi thought about it, several months had gone by since their trip to Yakushima without anything special happening. This was the biggest and final event of the year— there was no way he could pass up a perfect opportunity to get just a little bit closer to Belldandy. As his imagination soared, he began to get more and more excited.

"All right! This time I'm really going to kiss her!"

"Kei-chan . . . you still haven't kissed?"

". . . !"

The golden leaves of the ginko tree rained down like traditional dancers' fans as the warm autumn evening sun faded toward dusk.

Ting! A delicate chime announced the lift's arrival at its destination floor.

"Even with a system administrator's license, there aren't many opportunities to come down here," Urd said to herself. How long had it been since anyone had been in here? Urd's footsteps were the only sound that broke the absolute stillness.

She pulled up a chair, looking first at the large console, then up at the distant levels above.

"When you really look at it, it's pretty spectacular."

This was the Universal Access Unit of Yggdrasil Central Main Control, Terminal 3. Located more than thirty levels below the system operation room where Urd and the operators normally worked, it was one of the oldest device rooms of the Yggdrasil System. In order to defend Yggdrasil from the ongoing threat of bugs, the system was constantly being upgraded. As a result, many of its old programs and devices were now obsolete.

"Hope I can get this thing to work for me . . ." Urd's fingers danced elegantly over the panel.

Although they'd outlived their usefulness, these older technologies couldn't be casually discarded. Careless deletion or disposal was likely to cause negative aftereffects. For that reason, it was common practice simply to abandon them as they were.

"Is the answer I'm looking for here?" Urd wondered.

A flurry of lights flashed, illuminating the console. Urd overlayed an image of the specter against those lights.

When I battled that thing on the roof . . . the psychic waves I felt it emit were definitely demonic . . . and not from just any demon, either.

Urd still remembered the sensation—she couldn't forget even if she'd tried. That was precisely why she'd returned to Heaven to confirm her suspicions . . . but so far, she'd been unable to come up with anything.

"In any case, based on time-axis algorithm analysis, there've been irregularities in the balance between the occurrence of uncertain elements and the area-occupation rate of time-continuum certainties ever since the system restore."

Urd reviewed the facts she was sure of aloud, tossing back the silver locks that rested on her shoulders.

Unless . . .

Her bracelets tinkled.

On the day when the heavens had collapsed . . . perhaps the program Skuld created was incomplete . . . or maybe the system collapsed slightly sooner than we anticipated . . . As the thought occurred to Urd, she began to input new data into the console, but then stopped herself.

These were only hypothetical possibilities. Now that the reset had been implemented, the fastest shortcut was to run a simulation of the conditions at that moment when the restore program was run—with the assumption that Skuld's program and the timing of the system's collapse had all been correct.

"I'll think about the implications afterward."

Urd's fingers resumed their work.

She'd conducted exhaustive investigations at numerous locations, under the auspices of "systems maintenance work," but had failed to identify a single problem. The only avenue left to explore was this ancient relic: the Terminal 3 Universal Unit. Urd felt a complicated mixture of worry and anticipation as she set to work checking over the system.

Beep-beep-beep . . .

Suddenly, a signal flashed amid the flood of streaming data.

"...?..."

Urd switched over to the monitor to confirm what she'd seen. Oddly enough, it was an indication from Yggdrasil's very first unit.

"Why would this unit . . ."

Even though it was old enough to be a fossil, there was evidence that the unit had been active quite recently.

"Why did it start up?"

Immediately, Urd set about excavating the relic. But while it showed an indication of having responded during the system restore—when Yggdrasil had been rebooted—it was completely unresponsive now.

"Don't clam up on me now . . ." Urd rebuked it.

She tried everything she could think of, but to no avail. There was no way even to tell whether or not there had been a problem.

"Great . . . if I have to restore this system, it could take ages . . ."

"It sure would."

Urd spun around to locate the source of the sudden interruption. "! . . . Peorth!"

A Goddess First Class with lustrous black hair smiled back at her. Urd had been so absorbed in her work, she hadn't even noticed Peorth's presence. How could she have been so oblivious?!

"You've been behaving so uncharacteristically, I took it upon myself to follow you, *chérie*."

This only made Urd feel worse. She hadn't realized she'd been so obvious!

"Great. That's really depressing," she muttered.

But Peorth paid her no mind.

"Urd, you're prone to reckless behavior, but you aren't completely insensible, *n'est pas*? When you throw yourself into your work with such fervor, it's obvious that something out of the ordinary is afoot."

"Is that a compliment or an insult?"

"Take it however you prefer, *chérie*."

Peorth chuckled softly and peered over Urd's shoulder at the monitor.

"I've never been down here before either. I suppose you never know when this sort of knowledge might come in handy . . ."

"Yeah, whatever." Urd decided to cut her losses. She turned her back on Peorth and returned to her work.

She tried a number of tactics, but still the unit refused to respond. After descending more than thirty levels to reach this place, the only thing she'd learned was that this unit was part of some sort of network and that for some reason, it had responded when the Yggdrasil System had rebooted. Hardly what you could call satisfying results.

All right then . . . the only thing left is to conduct a time index search up until the point at which that menace touched Keiichi . . .

It seemed that the fastest remaining tack was to investigate all of the apparition's appearances, one by one, starting from the restore point and ending with the encounter on the roof of the South Building. And that would take forever.

"Peorth . . . as a Goddess First Class, I'd like to ask for your help with something."

Peorth stopped poking around and swiveled dramatically toward Urd.

"Oh, is that so? And what might that be?"

"Would you give me a foot rub?"

"What . . . ? . . ."

"Well, since it seems like you've got nothing better to do . . ."

". . ."

Out of nowhere, a whirlwind of red roses began to swirl in the air.

"I didn't come down here . . . to tolerate your insolence!"

Peoth's white arms danced gracefully in the air.

"Special Attack—Rose Hurricane!"

As the stems shot out of Peorth's back, petals and thorns flew at Urd like shrapnel.

"AI-YIIIIIIIIIIII!"

The frenzied storm of roses filled the Universal Terminal of Yggdrasil Central Main Control Terminal 3 with crimson.

Plip!—something landed on Keiichi's cheek.

At first, he was too absorbed in his work to notice. But in no time at all, the scattered drops evolved into a heavy shower.

"It *is* raining! Good old Belldandy," Keiichi murmured to himself.

It had been a beautiful morning, and the weather forecast had promised a zero percent chance of rain. But when Keiichi had left the house, Belldandy had handed him his rain slicker. Keiichi had wondered why, but he'd tucked it into his bag anyway.

Then, that afternoon, the weather had shifted. Black, ominous clouds had gathered suddenly across the sky, and now, finally, the rain had come.

Keiichi pulled the slicker out of his bag and quickly put it on. He had a lot of work lined up, and the last thing he needed was to catch a cold.

"Hey, kid! After we finish assembling this one, we'll wrap it up."

"Okay!"

Keiichi exhaled deeply, his breath white. Otaki had set him up with this part-time job installing guard rails. On the prefectural road by the Nekomi Sea Life Aquarium, the workers buzzed about their trucks, hurrying to finish up for the day.

Now the rain was coming down in earnest. The droplets mingled with the ocean wind, and Keiichi could feel his hands and feet quickly growing numb.

Using the air ratchet, he carefully installed the last rail and shut off the motorized compressor.

"All right. Load the tools and the compressor onto the truck and we're done for the day. Good work, everyone."

"Got it."

Keiichi quickly gathered up the scattered tools and put them away, and with the help of the other workers, managed to hoist the compressor up onto the bed of the truck.

"All right, see you tomorrow. Be here at ten-fifty, sharp!"

"Right. See you then."

Keiichi watched the convoy of trucks leave and let out a deep breath, glancing up at the large animatronic clock on the arch at the aquarium's entrance.

"Just a little bit more than four hours until my next job . . . good. I've got time to pop home and have dinner first, just as I planned."

Keiichi rubbed his frozen hands together and started the ignition of his BMW. The hum of the engine drowned out the rain, and a cloud of white smoke drifted up from the tailpipe into the darkness.

"I hope it lets up soon . . ." Keiichi prayed earnestly as he pressed his hands against the body of his motorcycle for warmth. His night-shift job—another of Otaki's hook-ups—was directing traffic at a construction site. Manual labor was hard on the body, but it was easy to get chilled to the core doing that kind of work, since you had to stand still in one place for hours on end. It would be far worse in the rain.

"Better get rolling."

His bike finally warmed up, Keiichi was just about to give it the gas when he noticed a woman walking toward him. She had no umbrella, and she tottered forward unsteadily through the downpour.

". . . ?"

Keiichi knew very well that at times like this, it was best to mind his own business. But for some reason, he couldn't quite look away. Suddenly—perhaps she'd felt his eyes on her—the woman stopped short. Her gait suddenly became surprisingly surefooted as she made a beeline for Keiichi.

"Yikes! This is bad!"

Keiichi reached for the gas and was just about to pull out into the road when the woman let out a commanding shout.

"Hold it right there!"

Without thinking, Keiichi let go of the gas. The woman's hair was drenched and disheveled, but she exuded an imposing aura . . .

Keiichi gagged.

It was Sayoko Mishima, the queen of the Nekomi Institute of Technology.

She strode over to Keiichi, grabbed him by the collar, and began to interrogate him.

"Who're you? Do you go to N.I.T.?"

"Y-yes."

"Your name and year."

"Keiichi Morisato, second year, mechanical engineering department!" Keiichi shouted with a rigid salute.

Wait, this isn't the army, he reminded himself, embarrassed.

Sayoko stared at him, then suddenly pounded her fist into her hand as if remembering something.

"Morisato . . . You're the guy who brought *that girl* . . ."

"That girl?"

"You were with Belldandy . . ."

Her aura pulsed with emotion—and for some reason, as she

mentioned Belldandy's name, rage.

"Huh?"

"That's right . . ."

As she focused that rage on the flustered Keiichi, Sayoko's eyes gleamed.

"I'm glad I ran into you. Come with me. It's the least you can do, after all!"

Delicate fingers clamped down on Keiichi's arm. He nodded, helplessly.

The upscale bar, not far from the aquarium, was housed in a pretty building with white walls and a homey atmosphere. There was no sign at the entrance, and it would have been easy to mistake it for a private residence. It was an establishment for insiders only.

"Good evening."

"Why, Mademoiselle Sayoko! You don't have your car today?" the proprietor asked in astonishment.

Sayoko was so wet, she looked like she'd gone for a swim fully clothed. Traveling by motorcycle in the pouring rain was a quick way to get drenched to the bone.

"Please change into this robe, Mademoiselle. I'll have your clothes dry for you when you leave."

Naturally, she got the full celebrity treatment.

"Shall I escort you to your usual table?"

Now clad in a soft silk robe, Sayoko glanced toward the tables by the window. Two-person tables lined the huge window overlooking the ocean, and at the very far end there were two four-person tables. Apparently, this was where Sayoko normally sat.

But Sayoko shook her head and turned away.

"I have no desire to look out at the ocean on a day like this. We'll sit at the counter."

"Right this way, please."

Keiichi was still standing by the entrance, unable to speak. He felt profoundly out of place and awkward, and wanted more than ever to go home.

"What are you doing?" Sayoko said in a stern voice. "Sit!"

But the queen also had other ideas. Keiichi allowed the proprietor to relieve him of his slicker and backpack as he sat down reluctantly at the counter.

"Do you have Krug?" Sayoko enquired.

"Of course, Mademoiselle. We have a complete selection."

"Of course you do. I'll have the Klos du Mesnil, please."

"Right away, Mademoiselle."

Softly, the barkeep set down an elegant jade-green bottle with an ornate golden label in front of Sayoko.

Klos du Mesnil was a Krug champagne made only from a particular species of grape in a particular field in a particular year. The quantity produced each year depended on the vintage, but was generally quite small—only nine thousand to seventeen thousand bottles. Naturally, it cost an arm and a leg.

"Be thankful for the opportunity to drink with me—my treat," Sayoko informed Keiichi.

The sparkling liquid glittered with bubbles like pearls as the bartender poured it into two glasses—so this was what they meant by "champagne gold."

"Cheers."

Their glasses clinked musically, and Sayoko downed the champagne as if it were water.

"Ahh . . . delicious!"

As she savored her drink, Keiichi remained frozen with his glass in the air. He had to ride his motorcycle after this—there was no way he could drink alcohol. At the same time, he didn't feel comfortable asking for something else.

"Is the Krug unsatisfactory, Monsieur?" the bartender inquired in a whisper.

Keiichi set his glass down apologetically. "It's just that . . . I'm on my motorcycle . . ."

"Please pardon me, Monsieur."

The bartender smiled and quickly brought Keiichi a replacement. He poured the amber liquid over large chunks of ice in a gleaming crystal glass.

"It's oolong tea."

To the casual observer, the drink looked like whiskey. This way, Sayoko wouldn't take offense.

"Morisato-kun . . . are you drinking?" Sayoko asked, as if on cue.

Keiichi pointed at his glass.

"That's right . . . drink up!"

Sayoko smiled in satisfaction. Her cheeks were bright pink, and the area around her mouth looked a little bit rosy, too. But

that was hardly surprising, considering that she'd already hit several bars that evening.

"Listen . . . I should really be going soon," Keiichi said. "I have to work later . . ."

Perhaps Sayoko was in the middle of some kind of major personal crisis, but Keiichi had neither the time nor the money to keep her company just now. With every passing minute, he was running out of time before his next job began.

"Why don't you phone home and have somebody come pick you up? If I take you on my motorcycle, you'll just get soaked again."

Keiichi was doing his very best to be nice, but once again, Sayoko glared at him.

"It's Belldandy, isn't it?"

"Huh?"

How did Belldandy get dragged into this?

"You'd rather be with her, wouldn't you?"

"What?!"

This hardly seemed a relevant question. When Keiichi had first come to N.I.T., like so many others, he'd worked up the courage to ask out Sayoko to take in some museums. She'd shot him down immediately. Now, he hardly knew how to react to her sudden attentions.

"Belldandy, Belldandy! She's all anyone ever talks about anymore . . . even though *I'm* the queen of the school!"

By now, Sayoko had polished off the bottle of Krug and switched to Bombay Sapphires on the rocks. She was already on her third.

"I can't take it. How am I supposed to compete with a rival who isn't even around?"

So that's why she resents Belldandy!

Ever since the MMG Survival Game, the stories of an angelic Belldandy dressed in white had become legendary—no, *mythological*, even. Her popularity was out of control, and Sayoko's frustration was similarly uncontainable.

"I thought it might take my mind of things to go on a date with a young businessman . . ." Sayoko recounted.

Her date that night had been a winning pick by every measure: handsome, an excellent student, and from a family of means. Sayoko had enjoyed his attentions and had been actually looking forward to their date. First, he'd come to pick her up in an Aston Martin. They'd had a lovely lunch at a well-reputed French restaurant and high tea at an open-air café overlooking the ocean. Sayoko had been pleased with her date's selection of venues, sophisticated repartee, and impeccable manners.

"But the true measure of a man is how he deals with a crisis," Sayoko continued.

"Ah . . ."

It happened in the parking lot. Space was tight, and the young man had been so focused on not hitting the other cars that he'd grazed the side of the Aston Martin against a low decorative planter. That was when the whole evening had gone down the drain.

It turned out that the fancy British car belonged to the boy's father and that he'd borrowed it without permission for their date. Disaster! His father would disown him for taking out the precious car without permission and bringing it home damaged! All at once, the boy's flawless poise crumbled, and he burst into tears right there in public.

"I can understand why he was upset . . ." Keiichi sympathized.

From the car's perspective, the injury had to have been a traumatic ordeal. And as for the driver, the cost of repairs would be equally painful. As a fellow machine-lover, Keiichi nodded with compassion over the poor Aston Martin, but Sayoko wasn't swayed.

"But he wouldn't stop bawling! Talk about pathetic!"

Completely disillusioned by her date's reaction, Sayoko had abandoned him on the spot and headed for the bar. Three bars later, she'd been wandering through the rain when she'd run into Keiichi.

"Turned out he was just a big baby putting on a show," she lamented.

She drained her glass and let out a deep sigh. The chunks of ice in her tumbler clinked musically.

"One more," she called to the bartender.

The bartender removed her glass, exposing the slightly damp coaster. Sayoko pulled a deep red jewelry box out of her Fendi bag and set it atop the coaster.

"What's that?" Keiichi asked.

"Oh, you don't know? It's called a 'love ring.'"

"Ah . . ."

The ornately patterned ring glimmered in the light. Now that he thought about it, Keiichi had been so busy working himself half to death that he hadn't thought about what he was going to buy with the money. *And Christmas is right around the corner . . .*

As Sayoko knocked back another drink, Keiichi asked tentatively, "I guess it makes a girl pretty happy when a guy gives her a ring, huh?"

"Oh, yes . . ." Sayoko's expression softened. "There's all kinds of jewelry . . . but a ring is really special."

She smiled dreamily, gazing off into space. "Even more so if it's from a guy you really care about."

"Ah . . ."

It was a dramatic shift from her usual snooty, aristocratic manner, and Keiichi was slightly startled.

She's a girl, after all . . .

As Keiichi gazed at the twinkling ring, an indescribable feeling came over him. His face reddened and his heart sped up as he imagined Belldandy's smiling face in its sparkle.

A ring . . . that's a great idea.

Belldandy would probably love it if he gave her a ring like this. He imagined himself blushing slightly as he slid it onto her ring finger . . . and then . . . and then . . .

For a moment, Keiichi's fantasies ran wild, but he forced himself to return to reality. That was when he noticed the smooth jazz playing on the sound system.

Ha-ha-ha . . . it must have been the music!

Intoxicated by the atmospheric strains, he gazed at the deep crimson box once more. He knew nothing of the cost of precious metals, let alone what such a ring might cost.

"By the way . . . how much does something like this . . ."

He began to ask Sayoko—just for reference—but when he looked up, she was gone.

"Where . . .?"

"Mademoiselle Sayoko retired to the powder room. Her garments were dry, and she went to change," the bartender informed him.

"Oh."

Apparently, time had continued to move in the real world while Keiichi had been lost in fantasy land. He picked up his glass, now wet with condensation, and gulped down the oolong tea.

If Sayoko had gone to change, she was probably ready to go home. Keiichi would finally be liberated. He glanced at his watch . . . less than two hours left until his next job.

If I rush straight home I might still be able to wolf down some dinner . . .

But that vain hope was to be cruelly shattered.

Sayoko emerged from the back wearing her clothes and coat. In spite of how much she'd drunk, she was still steady on her feet. The girl had class.

"The check, please . . . and Morisato-kun, I'll be needing a ride home."

"What?" Keiichi wondered if he had heard right as Sayoko

settled the bill with her gold card. "You want me . . . to give you a ride?"

He felt his dinner, and Belldandy's smile, recede into the distance.

"Why? You can take a taxi! I told you, I have to work . . ."

"But I had a date tonight so I only have my credit card on me."

"So?"

"So I don't have any cash."

"What?!"

"So I need a ride."

Keiichi was tempted to continue debating this princess-logic, but a pushover like him was no match for the likes of Sayoko. He wound up driving her home in the sidecar of his BMW.

Keiichi sighed deeply.

The moonlight shone on the wet pavement as he pulled up to a phone booth and removed his helmet. The hands on his watch had moved quite a bit since the last time he'd checked . . . he had less than fifty minutes left.

"Crap! Sayoko Mishima totally screwed up my schedule!"

He rummaged in his pocket for change but came up with nothing but silvery coins—at any other time, that would have been a good thing.

"No tens?"

He tried the other pocket and finally found a single ten yen coin. Glancing at his watch one more time, he slowly dialed the phone.

After I told Bell I'd be home for dinner . . .

Keiichi had never been so nervous calling his own house. After six rings that seemed to last an eternity, he heard someone answer.

"Belldandy, I'm so sorry!"

Keiichi began to apologize immediately. But the voice on the line wasn't the one he'd hoped to hear.

"Oh, it's just you, Keiichi."

"Skuld?"

Keiichi felt the strength drain from his body. Belldandy always answered the phone—it *would* have to be Skuld at a time like this.

"Um, can I speak to Bell . . ." he was about to ask Skuld to put Belldandy on, but remembered that his ten yen coin wouldn't last long. He'd rather talk to Belldandy, but if time ran out just as Skuld was calling her, all would be lost. He'd have to ask the little goddess to take a message.

"Tell Belldandy that I'm going straight to my next job and I'm sorry. I won't be home until morning so tell her not to wait up. And I'm sorry for missing dinner . . . I'll apologize properly when I get home."

"Fine. Bye." Skuld hung up abruptly, leaving the phone buzzing in Keiichi's ear. A blast of frigid air assailed him when he opened the door of the phone booth.

"Brr!"

Quickly, he turned up the collar of his jacket.

"Is that . . . snow?"

The rain had resumed once more, but now white crystals were beginning to replace the clear drops. Keiichi took a deep breath to restore his wilting determination and turned the ignition key. His sigh condensed into a white cloud and faded into the darkness.

"I just can't concentrate today!"

World Inventions Journal, a documentary show that chronicled epoch-making inventions and the great luminaries who had developed them, was approaching its climax. Against a background of placid classical music, the featured inventor was about to perform his final experiment. Normally, Skuld would have been on the edge of her seat, furiously scribbling notes, but not today. Her eyes gazed at the screen, but the information completely failed to reach her cerebrum.

"Booooring . . ." she complained, hugging her knees.

Riririririririri! The telephone in the hallway rang shrilly.

"Urd . . ."

For some reason, Skuld was sure the call was from Heaven. She made a wild rush for the phone and grabbed the receiver.

"Hello?" she squeaked with excitement.

"Belldandy, I'm so sorry!"

The voice at the other end wasn't the one she had hoped to hear.

"Oh, it's just you, Keiichi." Skuld wilted like a deflated balloon. But Keiichi took no notice of her reaction, babbling on about giving Belldandy a message.

Gimme a break!

Skuld felt her irritation mount.

"Fine. Bye," she said brusquely when Keiichi had said his piece. Then she slammed down the receiver.

Would it kill Urd to at least check in like that? Skuld pouted, glaring at the black telephone. Just then, she heard a gentle voice call her name.

"Skuld . . ."

"Oh . . . Belldandy!"

Belldandy stood behind her wearing an apron and a worried expression. Skuld felt a rush of embarrassment—Belldandy must have seen her taking out her frustrations on the phone.

"Who was that?" Belldandy asked.

"Keiichi. He says he's going straight to his next job. And that he's sorry he won't make it home for dinner."

"Oh . . ."

For a moment, the hallway fell silent apart from the faint sound of the television. *World Inventions Journal* was drawing to a close.

"Skuld, you were watching in Urd's room again, weren't you?" Belldandy said, looking perplexed. The door was open a crack and she could see the light of the TV.

Without Urd around to battle tooth and nail over television rights, Skuld had a complete monopoly over the TV in the tea room these days. But for some reason, she was completely uninterested in watching it. No matter how many times Belldandy scolded her, she watched the one in Urd's room instead.

"Skuld . . ."

Belldandy knew Skuld would sooner die than admit that she missed Urd. She put an arm around her stubborn little sister's shoulder and gave her a warm smile.

"Would you like some ice cream?"

Skuld nodded wordlessly.

In the warm tea room, a rice bowl and dishes of Belldandy's cooking waited on the low table. Belldandy covered the food with plastic wrap and took it back into the kitchen.

"After you went to all that trouble . . ." Skuld lamented.

"I don't mind, Skuld," Belldandy said softly, shaking her head. She returned to the tea room with Skuld's ice cream, then laid her dish towel over the rice bowl and reached for her knitting.

"It's just . . ." Skuld frowned, her spoon in her mouth. As far as she was concerned, anyone who wasted her beloved sister's home cooking deserved capital punishment. But Belldandy just smiled wanly.

"I'm the reason . . . Keiichi's working so hard," she said after a moment's hesitation.

"You are?" Skuld was taken aback.

". . . Yes."

Belldandy smiled, and a look of nostalgia came over her face.

When a year had passed since she'd first come to Earth and sealed her contract with Keiichi, Keiichi had presented her with a ring. He'd slaved away day and night, even depriving himself of sleep. And now, he was doing the same thing again.

"Well, that's a good thing . . ." Skuld's round, dark eyes peered into Belldandy's. ". . . Right?"

If Keiichi was going to give her a present again, Belldandy should have been happy—but she seemed to have a bad case of the blues. Skuld cocked her head.

"So how come you look so down in the dumps?" she asked.

For a moment, the look in Skuld's eyes reminded Belldandy of Keiichi. So full of worry, uncertainty, and irrepressible anticipation . . .

Oh, Keiichi! Belldandy looked away, unable to maintain Skuld's gaze. *Of course I'm glad . . . it's just that . . .*

Belldandy felt the turmoil rise in her heart, and she bit her lip to contain it. In the back of her mind, she could still hear Urd's voice.

"You want to see Keiichi's smile, don't you?"

Of course, Belldandy wanted nothing more. But what would really make Keiichi smile was if she could let down her guard.

"I understand, sis!" Without warning, Skuld grasped Belldandy's hand.

"Skuld . . ."

"Maybe it's important . . . and maybe they're working really hard . . . but both Keiichi and Urd should think about how it feels to be the one waiting at home all alone!"

Skuld seemed to have interpreted Belldandy's troubled frown as an expression of the same loneliness she was suffering. She nodded emphatically, her dark eyes moist with tears.

Yes . . . sometimes it isn't enough just to watch over someone.

Sometimes you need to respond to their feelings, too.

Softly, Belldandy placed a hand on Skuld's back. Keiichi must be feeling the same way—the same sadness of longing for someone just out of reach. As a Goddess First Class, Belldandy's mission was to bring Keiichi happiness. If she was causing him unhappiness by being overly cautious, she was putting the cart before the horse.

I wish I could make Keiichi smile from deep down inside.

Belldandy's heart throbbed. It was almost Christmas. On a day when people were so filled with happiness, perhaps she could afford to loosen up a little bit. It couldn't hurt to respond to Keiichi's feelings on just one day of the entire year.

A slight pink flush rose to Belldandy's white cheeks as she came to a decision.

"Skuld!" she said cheerfully. "Let's have a party on Christmas Day!"

Skuld looked up in surprise. "Do you mean it, Belldandy?" Her puppy-dog eyes sparkled. "Then . . . can we have a cake and a tree? And exchange presents . . ."

"Exchange presents?" Belldandy echoed.

"Yes! I read about it in *Flower Girls*. You decorate a tree, eat cake, and exchange presents by candlelight. Christmas is a very important holiday for sweethearts."

Skuld's melancholy vanished completely and a bright smile bloomed on her face as she lost herself in the world of her beloved *Dobon*. Belldandy looked on, smiling, when a startling realization occurred to her.

Come to think of it . . . I've never given Keiichi a real present!

Counting the past, she and Keiichi had spent more than four years together, but they'd never actually exchanged gifts. Once— though not for any particular occasion Belldandy had knit a sweater to give to Keiichi. But thanks to a bit of interference by Sayoko, Belldandy had missed the opportunity to present it to Keiichi in person. Ultimately, the sweater had found its way to Keiichi—but Keiichi had sort of missed the actual experience of receiving the gift.

Maybe I'll make him another sweater to give to him myself this time. I'll knit each stitch with love . . .

But immediately, she rejected the idea. If she put too much affection into the gift, it might cause trouble . . . she raised her head decisively.

Better make it something else . . .

But for some reason, that something else eluded her. She stared off into space, racking her brains.

"Belldandy . . . ? Are you okay?" Skuld asked gingerly.

Slowly, Belldandy turned her head.

"Skuld . . . What sort of present do you think Keiichi would like?"

"I Iuh?" That was a puzzler. Now it was Skuld's turn to freeze. "Keiichi?"

Really, Skuld hadn't the faintest idea. She'd never thought about it—to be quite honest, she never wasted much time thinking about Keiichi. But if something was troubling her beloved sister, far be it from Skuld to turn a deaf ear. It was a tougher challenge than math problems or debugging, but Skuld tackled the question head-on.

"Keiichi, huh? Keiichi . . ."

She fell silent, her eyebrows knit tightly as she struggled to recall things Keiichi had said and done.

"Now that you mention it . . . he did say that he chipped his screwdriver," Skuld mumbled, staring up at a spot on the ceiling.

The Phillips screwdriver Keiichi had chipped while working on his bike . . . Skuld had recommended that he buy a new one, but Keiichi had stubbornly refused. "Scratches are history," he'd said. "That goes for everything we use, including tools. Even when they get chipped, or worse, broken . . . when you've used something for a long time, through good times and bad, that makes that something one-of-a-kind. It makes it irreplaceable."

"A screwdriver . . ."

Gradually, Skuld coaxed the incident out of her large pool of slumbering memories. She could see it all still in the back of her mind. Keiichi's every gesture and word brought a feeling of deep warmth to Belldandy's heart.

"Oh . . . but that was before the reset!" Skuld remembered.

Great—she'd gone to all the trouble of remembering only to realize that the event bore no relevance to this reality. Skuld sat up and stretched deeply, trying to revive her flagging concentration. She opened the shutters, hoping to clear the air a bit.

"Ooh!" Skuld exclaimed. A white veil blanketed the landscape. "Belldandy, it's snowing"

A sprinkling of pure white dusted the paving stones, cherry trees, and ginkgos, transforming the familiar yard into an entirely different landscape.

"Oh, how lovely!"

Belldandy brought her face up to the glass and gazed out.

The snowflakes fluttered down from Heaven, evenly blanketing the earth. The delicate, white snow-fairies were as pure and beautiful as Holy Bell's wings.

With dazzling lights and twinkling Christmas tree ornaments, the holy and romantic night leading up to the big holiday was a white Christmas Eve. Every nook and cranny of the landscape was covered in snow. It was an enchanted, silvery world.

The streets were filled with bustling crowds, and "Jingle Bells" played cheerfully in the shops . . . or at least, that's how it should have been. But the snow hadn't let up for even a minute since it had begun falling a week ago, and the streets were deserted.

Today, too, the celestial emissaries poured tirelessly out of the sky.

"Ugh! Clearing the roof, I see . . ."

Megumi's breath made white puffs as she climbed the stone steps to Tarikihongan Temple. Directly ahead of her, she could see Keiichi up on top of the roof.

"Heave-ho!" Keiichi shouted, cheerfully absorbed in his work.

"How can he enjoy that?" Megumi let out a half-exasperated sigh as she made her way across the already-cleared stone walkway. Snowmen and snow caves dotted the yard.

"Oh, Megumi! What're you doing here?" a voice asked suddenly from above. Keiichi had finally noticed her presence. He wiped the sweat from his brow and waved.

"I brought you something from Takano." Megumi held up the plastic shopping bag she was carrying. The bag looked like it might give out at any minute under the weight of its lumpy contents.

"No, I mean, what are you doing *here*? What happened to your trip?"

"Oh . . . *Ah-ha-ha-ha!*" Megumi grimaced. "It got canceled. Because of all the snow."

Megumi had been planning her trip since autumn and had sold her camera to Keiichi for 30,000 yen to pay for the reservations. It had promised to be quite a treat—a scenic drive to the inn, hot springs, and a fancy dinner—but the unforeseen snow had ruined everything. First, Megumi's friend had been afraid to drive on the snowy roads, so they'd switched to rail travel at the last minute. Just as they were beginning to look forward to traveling by train, the rail lines had been fully suspended. The only options left to them were walking and flying, and two days ago they'd finally called in their official cancelation.

"Jeez, that's too bad."

"Yeah, well, what can you do? You can't argue with nature. Besides, they made a special exception and waived the cancellation fee. The travel agency's giving us back half the money, too."

"Wow."

"Well, there's never been a snowstorm like this before, ever. I guess a bunch of other customers raised a big stink. So they're returning our money as long as we sign up for another package. We've already made reservations for next spring."

"Good work." That was Keiichi's little sister—she was no pushover.

"Besides, I managed to get one of the last slots in the special intensive course at school. So I guess it was a blessing in disguise."

For the past few years, it had become a holiday tradition to hold a special class on Christmas day that was especially popular with the students.

"What're they teaching this year?"

"Aerodynamics!" Megumi chuckled triumphantly.

That did sound like a stroke of luck. So much so that Keiichi was a little envious. Megumi always got all the breaks, and Keiichi felt a sudden urge to mess with her a little bit. He scooped up an extra large shovelful of snow and tossed it down. It made a heavy crunching sound as it collided with the snow below.

"All right, then, you can help me clear the roof!"

"No way!" Megumi's refusal was immediate. "Forget it! I did plenty of roof-clearing up until last year!"

Megumi hated snow. More specifically, she hated the way it accumulated needlessly on the roads and rooftops. You had to clear the roof or it would damage your home, and you had to clear the streets in order to get anywhere. More than anything, it bothered her that the snow made such a royal nuisance of itself and then disappeared in the spring as if it had never existed. Not that she would have preferred for it to stick around all year long, but there was something unspeakably irksome about having all that wintertime hard work completely nullified.

"I'll leave it to you, since you seem to be having such a blast. Besides, I need to talk to Belldandy." Without giving Keiichi a chance to respond, Megumi hurried off toward the house at a faster clip than before.

Ha! What a hypocrite! Back at home, Kei-chan hated shoveling the roof, too!

The handle of the plastic bag was digging into Megumi's fingers and she transferred it to her other hand as she opened the front door.

"Helloooo!" she called. Megumi treated the temple like her own home.

"Yes?"

The paper door at the end of the hallway slid open. The aroma that wafted forth was so tantalizing that it made Megumi's stomach rumble.

"Oh, Megumi! Come in!" Belldandy emerged wearing an apron and oven mitt.

Ah . . . they're having a Christmas party!

Now it all made sense. No wonder Keiichi had been in such high spirits.

"Looks like I brought these at just the right time," Megumi said, plopping down the heavy bag.

"What are they?" Belldandy kneeled and peeked into the bag. A smile spread across her face. "Oh, potatoes!"

Stuffed full of plump tubers, the bag gave off a pleasant, earthy smell.

"These are all for us? Are you sure?"

"Takano . . . our mother in Hokkaido, sent a whole box from home. I'll never get through all of them alone, so I thought you could help."

Even now, Megumi still had more than half a box left. She'd eaten a few, but she lived alone and her repertoire of potato recipes was limited. She could only make potato salad or baked potatoes . . . and maybe potato croquettes if she really pulled out all the stops.

"If it weren't for all this snow, I would have brought you the whole box . . ."

The truth was that Megumi much preferred for Belldandy to cook the potatoes so that she could come over and eat them. It seemed like that was kinder to the potatoes, too. Belldandy smiled—she could tell what Megumi was thinking.

"I'd better cook up a storm and you can help us eat them!"

"Hooray! Belldandy, you're the greatest!" Megumi threw up her hands with joy, just as the roar of an engine drowned out her cheers.

"What's that?" She turned in surprise just as the front door flew open.

"I'm home, sister dearest!"

Skuld burst into the room, her arms laden with packages. She plunked them down on the floor. The shopping bags overflowed with party goods: everything from poppers and party hats to lights, garlands, and tree decorations.

"Wow, what a haul!" Megumi marveled.

"Yeah, well, it's going to be a spectacular party!" Skuld removed her snowy goggles. "There's more outside. Come help!" She grabbed Megumi's hand and dragged her outside without giving her a choice in the matter.

"Whoa! What on earth . . . ?"

Megumi gaped at the futuristic vehicle parked just outside the front door. Skuld puffed out her chest with pride at Megumi's surprised reaction.

"Isn't it fabulous?" she clucked. "It's the 'Banpei-kun Cold Climate Attachment: Snow Rider V3,' or the 'Banpei-kun V3' for short."

For short? Megumi wondered. Its shape resembled that of a snowmobile but Banpei's round head stared out from its prow, creating an effect that was somehow cute and disturbing at the same time. The V3 was painted red, white, and black. Skuld grew increasingly pleased the longer Megumi stared at it.

"I'll give you a ride on it sometime."

"Uh-huh . . ." Megumi responded noncommittally, smiling politely and nodding. Skuld thrust a load of packages into her arms.

"Here, take these."

She must have bought out half the store. These bags were full of ornaments and artificial holly.

"Time to start decorating!" Skuld scampered energetically into the house with another armload of loot. Megumi burst out laughing—Skuld reminded her of a busy worker bee.

"Sorry about that!" Megumi's felt her load lighten. Belldandy stood in the spot Skuld had just vacated, holding the packages Skuld had dumped on Megumi.

"No problem. You guys are really going all out, aren't you!"

"Yes! It's our first Christmas party, you see . . ."

Celebrations were always fun, no matter what the event. Especially for kids—not that Megumi would have expressed that sentiment to Skuld's face.

"You should join us, if you like!" Belldandy offered.

Megumi was about to nod, seduced by Belldandy's kind lavender eyes and the mouthwatering smell of her cooking. But just then, she heard another shovelful of snow plop down from the roof and stopped herself.

I'd better not.

It sounded like Keiichi was clearing the other side of the roof now. Megumi could hear the loud crunch of snow from behind the house.

This is Kei-chan's big day.

Megumi shook her head instead. "Sorry . . . I've got plans with a friend," she said lamely. "I'll take a rain check."

"Oh!"

For some reason, Belldandy's warm, guileless smile made

Megumi's conscience prick. *Geez, it's really hard to lie to her!* she thought.

". . . Later!" Megumi called, quickly making her exit.

Little mountains of snow surrounded the house, promising more snowmen to come. A new dusting of snow was already accumulating on the freshly exposed roof tiles.

Good luck, Kei-chan! Megumi sent a silent cheer of encouragement to her brother as she trotted down the stone steps.

Wonder if he'll manage to kiss her . . .

She fired up the engine of her KSR, tossed back her hair, and donned her jet helmet. Chuckling softly, she gave it the gas and executed a deft turn—she'd been raised in snow country, after all. The KSR purred happily as it disappeared down the snowy road in a puff of white smoke.

"I now present . . . the One-and-Only Skuld Shining Christmas Illumination Ceremony! And now . . . Switch Number One!"

An incredible display of ornaments and silver and gold garlands adorned the towering Japanese maple. As Skuld's finger flicked the switch, the entire tree lit up, including the star at the very top.

"It's beautiful!" Keiichi marveled, grinning from ear to ear.

"That's just the beginning! Switch Number Two—ON!"

This time, every tree in the compound lit up.

"And finally, Switch Number Three!"

The snowmen and snow huts that populated the yard flickered with colored lights. It was almost like the electrical parade at Disneyland.

"Oh, wow!"

The lights twinkled in the darkness, making the snow sparkle.

"What a fantastic party! The three of us are going to have a blast!" Keiichi cheered.

A lace tablecloth covered the low table, piled with fried chicken, potato gratin, green salad . . . and so many other dishes that it was hard to know where to begin.

"Fantastic!" Skuld cheered, flinging her fists up in the air. She was wearing a pointy party hat. "Merry Christmas!" she shouted.

She was trying so hard. "Don't worry," Keiichi said gently. "You know how much Urd loves a party. I bet she'll show up any time now."

Skuld inhaled sharply. "I wasn't . . ." her fists fell limply to her sides. "It doesn't matter to me!" she insisted, turning her face away and fidgeting with a party popper.

Urd had gone back to Heaven more than a month ago. Skuld had harbored faint hopes that she might make it home for Christmas, but there was still no sign of her return. Apparently Santa was deaf to a goddess' Christmas wish.

"I don't care. I'll eat Belldandy's special homemade cake all by myself. And I won't save any for Urd!" Skuld wiped away the tears welling up in her eyes and began to place candles in the cake resting atop the TV.

"That's right. The three of us are going to live it up! And since it's a special occasion, there's champagne for you, too, Skuld!" Impressed by the little goddess' machismo, Keiichi reached into the cooler and pulled out a small bottle of champagne rosé. The bubbly drink sparkled like a pink tourmaline.

But Skuld glared back at him. "Wait. You were treating me like a kid just now!"

"No!" Keiichi was trying his best to be kind, but somehow he'd offended her.

"Besides, alcohol doesn't get me drunk, you know!"

"Huh?" This was awkward. Keiichi was afraid that if he tried to backpedal, he'd only make things worse. Just then, the kitchen door slid open, rescuing the cornered Keiichi.

Smiling warmly, Belldandy emerged carrying an hors d'oeuvre plate loaded with meat and cheese. "Thank you for waiting!"

"Sister dearest!"

"Skuld, would you give me a hand?"

Just in the nick of time! But Keiichi's relief was soon eclipsed by astonishment. Hand-rolled sushi, croquettes, an entire roasted chicken . . . dish after dish came parading out of the kitchen.

". . ."

Belldandy had shut herself in the kitchen for so long that Keiichi had anticipated a feast . . . but this was beyond his wildest imaginings. There was more food than could fit on the table, and already the platters were spilling over onto the tatami mat floor.

"I made fruit punch, too!"

The pièce de résistance. Colorful chunks of fruit floated cheerfully in a great glass bowl. There was also fried shrimp,

Chinese pork dumplings, pasta, and pizza . . . Keiichi found himself growing faint as he gaped at the grand symphony of Japanese, Western, and Chinese delicacies in quantities worthy of an eating contest.

"I wonder if I'll be able to eat it all . . ."

As the space in the tea room was gradually crowded out by plates of food, a hearty yell resounded through the air. It was the last voice in the world Keiichi had hoped to hear at that moment.

"YO! MORISATO! MERRY CHRISTMAS!!"

The front door burst open.

". . . ?!"

Keiichi almost toppled over in surprise—was he hearing things? He ran toward the front door, praying that he was mistaken.

"T-T-Tamiya?"

But his prayers went unanswered. It was Tamiya, all right. And not only him . . . it was also Ōtaki and the entire Motor Club.

"Wh-wh-why . . . ?" Keiichi stammered in disbelief.

Tamiya grinned down at him disdainfully, waving a mostly full bottle of sake. "Lookee whut I brought!"

". . ."

As Keiichi struggled to overcome his own stubborn disbelief, his mind searched desperately for an escape route. But his efforts were interrupted by Skuld's belated appearance.

"They really came!" she marveled softly.

"What?"

"I ran into them down at the shopping center when I was out buying stuff . . . and I told them we were having a Christmas party . . ."

"And?"

"They looked like they really wanted to come, so I said, 'why not stop by if you're not doing anything' . . ."

"You said that?!"

"I never thought they'd actually come!"

"Skuld, think of who you're talking about here . . ."

Ever since Tamiya and Otaki had been banned from the Motor Club, they'd been bored out of their minds. A Christmas party at the Morisato place was the perfect opportunity for them to cut loose—there was no way they'd pass up the invitation.

"We's gonna party it up tonight!"

The whoops and cheers of the Motor Club members echoed across the temple grounds.

There goes my romantic night . . .

Keiichi sank weakly to the ground, wondering if the earth would swallow up his limp body.

"Number 37, Toraichi Tamiya! I'll be singing 'Ship of Cousins'!"

"Yo, Den-chan! We've been waiting for this moment!"

The room filled with cheers as Tamiya struck a pose, brandishing the portable karaoke machine's microphone.

"Excuse me! Is there any more ice?"

"Coming right up!"

The Motor Club had annihilated the mountain of food. In no time at all, every last bite had disappeared into their stomachs, leaving behind a trail of empty plates. The large bottle of sake they had brought rolled on the floor, and the other sake they'd run back out to buy was already half gone.

"I'm sorry, Belldandy!" Keiichi apologized, bowing his head as Belldandy ran back and forth tending the guests.

"There's nothing to be sorry about! I'm having a wonderful time!" Belldandy surprised Keiichi by flashing a smile of genuine happiness. "We're all here together for Christmas—and best of all, Skuld's having so much fun . . ."

Skuld was playing cards with the Motor Club members and laughing up a storm. It had been a long time since she'd been in such high spirits.

"That's true."

Keiichi couldn't help smiling. His romantic Christmas hadn't materialized, but maybe a Christmas of wild festivity wasn't such a bad thing either.

The boisterous laughter and singing lasted into the wee hours of the morning.

Just when it seemed like it might never stop, the snowfall dwindled to a halt. The heavy clouds that had blanketed the sky vanished, and a bright silver moon lit up the sky.

Keiichi sat down alone on the edge of the veranda, enjoying the bracing winter air as it cooled his flushed skin.

"Everyone's fallen asleep."

Keiichi turned—he hadn't heard Belldandy's approach. Her fair skin shone in the moonlight.

"You must be tired . . . that was quite a Christmas party!" Keiichi commented.

His heart raced, but he willed himself to act natural.

"You must be tired, too, Keiichi!"

Belldandy smiled, her pale yellow dress fluttering in the breeze. She'd finally removed her apron.

The temple grounds twinkled with Skuld's Christmas lights.

"Keiichi . . ."

". . . Yes?"

"May I sit . . . next to you?"

"S-sure."

Without making a sound, Belldandy sat down so close that Keiichi could feel her shoulder against his. He thought he detected a sweet fragrance, like the perfume of flowers. Her chestnut hair brushed against his cheek, and Keiichi felt like his heart might explode.

"The snow stopped . . ." he observed.

"So it did."

Keiichi felt his hands grow clammy with sweat as the inside of his mouth dried up, making it hard to talk.

"The moon is really beautiful."

"Yes."

He was having a hard time getting a conversation going. Just then, he felt a gentle weight against his shoulder.

". . . !"

Belldandy was leaning her head against him!

"~~~~~~~~~~~"

Keiichi was so elated he thought he might die. Adrenaline surged through his body, and tears of joy filled his eyes.

Man, I'm glad to be alive!

As Keiichi's heart roiled with turbulent emotion, he gazed up at the heavens. The frozen night sky was absolutely pure, and the glittering white earth was absolutely quiet.

"Keiichi?"

The warmth left Keiichi's shoulder after what seemed both an eternity and a heartbeat. Belldandy straightened up and peered into his face.

"Wh-what?" Keiichi asked, unable to conceal his disappointment.

Belldandy thrust a large package tied with a red ribbon into his hands.

"Merry Christmas!"

"Oh!" At first, Keiichi was surprised, but then a slow grin spread across his face. "Th-thank you!" he stammered.

Keiichi had never imagined that Belldandy might give him a present. He grasped the large, weighty package in both hands as happily as a child. "Wow! You really shouldn't have!"

The grin on his face filled Belldandy's heart with happiness.

"Can I open it?"

"Yes."

The ribbon fell away.

"I hope you like it . . ."

Belldandy's heart raced. What a peculiar feeling! She hadn't realized that giving someone a present was exciting for the giver, too. For the first time, she was filled with the satisfaction of handing someone a gift.

Keiichi unwrapped the box and opened the lid. He let out a whoop of excitement.

"Oh, wow!"

A total of six pro-style screwdrivers lay nestled in the box, three Phillips and three standard ones, arranged in an alternating pattern. Keiichi couldn't take his eyes of their handles. Nowadays, plastic or hard rubber handles were the norm, but these drivers had wooden grips. The wood grain of the Phillips drivers was stained a deep maroon, and the standard drivers were a dark ivy green. They were so elegant and beautifully crafted, they seemed more like works of art than mere tools.

"They're so different from the ones you normally use that I wasn't sure . . . but I was drawn by the warmth of the wood . . ." Belldandy said shyly, and Keiichi felt his heart fill with affection.

It must have been difficult for Belldandy to pick them out—she was no screwdriver aficionado, after all. She'd gone to all the trouble of finding them, just for him. That alone was enough to make Keiichi's heart grow hot.

"Thank you, Belldandy. I love them!"

"Do you really?"

"Yes! These are made by a company called Suzuka Circuit, and I've been curious about their products for a while."

Belldandy had decided on the screwdrivers after hearing Skuld's story and giving the matter a great deal of consideration. When she saw how happy Keiichi looked as he gazed down at them, she was overcome with relief.

Thank goodness he likes them!

The moon was beginning to hang low in the sky as dawn approached. In the northern sky, Polaris shone almost as brightly as the full moon.

"You know something strange? I had a dream that someone gave me a screwdriver." Keiichi remembered suddenly as he looked down at the gleaming tools.

"A dream?"

"Yeah . . . it was when I was unconscious, after the ghost hunt incident."

Keiichi had dreamt that he was still living in the N.I.T. dormitory. One day as he was doing homework in his room, he heard a sudden knock at the door. When he went to answer it, there was nobody there. But a strange machine sat on the floor of the hallway. This seemed odd, but Keiichi picked up the machine and examined it. Immediately, he was entranced. Its inner workings were full of beautiful, arcane machinery—he had never seen anything like it. There was a part that was broken, and Keiichi couldn't bear to leave it that way.

"I simply had to fix it," he explained to Belldandy.

It was difficult fixing an unfamiliar machine, but somehow Keiichi had managed it. He'd returned it to the hallway where he'd found it and, satisfied, had gone to sleep. When he awoke—still in his dream—he'd opened the door again only to find that the machine was gone. In its place was a single screwdriver, as if it had been left for him as a thank-you gift.

"It must have been déjà vu—no, wait, I mean, a premonition—that you were going to give me these . . ." Keiichi concluded cheerfully.

But in contrast, Belldandy's smile had faded.

A Machiners dream . . .

It was hard to be sure simply from what Keiichi had just told her, but Belldandy was fairly certain. Machiners were actually a type of mysterious creature that resembled machines. They were very rare and goddess magic had little or no effect on them. For that reason, it was difficult for even Belldandy to help them when they were hurt.

One day, the Machiners would seek Keiichi out for his unbridled affection for all things mechanical . . . but that wasn't due to happen until much later. Before the system restore, this had taken place around four years after Belldandy and Keiichi had first met.

Had time become somehow distorted?

But this was a dream, not an actual event. Perhaps the apparition that had nearly caused a spacial rupture had enabled Keiichi to glimpse the future somehow.

Everything's fine . . . just fine. As long as I'm careful . . .

Belldandy assured herself, trying to quell the panic welling up inside.

Just then, Keiichi extended a small package toward the frowning Belldandy.

"Er . . . Merry Christmas, from me."

Stiff with nervousness, Keiichi proffered the gift with trembling hands. From the anxious smile on his face, it was evident that he'd noticed the shift in Belldandy's mood.

"I just want you to know how grateful I am to you, every single day . . ."

Keiichi had been waiting for the right moment to give Belldandy her gift, and now he felt slightly embarrassed that she'd beat him to the chase. He plowed ahead anyway, gripping the pretty little box tied with a gold ribbon with heartfelt emotion. "Belldandy . . . I hope you'll stay by my side forever."

As he repeated the words he'd said to her when they'd first sealed their contract, Belldandy looked straight back into his eyes.

She knew she should be happy to receive his present, but her emotions were in turmoil. Perhaps it was because of her anxiety at hearing about the Machiners dream. No—it was more than that—it was also her ambivalence about allowing Keiichi to get too close.

Should I really go ahead and accept it? She wondered as tears sprang to her lavender eyes.

"Um . . . Belldandy?"

Keiichi's dark eyes filled with sadness, and Belldandy knew she'd upset him.

"I'm sorry," she found herself saying. She smiled through her tears. "I'm sorry . . . I'm just so happy . . ."

Immediately, Keiichi's anxiety melted away.

"Oh, good! I . . ."

His cheeks flushed a bright red, and he held out the present once more.

It's just that I swore I'd protect you.

Belldandy gently accepted the tiny box and gazed at it tenderly. Keiichi looked on, his heart pounding.

"May I open it?"

"Yes."

She carefully undid the ribbon and opened the lid of the box. A beige ring case rested inside.

"I hope you like it . . ."

Delicately, she opened the lid. Inside, a gold tiara-shaped ring glittered with tiny diamonds.

". . . It's beautiful!" Belldandy exclaimed. When Yggdrasil had been reset, everything in the previous world had ceased to exist and everything that existed now was different. But still, the ring filled Belldandy with a feeling of nostalgia.

"I really don't know anything about brands or anything, so I looked at a lot of different types—but I thought this tiara design suited you the best," Keiichi explained bashfully.

"Thank you, Keiichi."

How many shops had Keiichi visited to find this delicate, ornate little ring? Belldandy imagined him combing the jewelry shops as he hustled from job to job.

"Will you put it on for me?" Belldandy said, gently handing the case back to Keiichi.

"Oh!" Once again, adrenaline surged through Keiichi's system. It was almost unnerving to have his dreams play out exactly as he'd imagined. *Yikes! It's just like my fantasy!*

He swallowed.

"Really?"

"Yes."

Keiichi could feel every pore in his body dilate. Softly, he took a deep breath and picked up the ring. Awkwardly, he took Belldandy's left hand.

Oh, geez! It's like a wedding!

He felt himself breathing harder as he slowly slid the ring onto Belldandy's ring finger. The tiara sparkled against her fair skin.

"Merry Christmas, Belldandy."

"Merry Christmas, Keiichi."

The Christmas lights glittered like the stars of the Milky Way above, illuminating Keiichi and Belldandy's faces as they smiled at one another. But just then, a shadow fell across their faces. Out of nowhere, black clouds appeared in the sky, shrouding the moon in darkness.

A gust of wind blew through the trees, scattering the snow accumulated on their branches.

Belldandy's ring sparkled as she brought her left hand to her heart and squeezed her right hand into a fist. The icy air chilled the silent night.

*　　*　　*

K A Z A B A N A — W I N D F L O W E R

"What a glorious day!"

Keiichi slid the glass door open with a vigorous thrust. A gust of frigid air blew into the room, chilled by the frozen landscape. Keiichi took a deep breath, ignoring the cold jolt to his sinuses. It was incredible how fantastic it felt to see the sun for the first time in weeks.

"All right! Here we go!" he shouted, full of energy. Wearing a headband fashioned from a twisted towel, he stretched up to his full height in front of the blue sky as he hoisted a broom in one hand, a garbage bag in the other. Even the chirping of the swallows as they darted cheerfully back and forth between the roof and the trees sounded like a rousing fight song to his ears.

"Sheesh! What're you so happy about?" Skuld muttered sullenly. The room was a shambles, littered with empty cans and bottles and food wrappers as far as the eye could see. The fun was over, and Skuld couldn't see any reason to be excited now.

"Oh . . . *ah-ha-ha-ha-ha!*"

Keiichi was full of exuberance today. He broke into a grin just thinking about exchanging presents with Belldandy the night before, and the world seemed like a wonderful place.

"There's nothing wrong with being happy, is there?" he said, and picked up a can near his feet to hide the fact that he was blushing. "The sun is shining, the birds are singing . . . it's a beautiful day to clean the house!"

"*What?*"

"*Ha-ha-ha-ha!*"

Skuld sighed. There was no point in talking to someone so happy that all they did was laugh.

"Idiot!" she muttered.

Out of the corner of her eye, Skuld watched as Keiichi cheerfully went to work picking up trash. Reluctantly, she retrieved the dustpan and looked around the room once more. The memory of singing and celebrating with everyone was still fresh in her mind. And yet . . .

"Those jerks!"

She threw down the plastic dustpan, and it bounced softly against the tatami mat floor.

Why should we have to clean everything up by ourselves? It's not fair! Skuld puffed out her cheeks indignantly.

After a few hours' sleep, the members of the Motor Club had skulked off before the sun was even up. Didn't anyone ever teach them to clean up their own mess?

"I don't want to clean up!" Skuld was too outraged to focus on tackling the mess.

The best option was to go straight back to her room, or to go out somewhere, but with her beloved sister leading the clean-up effort, Skuld couldn't bring herself to desert.

"I wish there was some easy way to clear this all up . . ." She mused, staring at the dustpan on the floor. Suddenly, she had a flash of inspiration.

"As long as the house gets clean . . . that's what matters, right?"

Skuld's eyes sparkled and her face brightened. It was hardly a challenge for a brilliant inventor!

"I'm a genius!" Nodding enthusiastically at her own idea, Skuld raced back to her room, humming a little tune.

Meanwhile, Keiichi continued to clean away, oblivious to Skuld. Now and then, he balled up a scrap of paper and posed like a pitcher on the mound before winding up and tossing the scrap into the bag of garbage.

"He throws the pitch!" Keiichi intoned, playing both athlete and sports commentator.

The ball of paper arced gracefully and dropped straight into the garbage bag.

"Strike one!"

Keiichi imagined a cheering crowd as he did a little victory dance. Encouraged, he picked up another scrap of paper and balled it up.

"It's the bottom of the ninth. The last batter steps up to the plate . . ."

Keiichi stood at the ready. He shook his head no several times at the catcher behind the garbage bag—he didn't want to throw a curve or a slider. He wanted this last pitch to be a fastball. He grinned at the sullen catcher, and finally nodded when the catcher gave him the sign for a straight pitch.

"The pitcher's getting ready . . . he winds up . . ."

Keiichi lifted his left leg high. "Here it comes!"

The paper baseball was just about to leave Keiichi's hand when . . .

"I guess we're doing our New Year's cleaning!" a sweet voice said behind him.

"Yikes!"

The paper ball slipped out of Keiichi's hand and curved listlessly through the air, losing momentum far short of the trash bag and landing at Belldandy's feet.

"Oh dear! You almost had it!" Smiling, she retrieved the scrap and dropped it into the garbage.

"B-belldandy!"

Flustered, Keiichi grabbed the dustpan and turned the other way. He was embarrassed that she'd walked in on him playing pitcher, but that wasn't the only thing making him flustered. All morning, he'd had a hard time looking her straight in the face.

"I rinsed out the cleaning rags. Here!"

"Oh, right!" Keiichi's heart thudded as Belldandy proffered the rag. She wore a Japanese apron, a kerchief in her hair, and the tiara ring glimmered on her finger. At breakfast, too, Keiichi hadn't been able to take his eyes off the ring whenever she was near. He was overjoyed that he'd managed to bridge the distance between them even just a little bit.

She's just handing me a rag. It's not like we're going to hold hands or anything . . .

Even though it was the most mundane of interactions, Keiichi felt strangely self-conscious. He could feel every capillary in his body dilate as he broke into a sweat. Belldandy's hair streamed down from her triangular kerchief like sunshine filtering through leafy trees. Just as Keiichi was about to touch her delicate hand . . .

"Hey, check it out, you guys!"

The youngest goddess came bounding into the room with her usual lethal timing. Keiichi was filled with a mixture of dejection and relief at being rescued from the final frontier of his self-control.

So close . . . and yet so far!

Keiichi's white-hot energy was not to be allowed to reach full incineration. Skuld barged in right between Keiichi and Belldandy, oblivious to the former's state of imperfect combustion.

"It's the Litter-Picker-Upper Tottoko Mark 2!"

She held up a lidded plastic container that resembled a garbage can.

What about Mark 1? Keiichi was about to ask, but he stopped himself just in time. Mark 1 had probably turned out unsuccessful, and Mark 2 was the improved version. In the past year, Keiichi had learned a thing or two about dealing with temperamental goddesses.

"I'll have this mess cleaned up in nothing flat!"

Skuld cleared her throat, satisfied that all eyes were upon her. She set down the Tottoko Mark 2 in the middle of the room and raised the antenna next to its lid.

"All systems go!"

Skuld hit the start button on her remote controller. A motor began to hum and the power light lit up. The machine rattled, its plastic lid vibrating. Suddenly, the lid popped open and multiple arms extended from the container. It looked like

Avalokiteshvara, the thousand-armed bodhisattva.

"Eep!" Keiichi backed away from the freakish machine. The Tottoko Mark 2 extended an arm straight toward him, plucked up a piece of garbage at his feet, and tossed it rapidly into the plastic can.

"Whoa!"

"And that's not all!"

That was when Keiichi noticed that the other hands were all performing separate tasks—one wielding a broom while another polished with a rag.

"Wow!"

Skuld cackled with satisfaction at Keiichi's amazement.

"Ho-ho! This place'll be gleaming in no time! What do you think?"

"It's wonderful, Skuld!"

Skuld basked in Belldandy's praise. "Tell you what . . . I'll finish cleaning the rest of the house!"

"Oh!"

As Skuld puffed out her chest and did a proud little dance, her invention had the room spic-and-span in under ten minutes.

"You can kick back and have a rest, sister dearest!" she crowed as she picked up the Tottoko Mark 2 and moved into the next room.

"Should we really?" Keiichi and Belldandy exchanged glances.

They could take advantage of Skuld's generosity and leave everything to her—but the weather was just too perfect. It would have been a waste to spend such a beautiful day lounging around. Keiichi tied up the bag of garbage he'd collected and tossed it outside.

"I think I'll take advantage of this sunshine and clear the snow around the great hall," Keiichi said. He'd already shoveled the area around the house, but the area near the great hall remained untouched. It could be treacherous if the deep snow turned to ice overnight.

"I'll tackle the kitchen and bathroom!" Belldandy announced.

The fir tree twinkled apologetically in the yard. Christmas was over, and the big New Year's cleaning was in full swing at Tarikihongan Temple.

It was amazing how dirty the refrigerator got just from the groceries. Belldandy wiped out the inside with a damp cloth to remove the grime and crumbs. She worked carefully and thoroughly, cleaning every last corner, but moving quickly so as not to let too much cold air escape.

"Thank you for always serving us so well."

Belldandy smiled as she closed the newly clean refrigerator door. The refrigerator's motor purred happily.

"Now for the sink!"

Belldandy's ring twinkled as she reached for the dishes in the dish drainer.

Keiichi's smiling!

The time they'd spent together the previous night was a happy memory for Belldandy, too. As she gazed at the ring, her heart filled with warmth.

Everything's fine—things are peaceful, and as long as I continue to be careful . . . everything should be all right.

Christmas Eve had come and gone without any major trouble. Belldandy was concerned about the Machiners dream, but for now, all she could do was wait and deal with things as they happened.

Keiichi's rice bowl was resting in the dish drainer. Belldandy was about to pick it up and dry it off when it slipped out of her grasp—as if of its own will—spinning in the air.

"Oh!"

The bowl shattered as it hit the floor. The fragments flew everywhere—it was a painful sight to behold. As Belldandy looked down at them, an unspeakable fear gripped her heart. Immediately, she dashed toward the front door.

"Keiichi . . . ?!"

She burst out of the house in a panic, but outside, the temple grounds were calm and quiet. White clouds floated in the blue sky like feathers, and the snow on the ground sparkled in the sunlight. An icy crust had formed on its surface, and clear footprints lead towards the Great Hall.

I don't sense any malevolent forces . . .

Carefully but quickly, Belldandy followed Keiichi's footprints. The persimmon tree's branches sagged under the weight of the snow. Suddenly, the snowy path toward the Great Hall came to an abrupt end. There was a small area—roughly the size of two tatami mats—that was clear of snow, exposing the paving stones underneath. This must be where Keiichi had been shoveling last.

"Keiichi . . . ?"

The footprints led back and forth from a small mound of snow but there was no sign of Keiichi. Belldandy circled around the other side, but found only a beautiful blanket of snow, with no indication of anyone's presence.

Where on Earth . . . ?

Belldandy glanced worriedly around the yard. How had he disappeared so suddenly? She gazed up at the roof of the Great Hall. Pure white snow blanketed the gently sloped roof in picturesque drifts. There was just one spot where the tiles were exposed. Directly below, there was a large mound of snow. Belldandy raised her hands toward the suspicious mountain.

It can't be!

As she focused her attention, a horrified expression rose to Belldandy's face. It couldn't be, but it was! She could feel Keiichi's presence distinctively from inside the mountain of snow!

"Holy Bell!" she cried sharply. There wasn't a moment to lose. The angel appeared immediately, scattering white feathers that blended perfectly with the snow. The two joined hands and their eyes met briefly as they began to sing in harmony.

"O Snow . . . rise up and dance in the Wind . . ."

A gust of wind began to swirl, sweeping up the nearby snow from the ground. But the mountain of snow remained untouched.

It's no good. Not enough power!

Compacted by gravity, the mounded snow was harder than she'd anticipated.

It may send Keiichi flying . . . but right now the important thing is to get him out!

Belldandy looked up at Holy Bell and nodded decisively. Then she summoned her energies.

"Holy Storm!"

The whirlwind turned into a powerful tornado, spiraling into the mound of snow like a sinuous whip. But even the raging funnel failed to disturb the mountain.

The magic of a Goddess First Class had no effect? Belldandy's eyes widened in disbelief.

Why didn't it work . . . ?

The image of the Jomon Cedar on Yakushima flashed into her mind. Nature was resisting her once again! But unlike before, this time she wasn't using a life-giving spell. The spell to clear away the snow was a simple one. Then why . . .

Desperately, Belldandy quieted the desperate fear in her heart and shouted at the top of her lungs. "Skuld! . . . Skuld!"

"What is it, sister dearest?"

The little goddess came running out, still carrying the Tottoko 2. She'd never heard such desperation in her sister's voice. In a flash, she was by the pale-faced Belldandy's side.

"Sis?"

"Please . . . I need your help, Skuld!"

"Wha . . . ?"

"Keiichi's buried under this mountain of snow!"

"What?!"

This was terrible. Skuld understood now why Belldandy was so frantic. But she still didn't understand why her sister needed her help. It should have been a snap with Belldandy's powers.

"Then why don't you use a spell . . ." Skuld began. As she looked up, she caught sight of the worry welled up in Holy Bell's eyes. Something was wrong. Skuld was seized with uneasiness. Belldandy's answer came as a tremendous shock.

"My magic isn't working."

"It isn't working?!"

Belldandy's magic was supremely powerful, even for a goddess. How could her spell fail? Skuld's mind raced.

Skuld couldn't believe that Belldandy could be at fault. That was impossible. In that case, Yggdrasil had to be malfunctioning. Now that Skuld thought about it, that troublemaker Urd was up in Heaven right now! She'd probably screwed something up! That had to be it . . . it all made sense.

"Got it, sis. Leave it to me."

The words tumbled readily out of Skuld's mouth, but she didn't actually have any brilliant solution in mind.

"Oh! I'll use the Banpei Riot Control Attachment . . ."

Her eyes fell on the immense steel form buried in the snow—extreme circumstances called for extreme measures. But immediately, she abandoned the idea. If she used too much force, she might end up hurting Keiichi. Besides, it could take hours to dig the thing out of the snow.

"And Banpei isn't charged up . . ."

Skuld had devoted the power supply to her Christmas lights display, and Banpei idled listlessly near the front door of the house, his red light threatening to die at any moment. The only machine left was the Tottoko 2 she held in her arms.

"Okay—let's give it a whirl."

Skuld set the Tottoko 2 down at the base of the snow mountain and opened the panel next to its container. Quickly, she rewired several connections and activated its power switch.

"That ought to boost its power . . ."

The machine's motor whirred a shade louder now as its arms extended from underneath the container's lid. It began to dig rapidly through the snow like a mole.

"Go, Tottoko 2!" Skuld cheered.

As the machine burrowed ferociously through the snow, the mound began to visibly crumble. A faint trail of smoke rose up as the device labored against its formidable task. It was then that a green windbreaker became visible in the snow—it was Keiichi's hunched form, crouching under the shield of his snow shovel.

"Keiichi!"

Carefully, Belldandy pulled Keiichi's limp body out of the snow. She leaned toward his icy cheek. His breath was faint but regular.

"Oh, thank goodness!"

Keiichi had managed to escape suffocation by crouching just

as the snow had fallen, creating a little bit of space, and his snow shovel had helped by shielding him from above.

The snow on the roof was beginning to drip, and chunks of it fell from the bent persimmon tree. The sun shone down benevolently as Belldandy hugged Keiichi's wet body.

"Belldandy . . ." Skuld looked up at her sister. She'd been waiting in the corridor.

"Everything's all right now."

Belldandy had tucked Keiichi into his futon, and he was snoring peacefully. His face had been blue when they'd dug him out of the snow, but now his cheeks were tinged with red and it was clear that his body was warming up again.

"He'll feel better by nighttime."

"Your healing magic worked?"

"Yes."

Skuld breathed a sigh of relief. She'd been more worried about Belldandy's well-being than Keiichi's.

"Thank you so much, Skuld. If it hadn't been for you . . ."

Belldandy embraced her little sister.

"I did it for you, sister dearest!"

As she basked in her sister's sweet fragrance, Skuld's dark eyes shone with pride. Now that the crisis was over, Skuld suddenly remembered her anger. She turned on her heel and strode down the corridor toward the telephone.

"I bet this is Urd's fault, sis! She must have crashed the system again! I'm going to get to the bottom of this . . ."

Skuld yanked the receiver from its cradle, determined to give Urd a piece of her mind for causing her beloved Belldandy such suffering. But a gentle hand stopped her.

"Sis . . ."

"Let me," Belldandy said as she took the receiver and slowly dialed the number.

If there was a problem with the Yggdrasil system, there would be various repercussions on Earth, and Belldandy would have to take certain measures. Besides, right now, she felt a desperate need to hear Urd's voice.

There's so much I want to tell you, sis . . .

Belldandy's heart raced with anticipation as the phone rang. After four or five rings, there was a click at the other end as somebody answered.

"Hello?"

"Why, if it isn't Belldandy! Long time no see, *cherie!*" the voice on the line crooned in honeyed tones.

"Peorth . . ."

Belldandy's heart sank. But she recovered quickly, and soon she was chatting with her old friend as if nothing was wrong.

"It has been a long time. How are things in Heaven?"

"*Très bien, très bien.* Everything's quiet and peaceful."

"Has Yggdrasil been functioning properly?"

"Why, first you telephone out of the blue and then you sound almost as if you expect something to be wrong! What on Earth is the matter?"

"Oh, just wondering . . ."

"Is that so? I certainly appreciate your concern, my dear, but at present everything is copacetic."

Not that Belldandy would have preferred to hear that there was something wrong . . . but if the system was functioning properly, that meant that the cause of the failed spell rested in Belldandy herself.

"Please excuse me. That's all I wanted to know."

She gripped the receiver tighter.

"That reminds me . . ." Peorth said. "There are a few things I forgot to say to Urd before she returned to Earth the other day. Tell her . . ."

Peorth was still in a snit over Urd's impertinence in Terminal 3 of the Universal Access Unit of Yggdrasil Central Main Control. She launched into a foul-tempered tirade on the other end of the line, emitting clouds of rosy perfume as she complained. But her rant fell on deaf ears. A tight knot had formed in Belldandy's chest.

In this world, every last event was significant—every action and every reaction, no matter how tiny. There was no such thing as simple coincidence—everything happened for a reason. But what did this latest development imply for Belldandy?

"Belldandy . . . ?" Skuld's voice brought Belldandy back to reality. Finally, she noticed the receiver's buzzing in her ear—the conversation was over. She hung up the receiver and forced her voice to sound casual.

"There's nothing wrong with Yggdrasil."

"Oh . . ." Skuld gave her sister a worried look. She would have felt better if there had been a problem with the system.

"What about Urd?"

"Peorth said she headed back some time ago . . ."

Traveling by teleport, Urd should have arrived home instantaneously. She sure was taking her sweet time! Skuld's temper flared. How could Urd be so irresponsible—off dawdling somewhere when Belldandy was having a crisis!

"That Urd! She's got some nerve . . ."

Skuld puffed herself up, but before she could launch into an indignant denunciation of her tardy sister, she was interrupted by a shout from outside.

"Kei-chaaaan!!"

The two sisters exchanged glances and ran outside.

Megumi was just arriving, pushing her KSR. Its tire was flat.

"Megumi . . . ?!"

Belldandy couldn't believe her eyes. The memory of *that day* flashed through the back of her mind. The day when Keiichi had given Megumi a ride to school and had been killed instantly in a traffic accident . . . the day his death had triggered the collapse of Yggdrasil.

It can't be. It's too soon!

Belldandy's lavender eyes filled with terror. Her body felt immobilized by an invisible force. But Megumi was oblivious to Belldandy's distress. Exhausted, she wiped away the sweat that streamed down her face as she parked the KSR near the front door.

"Jeez, what a drag!" Megumi's shoulders rose as she heaved a deep sigh. "I got too cocky, since I'm used to driving in the snow and all. I must have run over something sharp buried under the snow . . ." The KSR's rear tire was flaccid. "I thought I'd ask Kei-chan for a ride . . ."

"Ask Keiichi . . . ?"

"Yeah. There's a special Christmas lecture today."

"Is it . . . an aerodynamics class?" Belldandy asked falteringly.

"Exactly. Kei-chan told you about it, huh? Since my trip got canceled, I'm determined not to miss this class."

This is it.

Despite all of Belldandy's caution and attentiveness, destiny was determined to thwart her by plunging, unheeding, down the exact same path. Belldandy felt her knees threaten to buckle as a feeling of desperation and futility washed over her.

"Belldandy . . ." Skuld's fingers intertwined gently with her big sister's.

The Spiral Awakening Mandala had the power to synchronize the goddesses' memories. Although Skuld hadn't been on Earth at the time, she'd seen the events of that day through Belldandy's eyes. The terrifying memory of Yggdrasil's destruction came flooding back.

Skuld, too, knew that the events of that day had to be prevented from recurring.

"Where's Kei-chan? In his room?"

Once again, Megumi wiped her sweaty brow as she headed toward the house. The sisters were overcome by confusion and uncertainty . . . but time refused to wait. History would repeat itself if they simply stood and watched, their hearts full of fear.

As Skuld glanced toward the KSR's flat tire, her gaze fell upon the Cold Climate Attachment in the parking area.

That's it!

Quickly, Skuld checked Banpei's remaining battery power.

He should make it—just barely.

The battery was almost dead, but it should have just enough juice to get Megumi to campus. The return trip was another matter—but right now, the important thing was to get past the immediate hurdle.

"Hey, Megumi! I'll lend you the Snow Rider V3!" Skuld offered with a grin.

"Huh?"

"If you're in a hurry to get to school, the Snow Rider's just the thing! It could get you there in your sleep!"

Without waiting for a response, Skuld got straight to work outfitting Banpei with his Cold Climate Attachment.

"Um . . . uh . . ." Megumi stammered.

Yesterday, Skuld had made mention of lending her the Snow Rider at some point, but Megumi had never dreamed that the day would come so soon. She watched reluctantly as Skuld assembled the machine in less time than it took to make instant ramen.

"Okay! Hop on!"

"What?! But I . . ."

"Oh, go on!"

Skuld hustled Megumi aboard the Banpei Cold Climate Attachment: Snow Rider V3.

"Um . . . I really appreciate the offer . . . but I'm not sure I'll be able to ride this thing . . ." Megumi couldn't help feeling intimidated by the unfamiliar machine. She wanted to make her class—but not enough to risk life and limb. As she struggled to come up with a polite way of refusing, Skuld deftly circumvented her protests.

"Don't worry! It's fully automatic!"

"Huh?"

"All you have to do is sit there. Here, put this on."

Skuld jammed a helmet over the hesitant Megumi's head and quickly input "Inokuradai Building" into the machine's panel. One by one, the red lights turned to green.

"But Skuld, I . . ."

The motor hummed progressively louder.

"All right, Banpei! Show 'em your stuff!" Skuld shouted.

"Maybe I should . . ."

"Snow Rider V3, GO!"

As a "0" appeared on the electronic panel, the engine roared to life and a brilliant jet of flame spurted out of its tailpipe. The vehicle skidded forward, accelerating rapidly.

"AIIIEEEEEE!!!"

Megumi's scream reverberated through the yard as she battled the overwhelming g-force. In no time at all, the V3 had vanished from the temple grounds. The roar of its engine faded down the road, along with Megumi's shrieks.

"She'll be there in under twenty minutes," Skuld said. "Guaranteed."

As quiet returned to the garden, the only sound was the melting snow falling to the ground. Relieved of its burden, the cherry tree stretched its limbs toward the blue sky. As Belldandy stood gazing after Megumi, her legs buckled suddenly and she crumbled to the ground.

"Big Sister!"

Belldandy had been completely unable to act . . . but Skuld had been marvelous! Belldandy smiled affectionately as her sister's little hand clasped her shoulder.

"Thank you, Skuld. You saved the day again!"

"Oh, sis!"

The wind riffled through Belldandy's light-brown hair. Normally the voices of nature sounded like friendly whispers to Belldandy—but now they had a completely different ring.

Even if fate is determined to take Keiichi away . . . and to destroy Yggdrasil . . . I won't let it happen! I swear it as a Goddess First Class!

She couldn't afford to waste any more time quaking with apprehension. Belldandy stared boldly ahead, focusing her energy in the emblem on her forehead. Her long, beige velvet skirt fluttered in the air and, with a burst of light, transformed into her blue goddess uniform.

"Sis . . ."

Belldandy's golden bracelets gleamed. "I'm going to create the largest possible defense barrier shield," she announced.

The melting snow dripped into the puddles of water on the cobblestones, creating ripples that seemed to hint at what lay in store.

Ice cubes jingled in an empty glass. It had begun to sweat with condensation and form a wet ring on the table.

"More water, please."

Normally, on Christmas day, the Nekomi shopping district was swarming with so many couples and families that there was barely room to walk. But this year, thanks to the blizzard, there was almost nobody around. The festive strains of "Jingle Bells" echoing through the deserted boulevard only highlighted the emptiness.

"Here you are."

The man set a brimming pitcher of water on the table. The dry brown stains in the coffee cups bore witness to how long it had been since they'd been full.

"Some refills on coffee would be great, too."

"I'd be happy to take additional orders for coffee." Despite the dearth of customers, businesses had to carry on. As usual, the coffee shop in one corner of the shopping district had opened its doors at seven that morning. "If you want free refills, go to a family restaurant."

At first, the owner had been thrilled when a large group had filed in through the door . . . but four hours had gone by without any of them ordering more than a single cup of coffee. They did nothing but guzzle the free water, requesting constant refills, and the owner's patience was beginning to wear thin.

"But first, I'd appreciate it if you settled the tab," he added.

He brought their bill to the table to make sure they didn't run off without paying. Then he fetched them another pitcher of water before retreating into the back.

"Cool. All-you-can-drink water."

The twin pitchers of water reflected the sunlight that streamed through the window. Cable radio music played softly over the sound system.

"Man . . . All that drinking last night did me in, Den-chan."

Otaki poured water into his empty glass.

"Yeah . . . if we was still wandering through dat snow right now, we'd be popsicles for sure."

The ice danced in the water and melted slightly.

"That snow ain't no joke."

Otaki leaned back against the sofa and yawned deeply.

After a raging party and a short but pleasant sleep, the group had left Tarikihongan Temple at dawn . . . but after that, ferocious hangovers and barely passable snowy roads had left Tamiya, Otaki, and the rest of the Motor Club on the verge of collapse. The coffee shop had been their salvation. At first, they'd only intended to stop for a short rest, but now they were so comfortable that they hadn't been able to bring themselves to leave.

"Sure is nice out."

Warm sun streamed in through the window, and the shopkeepers of the nearby shops were out taking advantage of the beautiful weather to clear away the snow.

"The clubhouse probably needs clearing, too," one of the guys murmured softly as he watched them work.

"Yup. Duh roof."

The clubhouse—the Motor Club's home away from home—was a prefab building. It was definitely not constructed with frigid climes in mind, and the snow on its roof was probably a serious threat. Unfortunately . . .

"Too bad we's not allowed to even go near duh place now."

Tamiya and Otaki had yet to be relieved of the ban imposed on them after their survival game shenanigans.

"What a tragedy, Den-chan!"

"A crying shame, Dai-chan!"

The pair collapsed into despondent sobbing.

One of the motor club members raised his hand with a suggestion. "Why don't we ask the interim club president to do it?"

"Oh! Morisato!"

Come to think of it, both the grounds and the roof of Tarikihongan Temple had been immaculately clear when they'd visited yesterday.

"Morisato, our savior!" Tamiya declared, and the rest of the gang nodded eagerly. They fished handfuls of change out of their pockets and scattered it across the table.

"Right. We'll ask Morisato to do it," Tamiya confirmed.

"The rest of you, be sure to show up later and give him a hand," Otaki instructed.

"Right!" The gang responded enthusiastically—though it remained to be seen whether or not they would follow through.

Coins in hand, Tamiya made a beeline for the pay phone near the shop's cash register.

"All right . . . last one."

Wearing the red and white skirt that was the uniform of a Goddess Second Class, Skuld used a hammer and stakes to chart out a mandala in the ground. Her tiny angel, Noble Scarlet, peeked out from behind her back, darting this way and that as she did everything she could to help.

Skuld plotted out the complex design with great care. As she finished drawing the final line, she looked up proudly at her sister in the sky.

"It's finished, Big Sister!"

The ground sparkled like white sugar candy, contrasting beautifully with the clear blue sky. A gust of wind stirred the air.

"I'm not sure whether or not this is right . . ." Belldandy gazed down at the temple from her perch on Stringfellow. A pair of gentle blue eyes peered into Belldandy's stern face.

"Holy Bell . . ."

White feathers danced in the wind. Wordlessly, the angel smiled, nodding supportively as she gazed heavenward.

"You're right . . . we need to do everything we can right now," Belldandy agreed.

She raised her arms high overhead and began to sing, and Holy Bell did the same. As their voices blended, the harmony materialized as a sparkling golden light, etching a glittering mandala into the sky.

"That's amazing . . ." Skuld sighed in admiration as she watched from below. The rays of light whizzed through the air like shooting stars, rendering a working even more intricate and detailed than the one on the ground. Skuld looked on, hypnotized, until Noble Scarlet's frantic pointing drew her attention. The mandala was just one symbol from being completed.

"Oh, oops!" Quickly, Skuld, too, raised her voice in song. By synchronizing the mandalas in the sky and on the earth, they would create the strongest ward possible.

As Belldandy sang, her golden mandala sparkled even brighter. Skuld's song made the mandala on the ground glitter with a silver light, and its rays extended toward its sister pattern in the sky.

"Servants of Evil, Servants of Destruction, Keep Away . . . Protect those who take Refuge Within . . . Ultimate Magic Warding Mandala!"

The two songs mingled, echoing through the sky. The two overlapping mandalas glowed with white light, then scattered in a burst of glittering particles. They would prevent the intrusion of any being possessing harmful energy.

"Big Sister!"

Belldandy descended from the sky, followed by Holy Bell, landing lightly in the center of the garden.

"Thank you, Skuld. You've worked very hard."

It had been quite a challenging task for a Goddess Second Class. Belldandy caressed Skuld's slightly tired cheeks, affectionately drawing her little sister close.

"Let's have a break. Holy Bell and Noble Scarlet, you must be tired, too."

The angels retreated into dormancy, satisfied by a job well done. Once again, the wind was gentle, and Tarikihongan Temple was quiet and peaceful.

"Hey, Big Sister . . . now nobody can get in if they have even a little bit of evil in their hearts, right?"

"That's right."

"Too bad for Urd."

"Skuld, that's not nice!" The relieved sisters bantered cheerfully as they opened the front door.

Just then, Belldandy saw something that made her doubt her own eyes. Keiichi's shoes were missing.

"Keiichi . . .?"

A terrible premonition surged through Belldandy's body. Quickly, she ran to Keiichi's room and peeked inside. The futon where Keiichi had been sleeping earlier was folded neatly and put away in the closet. His jacket, too, was gone.

"No!"

It was clear that Keiichi had gone out. But why? *Why?* Belldandy's mind was filled with confusion.

"Big Sister . . . look."

Skuld held a note out to her dumbfounded sister.

"It was on his desk."

It was a short message, written in Keiichi's familiar handwriting.

> Tamiya called—they want me to shovel the roof of the clubhouse. I'm heading over to campus for a little while.
>
> —K1

How ironic—fate had snatched Keiichi away even as they were creating a working to protect him.

"Belldandy . . ."

But Belldandy only nodded, quietly. She returned the letter to the desk and turned toward Stringfellow, her eyes bright with determination.

"We'll go after him."

"What? You don't want to use a gate?"

"I want to keep watch on things from above."

Keiichi had died in a traffic accident—if fate had any hand, that was the risk they had to be the most wary of.

It had been just over ten months since the reset. The Jomon Cedar on Yakushima Island, the incident with the ghost at the South Building, and the avalanche of snow that had seemed to deliberately target Keiichi—Belldandy had attributed all of these phenomena to negative energy, or to weaknesses in her own spirit. That was what she had wanted to believe.

But she knew now that it wasn't so. Fate—this universe—was trying to correct the time glitch, by suppressing Belldandy's powers and conspiring to erase Keiichi's existence, regardless of whether or not he became a singularity. If destiny was attempting to correct itself by ending Keiichi's life, it was no wonder he had slipped past their barrier shield completely unhindered.

Then I'll do everything I can to fight it.

Calmly, and without the slightest hesitation, Belldandy made up her mind.

"Let's go."

As Skuld climbed on the back of the broom, Belldandy tightened her grip. A gust of wind swirled around them, and the broom zoomed upward into the sky. The cars and motorcycles on the streets below looked like toys.

The fact that we were able to execute a system restore has to mean something. There must be a way!

Belldandy was conscious of the great power this universe wielded—but nonetheless, she refused to give up hope. As she gathered speed, the wind grew stronger, rushing through her hair and clothing. Stringfellow carved a wispy trail in the sky as it raced toward the Nekomi Institute of Technology.

☙ CHAPTER FOUR ❧

K A M I T O K I — T H U N D E R B O L T
"I can see the school!" Skuld shouted to be heard over the roar of the wind.

They had scanned the ground attentively for traffic accidents as they flew toward the university, but now the N.I.T. campus was in sight and Belldandy's fears remained unrealized.

Keiichi . . . Still, Belldandy wouldn't be able to relax until she saw Keiichi. She was more vigilant than ever as she steered the broom toward the Motor Club headquarters.

Classes let out early for winter vacation, and thanks to the blizzard that had raged for seven days and nights, there was hardly a soul in sight. The glittering white snow remained pristine and undisturbed.

There, between the classrooms, a single track interrupted the snow's surface. Two thick lines that interlaced here and there, with a single line just off to their left. It was unmistakable: the tracks of a motorcycle with a sidecar.

He's here.

Belldandy tried to calm her racing heart as she decelerated and flew lower. She turned the corner of a school building, emerging into an open space. The prefab building was smaller than the trees that surrounded it, and it wore a heavy crown of snow that made it look like a snow hut.

"Keiichi!!"

There he was, as clear as day—buried up to his thighs in snow as he worked to clear the roof. Belldandy's heart leapt at the sight of him. She leapt down toward the building, too impatient to perform a proper landing. Her clothing billowed in the wind like wings.

"Belldandy . . .?"

Keiichi stopped his work, startled by the unexpected sight of a goddess descending from the sky. Quickly, he flung away his shovel and opened his arms wide to catch her. He knew very well that she didn't need his help . . . but somehow, she seemed strangely delicate and fragile, like a lost child.

"Belldandy!"

The moment their hands touched, Belldandy buried her face in his chest, embracing him tightly. He wanted to ask her what was wrong, but the words caught in his throat. Words might shatter the moment. He hesitated even to breathe.

Shyly but decisively, Keiichi drew his arms around Belldandy's thin form. The cool wind that tickled his cheeks carried a sweet perfume.

"AAIIIEEEEE!!!"

It also carried a screech that was more than piercing enough to shatter the mood. The cry echoed briefly before it was quickly absorbed by the snow.

"GRK!"

Skuld struggled desperately to control the broom, but she was no match for Heaven's fastest—and most stubborn—vehicle. After a descent that bordered on a free fall, Skuld made an impressive dive into the snowbank next to the clubhouse. The snow was a lot harder than it looked.

"Oh!"

Flustered, Belldandy pulled away at the sound of her sister's bloodcurdling yelp. Dismayed by this misfortune, Keiichi was momentarily unable to lower his arms.

"Oh, dear, what have I done!"

"U-uh . . ."

Their cheeks flushed with embarrassment, Belldandy and Keiichi hurried over to the side of the roof and peeked over.

"Skuld?"

"Are you okay?"

With her upper body lodged in the snow and her butt sticking up in the air, Skuld looked like a playful bear cub. Despite their concern, Keiichi and Belldandy burst into laughter. Belldandy raised her arms and intoned a spell.

"Rise up, O Snowflakes . . . Carry Thine Cargo to Me . . ."

Skuld's body floated up into the air. The broom, too, rose up out of the snow and traveled with Skuld up to the roof.

Snow crystals adorned Skuld's hair. Her face was red from

her dive, and her dark eyes brimmed with tears.

"Big Sister . . . how could you?!"

Now that the crisis was over, Skuld's panic was replaced by a flood of misery. It wouldn't be easy to forget the panic of being abandoned on the broom, or the terror of plummeting out of the sky.

"I'm sorry, Skuld!" Hurriedly, Belldandy cast a soothing spell on her sister. She felt terrible for having been so thoughtless and rash, especially after Skuld had been such a help to her that day.

"I would have been lost without you today, Skuld."

Lost without me?

Skuld swelled with elation at her sister's praise. The trauma of her fall quickly melted away.

"Keiichi, I should apologize to you, too. I'm sorry I startled you." Belldandy bowed slightly as the quickly recovering Skuld was turned away.

"Oh . . . well . . ."

Keiichi's cheeks grew red with embarrassment. He wanted to say something clever, like, *You're welcome to startle me like that anytime, babe,* but instead he found himself staring at his feet. Still, a smile spread across his face at the memory of Belldandy's warm body against his chest.

The winter afternoon was peaceful and quiet . . . but the mournful wail of a sudden gust of wind shattered the stillness.

"—?!"

The two goddesses stiffened, overcome by uneasiness.

"Belldandy . . ."

The melody carried by the wind shook them to the core. Skuld turned as white as a sheet and latched on to her sister's arm.

"What's wrong?" Keiichi asked.

But Belldandy didn't move. Ignoring Keiichi's question, she stared motionlessly off into space.

The wind sighed woefully.

"Urd . . ." Belldandy murmured softly, breaking the tense silence.

"Wish I could do this somewhere a little more discreet . . ."

After returning to Earth, Urd had gone straight to the Nekomi Institute of Technology without stopping at Tarikihongan Temple.

Just to be sure, she'd made a quick circle around the campus, but just as she'd feared, this was definitely the spot.

"Great."

There were plenty of empty areas on campus, including a large wooded grove, a big open field, and a parking lot. It was just her luck to wind up at the school dorm instead.

"Sorry about this."

Urd murmured a terse apology to any and all living things nearby before using a Localized Electric Wave to instantly clear the area of snow.

She waved her hands over the ground, which was still slightly damp, as she began to intone a low spell. It wasn't a cheerful melody, but a sutra-like incantation—soft and low. A ray of light darted across the ground as she sang, tracing an arcane mandala in the ground at her feet.

When she'd finished rendering the final symbol, Urd let out a sigh as she released her focus.

"Jeez, could they make the Space-Time Gate Opening Mandala any harder to draw?"

She tossed her hair as she looked slowly over the immense working. It gave off an eerie glow, glimmering enticingly.

"If I get caught this time I'll get worse than a suspended license . . ." Urd chuckled self-derisively.

The Space-Time Gate Opening Mandala was exactly what it sounded like—a working that transcended time to connect places and events. Opening such a door was extremely hazardous—it was difficult even for the most skilled sorceress to open the right door, and connecting to the wrong space-time or dimension could lead to the destruction of both worlds. For this reason, the spell was strictly prohibited by Heaven without a Level One Permit.

"All right . . . time to get started."

Urd glanced over the working and strode into its center. Her silver hair hung in soft waves, and her tanzanite-colored eyes shone brightly in the sunlight. She lifted both hands high in the air.

"O Faraway Past, Future of Antiquity . . ."

The air became absolutely still.

Out of nowhere, inky black clouds began to gather in the clear blue sky. The wind changed its pitch, and the sky suddenly took on an ominous cast. In no time at all, it had gone from blue to gray, obscured by layers of clouds.

"Across Billions of Days and Nights . . . I Call Upon the Myriad Doors . . ."

Blue-white lightning flashed through the clouds, writhing like a dragon-snake. Raging winds collided and howled.

"Sis!"

". . . !"

Urd spun around in time to see Belldandy, Skuld, and Keiichi come running toward her.

"How did you guys . . . !?"

Urd was unable to conceal her surprise. She hadn't expected her sisters to arrive so soon.

The spell she was about to use was forbidden. Naturally, Urd knew she would never be able to pull it off undetected—Belldandy was bound to come running the moment she felt the slightest waves of energy. That was why Urd had taken extra care as she returned to Earth and drew the mandala, trying to avoid her sisters' notice for as long as possible. Once the spell was cast, even if they discovered her, it would be too late for them to interfere. But now . . .

Urd cursed her carelessness.

"Step back, Belldandy! I don't want the three of you in harm's way!" she shouted.

"No, Urd!" Belldandy yelled. "Abort the spell immediately! I command you as a Goddess First Class!" Belldandy refused to back down. She knew that Urd wouldn't commit such an extreme violation without good reason—and especially not for her own benefit. That was precisely why Belldandy couldn't permit her to continue.

"The Space-Time Gate Opening Mandala is a forbidden spell! You know what the consequences are! Don't do it, Urd! I . . . I don't want to lose my big sister!"

Belldandy . . . Urd thought to herself. For a brief moment, she smiled and closed her eyes. Belldandy's words meant the world to her.

Then she opened her eyes again with renewed determination and waved her right hand lightly in the air. A stream of flame issued forth from her hand like a whip, licking Belldandy and the others' heels.

"Hey, watch it!" Skuld shouted indignantly. "Sis, say something!"

She looked to Belldandy beseechingly. But Belldandy's eyes were staring fixedly at Urd's hands and forehead.

"Urd . . ." Belldandy said, her voice barely a whisper, ". . . those jewels . . ."

Gauntlets of platinum filigree covered both of Urd's forearms, extending from her hands to her elbows, with pigeon-blood rubies that shone a deep crimson on the backs of her hands. The circlet on her head was half hidden by her silver hair, but it, too, was fashioned of finely wrought platinum, with a gleaming deep red stone on her forehead in the shape of a large flower.

"The Hlidskjalf Dusk . . ." said Belldandy.

The Hlidskjalf Dusk were not simply beautiful adornments.

They were the ultimate accoutrements—capable of amplifying their wearer's powers by a factor of hundreds, even thousands.

Anyone who wore the Hlidskjalf Dusk could obtain powers transcending even those of the Almighty, and in the wrong hands, they could easily bring about the end of the world. For this reason, it was forbidden even to touch them without permission from the Lord of Heaven—a taboo even stricter than that of the forbidden mandala.

"I won't miss twice," Urd menaced.

Urd, for her part, was no mere Goddess Second Class. She was half-goddess, half-demon, daughter of the CEO of the Infernal Realm. With the Hlidskjalf Dusk, her powers were immeasurable.

But Belldandy was not intimidated. She took another step forward.

"Belldandy!" Urd glared, and tongues of flame bloomed like flowers on the ground.

"Big Sister!" Skuld shouted.

"Watch out!" Keiichi chimed in.

The immense thunderclouds roared like a wild beast, and a ferocious wind tore violently at Keiichi and the goddesses' clothes.

"Because you're you, Urd . . ."

Belldandy touched the seal on her ear and quickly cast a spell. A pale light enveloped her as her chestnut hair turned to platinum blond and her eyes changed from lavender to a crystalline amethyst.

"Urd . . . I see now how strongly you feel." Belldandy would have been willing to suffer serious injuries to stop her sister. But she couldn't do that now—the fact that Urd was prepared to use not just the forbidden mandala but the Hlidskjalf Dusk made it clear just how determined she was. "In that case, I won't interfere."

She waved her right hand lightly, summoning a veil of light. The true powers of a Goddess First Class were immeasurably vast. They were so great that Belldandy ordinarily wore a seal on her ear to keep them contained. When she fortified her barrier shield with that protection removed, the wall of quiet completely shut out the raging storm.

"Are you all right, Bell?" Keiichi and Skuld regarded Belldandy with faces full of worry.

Belldandy bowed low. "I'm sorry, Keiichi, Skuld . . . I . . . ."

For the sake of their welfare, she really ought to take them away from this place immediately. And yet . . .

Sensing Belldandy's ambivalence, Keiichi and Skuld shook their heads.

"I don't really understand all of this, but I feel the same way you do, Bell," Keiichi said.

"Me, too! I don't want to leave Urd behind, either!" Skuld agreed.

Their kind words warmed Belldandy's heart. "Thank you," she said with feeling, and nodded silently. Then she rose to shield them as Urd continued her spell from the center of the mandala.

Sis . . .

The transformed emblem on Belldandy's forehead glowed with a blue light.

The sky trembled and roared. The wind raged still stronger, becoming a tornado and obliterating everything in its path. Bolts of lightning flashed across the sky, forming bands of light.

"Great River of Time . . . I Now Release a Flashing Arrow. Heaven and Earth Conjoin . . . Light and Darkness Conjoin!"

As Urd waved her arms, tangles of lightning danced at her fingertips like playful kittens. She began the last verse of her incantation. Red light streamed out of the mandala in time with her song.

"O Raging Electricity! Show your Power as a Key, connecting Time!"

From across the thunderclouds, strands of lightning gathered together in a single blinding band, focused on the center of the mandala.

"Time-Space Opening!!"

All at once, the energy flooded down into the mandala.

There was a moment of stillness.

Then, suddenly, the ground began to rumble.

"Keiichi—Skuld, get down!"

"AIIIEEEEEEE!"

"WAAUUGHH!"

The earth screamed and moaned. An earsplitting boom and a tremendous blast drowned out Keiichi and Skuld's screams.

The mandala glowed eerily, as if sucking energy from the cracked bedrock.

"Holy Wall!"

A wave of pure power washed over their feet. Immediately, the earth split and a dazzling wall of light appeared. The surge of power raged toward them like a tidal wave, rattling the shield like the leaves of a tree and threatening to swallow them.

"We're goners!" Skuld wailed.

"Hang in there, Skuld!" Belldandy shouted.

Beyond the shield, the world seemed to be coming to an end. The howling storm sank its jaws into the wall of light, creating shock-waves that leveled the dorm and the other nearby buildings, reducing them to rubble. A dragon-like clasp of thunder bellowed as a surge of lightning shot up from the ground toward the raging wind. Suddenly, the wind died down, as if the two forces had canceled each other out. Sunlight spilled down from between the clouds. After what had seemed like an eternity, the storm was over.

Gingerly, Skuld looked up. All was quiet.

"W-we're alive!"

Keiichi raised his head at the sound of Skuld's voice. The scene that met his gaze was completely unrecognizable. "Th-the dorm . . ."

Their surroundings were so barren that it was hard to remember what had been there before. Not a single blade of grass remained.

As Keiichi sat, stunned and unable to rise to his feet, he heard Belldandy say softly, "We have company."

Company?

Over where the dormitory had once stood, there was nothing but a cloud of dust still spiraling in the air. But Belldandy quietly released her shield and walked slowly forward.

". . . Ah."

Keiichi looked more carefully. As the sand dispersed, he was able to make out the form of what looked like a person. If Urd's mandala had been meant to summon somebody, what sort of being might it be? A monstrous giant? An ancient wizard? Keiichi's imagination raced as he stared toward the visitor.

". . . Huh?"

A string of bracelets tinkled musically on the newcomer's arm. She was neither a giant nor an old man, but a cute little girl who looked about ten years old.

Her shining hair was tied up on both sides of her head, and she wore a billowing piece of fabric like a miniskirt with a slit in it. Keiichi could tell from the red six-pointed star emblazoned on her tan forehead that, like the goddesses, she was no mortal.

"Who's that?" Keiichi whispered.

Skuld swallowed hard. The newcomer was someone she would never get used to, no matter how many times they met—someone that, quite plainly, scared her silly. Her expression rigid, she whispered her response. "It's Urd's mother."

"Urd's mother?"

"Yes."

At first, Keiichi was inclined to question how this young girl could be anyone's mother. But after all, these weren't human beings. He supposed that when goddesses were involved, anything was possible. Keiichi shifted gears mentally and moved on to his next question.

"So she's your mother, too?"

"No. She's Urd's mother." Skuld answered shortly.

This was somewhat confusing. Then *Skuld and Belldandy must be Urd's half-sisters* . . . he concluded.

This was news to Keiichi. Evidently, family relations among the divine could be just as complex as they were in the human realm.

"So she's a goddess, too?"

"No. She's the CEO of the Infernal Realm."

"The CEO of the Infernal Realm?"

"The leader of all demons."

"What?"

The Infernal Realm . . . the image that popped into Keiichi's mind was a scene from a traditional scroll depicting Hell, with hordes of demons, lakes of blood, and mountains of needles. From a human perspective, the two worlds seemed more or less the same to him.

"She's cuter than the devil . . ." he commented.

In contrast to Skuld, Belldandy smiled nostalgically as she approached the newcomer. The two of them had once pitted their skills against one another in a flying broom race.

"It's been quite a long time, Hild."

Hild glared back at her. "What the blazes were you goddesses thinking, pulling a stunt like that?" she roared. A gust of wind rushed past the goddesses.

The atmosphere was tense. "Then again, maybe she *is* scary," Keiichi murmured softly.

The sun shone down benevolently over the ravaged landscape.

"Excuse *me!* Is that all you can say, after all the trouble you've put me through?" Urd shot back, her jewels sparkling. Her voice was tired. Even aided by the Hlidskjalf Dusk, the Opening spell had been an exhausting ordeal.

Hild squealed with delight. "Urd, *baby!* We're so happy to see you!" Her ferocious demon-face vanished. She flung her arms out wide and threw them around Urd.

"Oh, for Pete's sake! I'm a goddess, remember?" Urd said, exasperated.

"Oh, but you're our daughter, all right. Well done, baby!"

Urd and her mother seemed to have an understanding of what was going on that the rest of them didn't.

"I think I get why Urd isn't crazy about her . . ." Keiichi said in a low voice.

"I know, right?" Skuld agreed.

Their whispered conversation drew Hild's attention. Ears like the devil, Keiichi thought—no, like a demon, he corrected himself. But Belldandy stepped forward, coming between them and Hild.

"Hild, what did you mean by that comment? Kindly explain yourself."

Belldandy's eyes were full of confidence—she hadn't done anything for a goddess to be ashamed off.

Hild chuckled softly. "You're just like your father, Bell-chan. We always liked that about him . . ." She smiled, her indigo eyes sparkling. "All right, Urd. Tell them why you needed to use a forbidden incantation to summon us instead of just picking up the telephone."

In truth, normally Heaven and the Infernal Realm were accessible by phone.

"I'm sorry to have been so secretive . . . But I wanted to be sure of things, first," Urd began, looking steadily at Belldandy. Belldandy looked confused. Urd exhaled deeply and tossed her hair.

"The first clue I had that something was wrong was when we went to N.I.T. for Megumi's exam—when we heard the rumor about the ghost that had destroyed the whale fountain."

Slowly, she recounted the events that had led up to this moment.

Urd observed that so soon after a system restore it wasn't natural for things to occur in this world that had never happened in the previous time axis. Even more so given that the goddesses hadn't had any hand in influencing those events. Still, she hadn't wanted to raise a fuss when there didn't seem to be any immediate danger. Urd filed her doubts away in a corner of her mind with the intention of keeping a watchful eye on the situation.

But during the Survival Game, something happened that made her unable to sit on her heels any longer. It was when she had first faced off with the apparition on the South Building rooftop.

"There was a huge blast of sparks when the thing touched Keiichi. During that brief instant, I felt something. Demon energy. *Her* energy."

"Hild's?"

"Yes."

Perplexed by this unexpected development, Urd had returned to Heaven to investigate. She had taken full advantage of her Administrator's License, ultimately discovering one clue: for some reason, the Universal Access Unit of Terminal 3 Yggdrasil Central Main Control had been active during the system restore. Unfortunately, she hadn't been able to discover why.

In the end, she'd been forced to conduct a Time Index Search—while she dealt with Peorth at the same time.

"Good work, Urd!" As a fellow technician, Skuld had to give Urd kudos for her hard work. Yggdrasil's memory included records of everything that happened in Heaven and every event that involved any goddess. It made Skuld lightheaded just imagining what an ordeal it must have been to comb through that extensive memory, isolating events pertaining to the brouhaha with the apparition.

"When I had all of the data, I ran an energy analysis. The results were . . . not good."

An energy analysis was a function within the Yggdrasil System that was capable of identifying an energy pulse—not unlike a DNA test. Every deity and every demon had his or her own unique energy pattern.

"There was a 99.2% correlation."

"Then, that apparition was . . ."

"Yes. *Her.*" Urd pointed to Hild, who smiled with pleasure.

"But why . . ."

"Yes, why, indeed? I decided to go to the Infernal Realm to find out."

Ever since she had made up her mind to live as a goddess, Urd had never once set foot in that forbidden realm. It wasn't an easy decision to make—but in the end Urd couldn't ignore the nagging feeling that something inconceivably wrong was afoot.

Steeling herself for the worst, Urd had arrived only to discover a demon realm that bore almost no resemblance to her expectations.

"I was honestly surprised."

The realm was subdued and quiet, its denizens completely inactive. Not only were there no attempts to gain market share on Earth—normally every demon's top agenda—nobody was even accessing the Earth at all.

Even Mara—a Demon First Class, rival, and childhood friend—was living a peaceful existence, despite the fact that in the past, she had been so determined to engineer the three goddesses' downfall as to use Sayoko as a human tool against them.

"And that included Hild, CEO of the Infernal Realm." Urd had found Hild completely transformed. No matter what Urd said, Hild did nothing but smile, offering no hint of the ferocity that lurked inside of her.

"Then, the Hild in the demon realm wasn't the same person

as the Hild standing here with us . . . ?" Belldandy ventured.

"Very good, Bell-chan! A-plus! We love how sharp you are, kiddo!" Hild grinned mischievously. "We tried so hard to get your attention, but you absolutely refused to notice! It was no fun at all!"

Finally, Belldandy understood why Urd had used the Space-Time Gate Opening Mandala. If Hild was in another dimension, clearly she wouldn't have been accessible by telephone.

But that led to a new question.

Why were there two Hilds in the first place? Belldandy had the feeling that this enigma was at the root of everything.

"All right, now it's our turn to explain." Hild peered at the goddesses as if trying to look straight into their minds. Her two ponytails swayed slightly. "First question. Did you know that the Universal Access Unit is an important line that connects to Nidhogg?" Nidhogg represented for the Infernal Realms much the same system as Yggdrasil did in Heaven.

"*What . . . ?*"

This revelation was so unexpected that for an instant, the goddesses didn't understand what Hild was saying. Simultaneously, their three faces grew rigid.

"Yggdrasil is connected to Nidhogg?"

"What do you mean?"

"I didn't know that either!"

Stunned, the three sisters exchanged glances. They were so surprised that they were unsure how to continue the conversation.

Hild gave a long sigh. "Just as we expected," she said, exasperated. Hovering in midair, she assumed a seated position. "Heaven really needs to improve its school system."

She cracked her knuckles loudly and a clear sphere appeared. Several bands of magic spun inside.

"The red line is the demons, the blue line is the gods."

The connection between Yggdrasil and Nidhogg harkened back to antiquity . . .

The battle for market share raged fierce between the demons and gods—not only on Earth but throughout Time-Space. Not only did the two races slaughter one another, but their powerful clashes occasionally disturbed other beings and realms.

Both realms knew that something had to be done, and in a god-demon summit, their leaders came to an agreement.

They called it the Doublet System.

Children selected from both realms would have their destinies intertwined, thus deterring lethal attacks on either side. The knowledge that killing an enemy would result in the death of a comrade would prevent battles to the death.

Moreover, in order to make the contract both fair and secure, it was agreed that a line would be established to connect the systems governing both realms. Allowing both systems to oversee the Doublet System would prevent any foul play.

The solution created an intimate connection between the two realms, despite their contrasting natures, thus deescalating the conflict. Equilibrium was maintained, and before long there was no more bloodshed.

But ironically enough, the new era of peace led many to forget about the line's existence.

"The Universal Access Unit . . ." Urd said.

Though largely forgotten, the line continued to connect the two realms, quietly but surely.

"Now that that's understood, question two: what do you suppose happened to that line after Yggdrasil was reset?"

"Um . . ." Unless someone had deliberately severed it, the obvious answer was that the line would have remained intact. "It's . . . still connected?" Skuld ventured tentatively.

"Is that so!" Hild focused an ice-cold glare on the youngest goddess.

"Eep!" Skuld grimaced, desperately fighting to hold back her tears.

Hild appeared satisfied by this. She peered now into her daughter's face.

"In that case, when you executed your system restore, what do you suppose happened to Nidhogg?" she asked.

". . . !"

Light and darkness . . . these contrasting elements were both essential halves of a single world. Unbeknownst to them, a line had connected the two realms—and when Yggdrasil had been reset, that line had been cruelly severed.

"Starting to get the picture?" Slowly, Hild uncrossed her brown legs, recrossing them the other way.

Like the two sides of a coin, like night and day, both elements were essential to the existence of their counterpart. But Yggdrasil had disappeared one day without warning, leaving Nidhogg to its imminent demise—unless something was done. Nidhogg hadn't hesitated to perform the only act it could to ensure its salvation: creating a new Yggdrasil.

"If Nidhogg hadn't performed the job so thoroughly, we probably never would have noticed," Hild said.

"Noticed what?" asked Urd.

"You."

"What?"

"In the Yggdrasil that exists as a counterpart to our Nidhogg, *you* don't exist."

"I don't . . . exist?" Urd repeated.

Urd was missing from Yggdrasil . . . from Heaven. The first to notice was Hel, the monstrous half-dead, half-alive beauty who governed Niflheim, the Realm of the Dead.

The dimension was accessible by a bridge that distinguished between the footsteps of the dead and the living. Tall gates loomed under various names as barriers dividing the living from the dead. The dark and shadowy realm of Niflheim was located right next door to the Demon Realm.

In the dusky hour when the dead are welcomed in, Hel was sorting souls as usual in her palace, along with Garm, the guard-hound of Niflheim. From here, the dead were sent off to their respective destinations.

But that day, Garm had bared his ferocious fangs in outrage. A soul was missing!

"Missing?"

"What, you don't understand? That human!" Hild pointed at Keiichi, who had been doing his best to stay out of the way.

"Who, me?" said Keiichi.

"Yes, you!"

Perturbed, Hel had climbed to the top of the World Tree to see what she could see, and had discovered that both Keiichi's soul and Urd's were missing. Immediately, she had brought the news to Hild.

"Honestly, we were a little bit hurt . . . that we had to hear it from Hel . . ." For a moment, Hild showed her maternal side. "We were about to come to you to find out what was going on, but the two of you had disappeared from Heaven as well!"

"Us?" Belldandy and Skuld exchanged glances.

"What was even stranger was the lack of reaction to your absence in Heaven. Even we weren't sure what to make of that!"

The three goddesses were unable to hide their agitation. Why hadn't there been a disturbance in Heaven?

The demon chief threw the foundering goddesses a lifeline. "A system restore means a reset, right?"

"Yes," said Belldandy.

"Then why did Urd retain her memory?"

"Huh?" Skuld wondered aloud.

Hild gave a little snort and recrossed her legs once more, softly rustling the fabric of her skirt.

"Because . . . of my blood . . . ?" Urd said. She had found it odd that she was the only one in Yggdrasil whose memory was intact, but had simply reasoned that it had to do with the unusual status of having half-god, half-demon ancestry.

"Now, come on . . ." Hild sighed, exasperated by her daughter's tidy but overly naïve and simplistic explanation. "Your memory was intact because Nidhogg wasn't reset! If your memory had been reset, too, *that* would have constituted a successful system restore!"

". . . !"

The three goddesses gasped.

Urd, with her memory intact, had never existed, and Belldandy and Skuld had disappeared at a certain point—because they had re-established their memories at Tarikihongan Temple.

To the Nidhogg that had been left behind when Yggdrasil was reset, beings who retained memories from prior to the system restore were a heresy. For that reason, Nidhogg had created a Yggdrasil that didn't include the three goddesses who had used the Spiral Awakening Mandala . . . and the Yggdrasil where they currently existed—the one that had been reset—had created a quiet Demon Realm, populated but non-operational.

Now, two Nidhoggs and Yggdrasils coexisted in separate dimensions.

"You understand how dangerous this is," Hild concluded.

Using the disconnected line, Hild had traced the restore point to the Nekomi dorm where Keiichi had lived. She had made a number of attempts to alert the three sisters—from the destruction of the whale fountain to the encounter on the South Building rooftop, barely succeeding in breaking through with a mere one-thousandth of her true self.

The situation wasn't sustainable as it stood, and if Hild hadn't succeeded in transcending time and dimensions to reach them, the current discontinuities might eventually have triggered the destruction of all of the affected realms.

It all made sense now, and the pain of it made Belldandy shut her eyes.

I finally see why the cedar tree on Yakushima wouldn't accept my magic . . .

Of course the most ancient life on Earth would refuse aid from a goddess who had disrupted nature's divine order. Belldandy was filled with remorse at the damage they had inflicted—even though their intention had been to save Heaven and, to that end, Keiichi.

That wasn't all. They had caused the creation of four realms. As goddesses whose purpose was to serve peace and happiness, this was a grave transgression.

I . . .

A gust of wind swept across the barren landscape.

Hild watched steadily as Belldandy struggled to come to terms with what they had done. She hopped down from her perch in the air, landing lightly on her feet.

"Why don't you and us go for a little walk, Bell-chan?" she suggested, gesturing casually with her thumb.

The wind howled mournfully.

"We held back as much as we could . . ." Hild said.

Urd's spell and Hild's arrival had completely ravaged the landscape. There wasn't a trace of snow left, and wreckage from the buildings was scattered here and there.

Belldandy walked along in silence. Gloomily, the two immortals approached what remained of the broken whale fountain.

"   Well?"

The wind riffled through their hair. Hild sat down on the remaining outside wall of the fountain, gave a little stretch, and looked up at the sky.

"You know what you have to do, don't you?" she said.

". . ."

Above them, the sky was an endless field of clear blue.

Belldandy hung her head, and Hild knew what her answer was.

The only way to restore the universe to normalcy would be to reset both Yggdrasil and Nidhogg simultaneously. But that meant that their memories would be completely erased.

Then who would prevent Keiichi from becoming a singularity again? Who would stop Yggdrasil's destruction? These feats could only be accomplished because of their retained memories.

They would be stuck in an endless cycle of destruction and rebirth. It was that reasoning that prevented Belldandy from taking the final step toward a total reset.

"You don't need to worry about that," Hild said softly, as if reading Belldandy's mind.

". . . ?!"

This time, Belldandy stared back at her without nodding, her amethyst eyes rapt.

"The survival of the universe is in peril." Her white garments fluttered, feather-like. "I don't understand how you can say that."

"Oh, really? So it's just the universe you're worried about?"

Belldandy stiffened. Her platinum blond hair danced in the breeze.

The clouds drifting overhead accelerated slightly.

Hild watched her for a moment. "All right, then, Bell-chan . . ." She extended a small hand toward the goddess. Her mischievous smile was just like Urd's. "There's something we want to show you. We'll take you there now."

Somehow, her small brown hand looked as large and gentle as a mother's. Belldandy hesitated for an instant, then reached out and took Hild's hand in her own.

"Back us up, now," Hild directed.

As the CEO of the Demon Realm began to chant, a blinding light enveloped the two beings. They disappeared, as if sucked up into the sky.

As the sun sank into the western sky, the shadows grew long.

MIZUKAGAMI—WATER MIRROR
Layers of clouds covered the sky in various shades of gray, shutting out the light of the sun. Dusk was beginning to fall.

"We knew this would be easy with the support of a Goddess First Class like you, Bell-chan!"

Hild and Belldandy had materialized amid thick clouds, and hovered like tiny boats drifting on a calm sea.

Hild had taken Belldandy by surprise when she'd plunged straight into another dimension after declaring that there was something she wanted to show Belldandy. And that wasn't all: before, the mighty CEO of the Infernal Realm had required the assistance of Urd and the forbidden Hlidskjalf Duck in order to open the correct inter-dimensional door—but now, the satisfied look on Hild's face implied that this was precisely the destination she'd had in mind.

"Hild? I thought it was difficult to travel to a specific place in another dimension . . ."

Hild responded to Belldandy's question without even turning her head. "Oh, yes, terribly! If you want to be able to influence events in that world, that is." They traversed a long tunnel of clouds, before finally emerging into a clear expanse of sky. "But just traveling by spirit is fairly simple, with the support of someone with powers like yours." A slate-blue sea stretched out toward the horizon, and seabirds winged busily across the distant sky like white specks. In the town below, scattered lights were already beginning to appear, like fireflies twinkling in the darkness.

Belldandy gazed down at the scenery below. *This place . . .*

For a moment, she wondered if it was only her imagination—but there was no mistaking such a familiar place. As she glanced around, just to make sure, her gaze met Hild's.

"You recognize it, don't you? Yes—this is the outskirts of Nekomi City. Only this isn't your universe."

"Oh!"

A feeling of uneasiness and confusion welled up inside of Belldandy as she realized that this town that felt so familiar was actually a strange, new place.

"This way." Hild changed direction suddenly, raising a hand to signal to Belldandy. The wind whistled forcefully through the quiet sky. Still frowning, Belldandy followed Hild's lead.

Under the glow of the streetlights, only the headlights of the occasional passing car interrupted the stillness of the road. In the darkness, rows of slumbering trees stood leafless and dead-looking. Belldandy and Hild passed through a neighborhood of tall apartment buildings before arriving at a large space by the side of the road.

"...!"

Belldandy broke into a smile when she saw the two conjoined shipping containers. An antenna and air-conditioning unit were installed on top of one, and a short flight of steps led up to an aluminum door in front. A large sign was mounted so that it was easily read from the road.

WHIRLWIND . . .

It was exactly like the one she and Keiichi had mounted together the day the shop had opened.

We had a hard time deciding on the design . . . the memory was as fresh in Belldandy's mind as if it were yesterday. Hild flitted in front of Belldandy like a little bird.

"This way, Bell-chan . . . we're going inside."

She sprang up onto the roof and then sank through it to

the inside. Belldandy had been about to head for the door, but instead followed Hild's example and entered through the roof.

She understood now what Hild had meant about not being able to influence events in this world: unless she made a conscious effort to plant her feet on the floor, they sank right through it. It was different from they way she often traveled through objects in everyday life—the sensation of slipping straight through things made her surroundings seem like a mirage. But Belldandy was so captivated by the scene before her that she hardly noticed.

The room was brightly lit and spic and span, despite its evident wear. The checkerboard wall was hung with a well-organized array of tools, and large crosses decorated the floor.

It's just the same . . .

Before the system restore, Belldandy had come here every day with Keiichi. As she looked slowly around the room, she felt a rush of nostalgia, as if returning to a long-lost home.

Even the small, square table in the center of the room was just as before. It was hard to believe that this wasn't the world she knew.

Keiichi's handwriting!

A battered pair of lockers stood in the corner of the room. Tenderly, Belldandy reached out a hand toward the nameplates that read "Fujimi" and "Morisato." Just as before, they were the shop's only employees.

"Phew! That wraps it up!"

Suddenly, Belldandy heard a familiar voice call out from the back of the shop—Chihiro Fujimi, the shop's owner and a former member of the Motor Club. She was generous, dynamic, slightly reckless, and beautiful.

Chihiro!

Belldandy turned, beaming . . . and then caught her breath. She didn't have white hair or wrinkles or anything as obvious as that—but the Chihiro that emerged carrying a cardboard box was clearly older now.

Finally, it was clear to Belldandy that this was an unfamiliar universe.

"Yearly warehouse cleaning: finished!"

The aluminum door swung open and a gust of cold air blew into the room.

Keiichi!

Belldandy stared as Keiichi entered the room, his breath white, and closed the aluminum door behind him.

Keiichi looked around thirty years old. He wore it well— thanks to his eternal baby face—but he was clearly no longer a college student, and he exuded an air of maturity based on self-assurance and a wealth of experiences.

"Sure is cold. Looks like it might snow," he remarked.

"That was a lot of work," Chihiro said. "Let's have a rest."

"All right."

As Belldandy watched the adult Keiichi hang the warehouse key on a hook on the wall, she felt a strange pang of emotion that was impossible to classify.

"Another busy year!" Chihiro gazed around the spotless room with satisfaction. Then she took out a calendar.

"Time for the calendar ritual?" Keiichi stood in front of the calendar with a slightly formal air.

"Care to join me, Morisato?" Chihiro asked.

"Sure. I do it at home now, too."

"Really?!"

Gently, Chihiro removed the current calendar from the wall.

"Okay . . . don't forget to wish."

She put up the new calendar, then replaced the old one on top of it. The idea was that if the year had been a good one, its luck would be transferred to the new year. If it had been a bad one, it would suck the bad luck out of the new year. It was Chihiro's unique custom, and she practiced it every year after the end-of-the-year cleanup.

"May next year be another good year!" Keiichi intoned, pressing his palms together in front of the two calendars. Then he and Chihiro bowed their heads once more, sending their thanks to the well-used appointment book, too.

"Calendar wish: finished," Chihiro declared with satisfaction as she turned away.

A tantalizing fragrance tickled their nostrils.

"Something smells fantastic," Keiichi exclaimed.

The coffeemaker hummed as a delicious aroma permeated the room. Hot water seeped through the grounds, and a thin stream of brown liquid percolated down into the pot.

"Blue Mountain coffee!" Chihiro chuckled.

"For real?"

"The director of the shopping district gave it to me as a New Year's gift."

"All right!"

"But first, let's take care of the year-end meeting," Chihiro directed.

"Gladly."

The rich promise of coffee made the prospect of a meeting more enjoyable. They sat down at the table in the warm room, savoring the delicious fragrance.

"Business as usual until the thirtieth . . ."

They both opened their respective appointment books.

"And on the thirty-first, we'll close at five p.m. like always. Agreed?"

WHIRLWIND was also known as the end-of-the-year E.R.

Most motorcycle shops closed their doors on the twenty-eighth or twenty-ninth of the month, but Chihiro made a practice of remaining open until the last day of the year.

A lot of motorcyclists eagerly anticipated their first ride of the year on New Year's Day. College students—not to mention business people—often waited for their winter vacations to begin before they started tuning up their bikes. This made it fairly common for something to need fixing right before New Year's, and Chihiro had initiated her policy of remaining open on the thirty-first out of the desire to respond to that need. By now, the institution had become famous, and even competitors sometimes took advantage of their services.

"Same as usual? No problem. We get a lot of those last minute requests, don't we? I love seeing those customers' worried faces break out in smiles when we fix their bikes." Keiichi nodded happily as he scribbled the note into his blank calendar.

Keiichi was always like that when it came to motorcycles—his eyes sparkled like a child's. Belldandy loved it when he got that look on his face.

Keiichi's just the same as ever.

Even if he was older, even if it was a different world, Keiichi was still Keiichi. Belldandy was overjoyed that he was no different from the Keiichi she knew.

And that wasn't all. She was relieved to see that his future was a sound one. It was sad that she wasn't there by his side, but she was glad that Keiichi was standing firm on his own two feet.

He's doing just fine . . .

Belldandy glanced back at Hild, who was leaning against the wall. But Hild looked away, avoiding Belldandy's gaze.

Hild?

Just then, the door burst open loudly. Belldandy inhaled sharply in surprise, then quickly looked to see who it was.

"Hi . . . You've been hard at it!"

A woman entered the room, breathing hard.

"I'm . . . sorry . . . I'm late!"

From the looks of it, she'd run over at top speed, and her words were choppy as she gasped for breath. She carried a beige down jacket under her arm—apparently, she'd been in too much of a hurry to put it on.

"Not again! You ran straight over here like that?" Keiichi scolded, taking her jacket and offering her a chair. But the woman refused to sit, turning toward Chihiro again and bowing low. She was still breathing hard.

"I'm sorry, Chihiro! After I promised I'd help with your big year-end cleaning!"

"Oh, it's fine! Forget about it . . . after all, you have a job too, Kozueko-chan."

The woman's cheeks flushed even pinker. "But I promised . . ." She screwed up her lips in frustration as she trailed off.

"You're always like this, Kozueko-chan! You have a strong sense of responsibility, I guess, and you're so stubborn! You and Morisato-kun are like two peas in a pod!" Chihiro let out a peal of laughter at the woman's earnestness.

"Huh?" Keiichi and Kozueko exchanged glances.

"You mean I'm like him?" and "You mean I'm like her?" they exclaimed simultaneously.

Now Chihiro was laughing uncontrollably. "You guys are the greatest, you know that?" Tears of mirth streamed down her face.

Now Kozueko's cheeks turned a bright red, and Keiichi chuckled self-consciously at their perfectly coordinated response.

Who is she?

Belldandy stood rooted to the spot, unable to tear her gaze away from Kozueko.

Her hair was slightly longer than shoulder-length, and she

wore it pulled back with an orange rubber band. Her skin was delicate and pale, and the only makeup she wore was a dab of lip gloss. She wasn't glamorous, but she had a fresh, gentle quality, like the first tidings of spring.

"In any case, have a seat, Kozueko-chan." Chihiro pulled out a chair when her laugher finally subsided. "I'm brewing up some Blue Mountain right now. Why don't you join us?"

"Mmm! That sounds fantastic!" Kozueko's eyes sparkled and her embarrassment vanished. Her expressions changed quickly, like those of a kitten. "Oh, I know! I have just the thing!" She reached for her orange tote bag and rummaged around inside. One after another, she pulled out an assortment of cute little packages of cookies and crackers.

"Leftover year-end gifts from the office. Winter vacation starts tomorrow, and there was no point in holding onto them until after New Year's, so we girls divided them up amongst ourselves."

Very practical.

"Oooh! I've heard of these—I saw an article in a magazine! All the stars are eating them!"

"Good eye, Chihiro! You're always up to date!"

The cookies Chihiro was pointing to were the latest celebrity favorite, appearing on television and the like.

"For your summer gifts, you had fancy bottles of wine," Chihiro recalled. "The city office doesn't mess around, does it!"

"It's true. Our vacations start earlier than most companies' and we know we can count on them. And I love that there's no overtime and that we get good benefits. When I graduated with a degree in electronics, I was sure I'd go to work for some big I.T. company—but I'm really glad I ended up at the city office instead."

Chihiro stuck out her tongue playfully. "You sure outdid me, Kozueko!"

The coffeemaker's motor fell silent. The long awaited Blue Mountain was ready. As Chihiro stood up, Kozueko rose to follow, but Chihiro waved her away. "I've got it! Sit!"

She winked playfully and disappeared into the kitchen.

As they breathed in the fresh aroma, Kozueko seemed to finally relax, letting out a soft sigh and leaning her head against Keiichi's shoulder.

"You're sure it's okay that you're skipping the year-end party with your co-workers?" Keiichi finally broke his silence.

"Mm-hmm. You know I'm good at weaseling out of those things." Kozueko mimicked Chihiro's wink. There was a relaxed, warm vibe between the two of them. "Besides . . ."

"Yeah. We have to tell her." Keiichi gave her hand a gentle squeeze, and Kozueko nodded bashfully.

What is this . . . feeling? Belldandy thought. She wrinkled her brow—her heart ached as if someone were squeezing it. Her body refused to move . . . she couldn't take her eyes off the scene in front of her, even to blink. Hild watched her, silently, from behind.

"Sorry about the wait!"

Chihiro waltzed into the room brandishing the coffee things on a tray, waitress-style. The fragrance of the Blue Mountain cast a magical spell over the white paper cups, making them seem as elegant and fine as Royal Copenhagen porcelain.

"Wow, talk about fancy!" Keiichi said.

"Mmm, that looks delicious!" Kozueko added.

"Enjoy!"

A cheerful evening tea party began, punctuated by lively conversation and laughter. Kozueko rolled up the sleeves of her loose beige sweater, attentively refilling the cups despite Chihiro's protests. Her cheerful, sincere smile was as dazzling as a sunflower in July.

She's beautiful . . .

The feeling came from the bottom of Belldandy's heart. Kozueko was no head-turner—she was fairly ordinary-looking— but she radiated honesty and joy, making the people around her feel comfortable and relaxed.

The window panes frosted over with white as it grew dark outside. Barely visible through the glass, a sprinkling of delicate snowflakes floated down through the sky.

"Chihiro, there's something we want to tell you," Keiichi said, sitting up straight. Kozueko, too, straightened up, as if she had been waiting for this moment.

"What is it, Morisato-kun?"

Chihiro, too, sat at attention, her expression suddenly nervous. A tense charge filled the air as the room fell momentarily silent.

"We wanted you to be the first to know . . ."

The only sound was the ticking of the clock on the walk. It seemed unnaturally loud.

"We . . ."

Keiichi's eyes met Kozueko's and he took a deep breath. Then he took the plunge, speaking slowly and deliberately. "We've decided to tie the knot this spring."

"Oh!" Chihiro's eyes widened, and in slow motion, a joyful grin took over her face. "Congratulations!"

She sprang to her feet so quickly that she almost knocked over her chair. First she threw her arms around Kozueko, then grasped Keiichi's shoulders tightly with both hands and squeezed. "Way to go, Morisato-kun!"

"Thank you."

Tears welled in their eyes as Chihiro congratulated the happy couple.

Belldandy stood frozen, her eyes fixed on Keiichi . . . and on Kozueko.

Tie . . . the knot . . .

She turned the words over and over in her mind. It took her a surprisingly long moment to realize that they were talking about marriage.

Belldandy had become quite accustomed to life on Earth, and she felt very familiar with how mortals lived.

And yet . . .

For the rest of his life . . . or for as long as Keiichi wished . . . Belldandy had intended to remain by Keiichi's side—as long as their contract lasted. To her, that was everything. Now, for the first time, she realized that although his wish meant living each day together, she had never considered the concept of marriage.

"Oh, I'm so relieved!" Chihiro flopped back into her chair like a marionette with its strings cut. "I've been so worried, wondering when the two of you would get married. I know it's unthinkable, but I was afraid just now you were going to announce that you were splitting up! For just a brief moment, a million thoughts raced through my head!"

"Ha-ha! Sorry!"

Now that the big moment was over, Keiichi, too, breathed a sigh of relief. He realized for the first time how nervous he'd been all day.

"We've come a long way since we first met when I was a sophomore in college." Keiichi recalled the day they'd met— almost a decade back.

As usual, the catalyst had been another of Otaki and Tamiya's crazy schemes. Rumors of a ghost had been circulating the campus, and Tamiya and Otaki had cooked up a plan for the Motor Club to hold a Ghost Hunt Survival Game.

They had ordered Keiichi to figure out where the ghost would appear, and reluctantly, Keiichi had headed over to the electronics department for help. For the most part, he was met with ridicule, but one student had been kind enough to hear him out: Kozueko Izumi, who was widely hailed as the girl-genius of the electronics department.

"It was so nice of you—agreeing to help me hunt for the ghost, even though I was a total stranger."

"I had to! I felt sorry for you!"

At first, Kozueko had casually volunteered her help. But as she spent more time with Keiichi, she began get into the project—and she found herself drawn to Keiichi . . . his enthusiasm and dedication to everything he did, and his sincerity, kindness, and warmth.

Keiichi, on the other hand, never dared to entertain the notion that he might have a chance with a girl like Kozueko Izumi, who was regarded as something of an unattainable prize by her many admirers.

When they were finished with their project, Keiichi had planned to invite Kozueko out to dinner to thank her for her help. Instead, Kozueko had asked *him* on a date.

"I was so nervous . . . I'd never asked a guy out before," Kozueko remembered.

"I was thrilled, though," Keiichi said. "Not to mention shocked!"

Kozueko had a strong sense of self but was also able to see things from other people's perspectives. She had guts and a warm heart. Who could say no to that?

From that day forward, slowly but surely, Keiichi and Kozueko had fallen in love.

"So, how many kids do you want?"

Chihiro knew it was none of her business, but she couldn't stop herself from asking the oldest question in the book. Kozueko's eyes sparkled, as if she'd known it was coming.

"I was an only child, so I think it's definitely important to have siblings," she said.

"Yeah, that's true. You fight sometimes, but that's part of the fun," Chihiro agreed.

"Right? But actually, I'm really in love with the idea of having twins . . . identical twins. I saw a program about it on TV—they have a sort of invisible connection, and sometimes they think and do exactly the same things. Isn't that bizarre? I love it!"

"Yeah, but have you thought about how tough they'd be to raise?"

"Huh?"

As Belldandy watched the joyful Kozueko, she found herself glancing down at the ring on her left hand.

Getting married . . . having children . . .

For human beings, it was the most normal thing in the world. Of course, new lives were born in Heaven, too. It was a goddess' duty, for all of eternity, to watch over and love every life unconditionally.

But the nature of this process was completely different from the human practice of getting married, making a home, working for a living, and raising children.

For a moment, Belldandy thought she could see Keiichi's smiling face in the sparkle of her tiara ring.

"You've got your work cut out for you, Morisato-kun! You'd better work hard to support your wife and kids!" Chihiro said.

"Yes. Speaking of which . . ."

Keiichi rose slowly to his feet and retrieved a small square box from his locker.

"I've been giving it a lot of thought, and I'd like to start from the very beginning."

The silver toolbox rested proudly on the table. Keiichi's air was just as dignified. His gaze was steady and determined.

"A second WHIRLWIND, huh?" Chihiro drew in a deep breath. She was filled with pride in how far Keiichi had come—she had always recognized his talents—but also a twinge of loneliness. "I have a great deal of respect for those tools . . . and for your skills."

Chihiro had long ago realized that Keiichi would outgrow her shop before long. He had the potential to be a national legend—a global one, even. The next Soichiro Honda or Carroll Shelby.

"I guess it *is* about time for you to strike out on your own," Chihiro said.

"Chihiro . . ."

"Very well. You have my blessing to open a second WHIRLWIND. On one condition: promise to make it even better than the first!"

Keiichi bowed his head deeply, thinking of what a sterling example Chihiro had always been, and all the knowledge she'd bestowed upon him.

"Thank you," he said. "I'll give it everything I've got."

Next to him, Chihiro, too, bowed low. She felt the same way Keiichi did.

Kozueko . . .

Keiichi was moved almost to tears.

When Keiichi hadn't had enough credits to graduate due to a minor misunderstanding, Kozueko had been nothing but supportive and cheerful. After graduation, when Chihiro had taken him on full time, Kozueko had encouraged him to follow his dreams, even though the job didn't pay much. Her gentle but strong presence and constant smile had become irreplaceable to him.

Keiichi reached for the tool box and opened its double lid. Inside, the tools were arranged neatly in two layers.

"By these tools, I hereby pledge not to waste everything you've done for me, Chihiro—from hiring me on part-time to making me a full-fledged employee. And Kozueko, you've always encouraged me tremendously. You're a goddess to me, and I promise to make you happy . . ."

". . . Keiichi-kun . . ."

Kozueko turned as red as a peach turning into a tomato.

The tools shone brightly in their box.

Belldandy turned and ran straight through the wall and out of the room.

Tiny snowflakes danced gracefully through the darkness. The headlights of cars illuminated the shop as they zoomed by, hurrying home.

Belldandy stood rooted to the spot, clutching her left hand to her chest above her heart.

Kozueko . . . you're a goddess to me . . .

Keiichi's words echoed in her ears. At the same time, she

remembered the words of their contract.

I want a goddess like you to be with me always.

From that day forward, Belldandy had remained by Keiichi's side, watching over him constantly. She supported his efforts and bestowed good fortune upon him, never doubting the happiness of their lives together.

And yet . . .

The tools in his silver tool box—they were unmistakably the ones from the Machiners.

Even though Belldandy didn't exist in this world, the Machiners had still visited Keiichi.

She remembered Keiichi's dream in their current world, not long after the system restore.

I should have known . . . nothing that happens is mere coincidence . . .

Tears ran down her cheeks.

Belldandy had always believed that in their previous lives, the Machiners and Keiichi had found each other because of there being a goddess in Keiichi's life. That *she* was the one who had brought them together.

But this world had proven her wrong.

It was an inevitable part of Keiichi's fate.

Human beings were all born with certain unique qualities. Qualities that could never be changed, no matter how or when anyone interfered.

Keiichi's love for machines—and their love for him—was an unchangeable part of his destiny.

Keiichi . . .

Somewhere along the line, Belldandy's desire to be with Keiichi had transcended her obligation to fulfill her contract. She had believed that being a goddess gave her the power to bring happiness to a mortal like Keiichi.

The tears streamed ceaselessly down Belldandy's cheeks and dripped down onto the ring on her left finger. Wet with tears, the golden tiara glistened faintly.

"Human beings . . . are so strong . . ."

Even in a world without any goddesses around, the Machiners had sought out Keiichi. And Keiichi had carved out a wonderful life for himself through his own hard work and dedication. With Kozueko, he would have an ideal partner forever by his side in life, old age, and eventually death.

As a goddess, Belldandy would never be able to bring Keiichi the same happiness.

Belldandy gazed tearfully up at the opaque black sky. The gentle snowflakes drifted past.

Meanwhile, Hild looked on in silence. Gently, she placed a small hand on Belldandy's back.

"Bell-chan . . . let's head back."

The light that spilled out of the shop's windows was tragically warm.

The dancing snowflakes twinkled in the darkness as a thin veil of white began to blanket the wet pavement.

*　　*　　*

Chunks of building lay strewn across the ground like a city of blocks built and demolished by a young child.

A small section of foundation, still buried in the ground, was the only reminder of where the N.I.T. dorm had once stood. There, Keiichi sat idly amongst the rubble.

The truth of the matter was that his mind had been temporarily paralyzed by the shock of witnessing events far beyond human imagination. But that didn't stop Keiichi from worrying about the well-being of the girl he loved.

I hope Belldandy's okay . . .

Belldandy had been led away by the CEO of the demon realm. True, she was Urd's mother—but that wasn't enough to reassure Keiichi.

But Belldandy's older sister Urd was lounging in the air, just as her mother had done earlier, and her younger sister Skuld was passing the time writing equations in the dirt with a hammer and stake.

Keiichi sighed. The two goddesses didn't seem very approachable at the moment, and Keiichi wasn't sure where to turn.

Just then, the youngest goddess let out a happy cry. "Big Sister!"

She was the first to sight Belldandy walking toward them through the wreckage. Like an adoring puppy dog, Skuld scampered forth to greet her sister.

"Belldandy!" Keiichi called, rising. But he was drowned out by the clamoring black-haired goddess as she threw herself into Belldandy's arms.

"Oh, Big Sister! I was so worried something might happen to you! I . . ." She clung to Belldandy, burying her face in her robes.

"It's all right, Skuld." Belldandy gave her little sister a warm smile and a gentle hug. The wind played with her platinum blond tresses.

"I was wondering what happened to you—since Hild went back quite a while ago." Urd, too, sauntered over, tossing her hair. She had felt the energy when the gate had opened. The deep red jewels of the Hlidskjalf Dusk sparkled in the sunlight.

"I'm sorry, Urd . . . I walked back."

"You walked?"

Belldandy could have returned in a heartbeat by teleport—if she'd chosen to walk instead, she must really have had a lot on her mind. Under Urd's worried gaze, Belldandy lowered her amethyst eyes, remembering her exchange with Hild.

"There—we're back, safe and sound."

The trip back to Belldandy's own dimension had been an easy one. They passed through the colorful interdimensional waves and landed in the exact spot they had departed from.

"Wonderful, Bell-chan!"

That took care of that. Belldandy took a deep breath as she shifted gears and readjusted to her world. Now that she was no longer a mere spirit, and she could feel definite sensations through her constantly regenerating molecules, the warm rays of sunshine felt good.

"Well?" Hild's indigo eyes probed Belldandy's. A breeze riffled through Hild's white hair and Belldandy's garments.

For a moment, Belldandy simply stood motionlessly where she'd landed, but now her expression grew resolute.

"Please lend me your help," she finally said, softly.

Hild smiled. "You're ready."

Belldandy nodded firmly. "Yes."

Nimbly, Hild hopped down from the ravaged fountain. Slowly, she raised her arms and began to sing an incantation.

Immediately, bits of light began to come together, forming shapes. These shapes assembled themselves into a three-dimensional figure that hovered above Hild's palms.

"A Nidhogg terminal . . ."

Immediately, Belldandy began to sing her own incantation, calling up a Yggdrasil terminal.

Light appeared in her palms, assembling into a mysterious form that was neither quite like a geometric pattern nor a motif from an ancient civilization. The formations that hovered above Belldandy's and Hild's hands were almost like Laputa, the legendary floating continent in the sky.

"This time we have to restore both Nidhogg and Yggdrasil," Hild said. "The main issue is timing."

"How about the moment the sun sinks below the horizon?"

Belldandy waved her hands, reconfiguring the pattern.

"Sunset? That's fine. The Earth will sleep, and Heaven and the Infernal Realm will finally awaken."

"I'd like to make Tarikihongan Temple the fundamental observation point," Belldandy said.

"Done," Hild agreed.

While goddesses and demons used different types of magic, the morphology of their formations was fairly similar. Belldandy and Hild input the Yggdrasil and Nidhogg information and access codes for the system restore before enclosing both data formations in magic globes.

All of the information needed for the amended restore operation was now contained in translucent spheres the size of softballs. All that remained was to insert the programs into their respective systems and run them simultaneously. This would fix the aberrations in the universe and reset everyone's memories.

"Give this to Urd, will you?" Hild handed over her magic sphere and gave Belldandy a little wave. Instantly, a working appeared on the ground.

"All right, we'll be going now."

She winked playfully and raised her hands to the sky. A gust of wind swept across the ground.

"Don't you want to tell Urd . . ."

But Hild shushed Belldandy, wagging her finger. "Things are better between us and Urd-chan this way."

"Hild . . ."

The wind pummeled Belldandy's body. Tufts of cloud spun in a circle, mixing with the wind and becoming a tornado. Before long, the twister extended high into the sky. Then, in the blink of an eye, Hild disappeared into its midst.

The sky returned to an aquamarine blue and a gust of wind blew past as if nothing had happened.

*　　　*　　　*

"She sure causes a commotion!" Urd sighed, ignoring the fact that from anyone else's perspective, her behavior was exactly the same.

"She said to give you her best." Belldandy smiled serenely, her amethyst eyes sparkling. She removed the magic globe from her pocket and passed it to Urd.

"Tonight at sunset," she said.

Now it was Urd's turn to feel torn, as she gazed at the flickering magic globe in Belldandy's delicate hand. She had braved numerous dangers to sustain this restored universe, for Belldandy's sake more than anything. If they executed another reset operation, this time all of their memories would be erased.

"Belldandy . . ." Urd was about to object, but she trailed off when she saw the look in Belldandy's pure, clear eyes. Urd didn't know what had taken place between Belldandy and Hild, but if Belldandy's mind was made up, there was no point in arguing.

"All right." Urd said simply and nodded, setting aside her reservations as she accepted the translucent globe. It glowed faintly in the palm of her hand. "Your friendly System Administrator will take it from here," she promised. She used the Hlidskjalf Dusk to apply a strong protection spell to the globe and then, without warning, grabbed Skuld in a headlock.

"W-what . . . ?" stammered Skuld, who had been quietly watching the proceedings.

"We're going back to Heaven . . . we need to hurry if we're going to get the system ready in time."

There were only a few hours left before sunset. There was no time to lose, since they would need to calibrate the Universal Unit that housed the critical line between Yggdrasil and Nidhogg as well as performing a variety of other checks and adjustments.

"Wait a minute, Urd . . . I still don't really understand what's going on . . ."

"I'll explain it to you after we get back."

"Explain it to me now!" Skuld struggled valiantly, but she was no match for Urd. With a graceful wave of one gauntlet-clad arm, a gate appeared instantly in the ground.

"Belldandy . . . !" Skuld wailed.

"I'll be back soon, too!" Belldandy promised.

"Then I'll stay with y—" Skuld began, but before she could finish Urd thrust her through the gate. "Not agaiiiiiiii . . ." Skuld's screams faded into the distance as she was swallowed up by the luminous portal.

"Geez, what a handful!" Urd sighed. She stood at the edge of the glittering gate, tossed her hair, and looked up at the sky. The sun set early in the winter, and already it was sinking low in the western sky.

"Keiichi," Urd said. Keiichi had been standing by rigidly, unable to take part in the goddesses' conversation.

"Huh?"

Belldandy had finally returned safely, but now Skuld was gone and Urd was about to vanish through the gate as well. It was more than he could keep up with. Still, he was doing his very best, and the sight of it made Urd smile.

"The rest's up to you. Got it?" she called.

Urd sank into the light as if her body was melting. The last thing to disappear was her hand, which she used to flash them a peace sign. Then, quietly, the gate closed.

Now only Keiichi and Belldandy remained. A gust of wind blew through, stirring up the sand.

"Um . . . Belldandy?" Keiichi managed to form the words as a strange sense of burning responsibility welled up inside of him. He wasn't sure what exactly Urd wanted him to do, but he would do his best.

Belldandy graced him with her most dazzling smile. "Keiichi, why don't we go for a drive?"

HAKUMEI — DUSK

The BMW with the sidecar purred happily along the seaside road, buffeted by the wind.

"That was unbelievable!" Keiichi exclaimed, still unable to get over his excitement at what he had just seen.

Keiichi had been met with quite a shock when he'd returned to the clubhouse with the intention of taking Belldandy for a drive as she'd requested. They found the prefab building in ruin, with half of its walls blown to pieces. Not surprisingly, the motorcycle Keiichi had left parked next to it was in no better shape.

"Totaled" wasn't the word for it—it had been reduced to smithereens. It was completely unrecognizable as a motorcycle.

Keiichi had slumped his shoulders in devastation. It was a double sucker punch, losing his beloved vehicle and being unable to fulfill the wishes of his favorite girl.

But his pain was soon soothed by Belldandy's beautiful singing.

The crystal-pure melody became light, diffusing all around them. Immediately, the bike's parts began to rise up out of the shadows and the rubble—some from a distance of several meters. Tiny screws, bolts, pipes . . . as if they possessed a will of their own, they swirled in the band of light, coming together in a dazzling flash. The BMW was whole again.

"The feel of the engine, the way it rides . . . it's all exactly the same!"

Keiichi had been concerned at first, but his fears were dispelled as soon as they began their drive. It ran as smoothly as if it had been restored by a top engineer.

"Your bike's happy, too," Belldandy smiled, gratified by Keiichi's pleased smile and the contented hum of the engine.

The smell of the surf filled their lungs as they turned down a side road toward the beach.

The golden sunlight sparkled on the ocean's waters.

"Keiichi!"

His goddess waved at him.

A swarm of ocean birds gathered around her, playfully fluttering their wings against her delicate hands, while the saltwater spray at the ocean's edge caressed her fair feet. Keiichi wasn't used to how Belldandy looked with her seal removed, but for some reason, she didn't seem in the least bit unfamiliar.

She's . . . so beautiful.

Keiichi sat watching her on the beach, dazzled by her loveliness.

Belldandy's laugh mingled with the roar of the waves. As the sunlight streamed through her platinum blond hair, she suddenly looked to Keiichi as if she were about to disappear.

"Belldandy!"

He ran toward her and grasped her hands.

"Keiichi?" Belldandy froze, surprised. A wave lapped at Keiichi's sneakers and withdrew.

Keiichi squeezed her hands. He didn't know why, but he was seized by a profound feeling of loss and the sudden fear that she would melt away into the ocean. He remembered reading Megumi the story of the Little Mermaid when she was small.

The mermaid turns into bubbles and disappears . . . he remembered absently as he gazed at his own reflection in Belldandy's amethyst eyes.

"Keiichi? Are you all right?"

"Oh . . ."

Immediately, Keiichi was yanked back to reality by the sight of Belldandy's gentle eyes peering into his face.

"I-I-I'm sorry! I-I don't know what I was doing . . ." quickly, he began to pull away, but Belldandy squeezed his hands back.

What's this?

His temperature soared. As Belldandy smiled sweetly at him, Keiichi was afraid she would hear the pounding of his heart.

"Are you cold, Keiichi?"

"I-I-I'm fine."

His body burned with the heat of a tropical sun.

"Shall we walk a little bit?"

"Y-y-yes!"

Amid the rhythmical susurrations of the waves, the two of them had the entire beach to themselves.

As they walked slowly along, Keiichi savored every step. The salty winter wind was piercing, but it was nothing compared to the warmth of Belldandy's hand.

"What about you, Belldandy? Are you warm enough?"

"Yes . . . I'm fine." A wave of happiness surged through her . . . how sweet of Keiichi to worry about the thin garments she was wearing! She rested her head against his slightly low shoulder and closed her eyes.

Keiichi . . . I'm so glad I met you . . .

The roaring waves reflected the sun's waves, glittering brightly, and the seabirds frolicked amongst them, converging and dispersing.

Off in the distance, the sea blended into the sky at the horizon line, forming a seamless world of blue.

For some reason, the ocean breeze carried the scent of springtime.

*　　*　　*

The sun sank low in the western sky, staining it a deep red. Still basking in the afterglow of a pleasant drive, the BMW hummed cheerfully as it pulled up to Tarikihongan Temple.

As Keiichi parked his bike, the first thing he saw was the snow around the Great Hall. The walkways were still blanketed in a thick layer of snow, unlike the neatly shoveled area around the house.

"Oops . . . forgot about that."

Between his accident with the snowdrift and the phone call about the clubhouse, Keiichi had completely forgotten his snow shoveling project.

Tonight, it would freeze solid, and once it iced over it would be no picnic to clear. But the afternoon drive had been such a joyful experience that it more than made up for it.

"I'll tackle it tomorrow," he decided lightheartedly. He even felt a surge of motivation.

Belldandy was silent.

Tomorrow . . . what a beautiful word.

She was filled with a renewed appreciation for how wonderful it had been to use the word "tomorrow" here on Earth without reservation.

But this world has no tomorrow . . .

The sun was about to set. She placed her left hand over her heart, as if to test her own determination, and smiled as she looked up at Keiichi from the sidecar.

"Keiichi . . . will you stay with me just a little bit longer?"

My last remaining task as a goddess.

Holy Bell emerged, spreading her arms, and Keiichi floated up into the air. In a cloud of white feathers, Belldandy and Keiichi landed gently on the roof of the house.

The view from the rooftop of the mountaintop temple building was spectacular. Below, lights began to glow in the town of Nekomi, and off in the distance the ocean was bathed in golden light.

"Wow . . . look at that!" Keiichi exclaimed with childlike exuberance. In the stirring glow of the setting sun, even the orange-tinted town looked happy. It was all because Belldandy was there by his side.

As Keiichi sat at the very peak of the roof, Belldandy stood still and silent, gazing out at the landscape.

"Keiichi . . ." she said softly after a moment. "Do you remember when we first met?"

". . . Of course!"

A year had gone by, but Keiichi remembered it clearly. It had been such a momentous occasion in his life that he could never forget it even if he tried. His phone call from the school dorm had connected to the Goddess Technical Help Line, and Belldandy had suddenly popped out of his mirror.

"It was the most fateful encounter of my life," Keiichi said. Conveniently, he'd managed to forget the embarrassing moment when he'd fallen flat on his rear end.

"It was an unforgettable encounter for me, too," Belldandy said. It was almost a miracle that she and Keiichi had found each other amid the myriad of living things in this universe. The system restore had bestowed upon them a second miracle. But now . . .

"Keiichi . . . there's something I need to tell you . . ."

Softly, Belldandy began to explain.

They had met for the first time four years ago. There had been various bumps in the road along the way, but Keiichi, Belldandy, and her sisters had lived happily together here at Tarikihongan Temple. Until one day, all of a sudden, it had all come to an end.

"Dead? Me?"

"Yes. You were protecting Megumi . . ."

It came as a major shock to Keiichi when Belldandy told him he'd died in a traffic accident. That wasn't surprising—few people remain cool and collected when informed of their death. Finally, Hild's words made sense to him now.

So that's why she said that there was a soul missing and pointed to me . . .

Keiichi processed the information with surprising composure, but was unable to conceal his surprise at the next thing Belldandy told him.

The destruction of the world . . .

Keiichi's death had triggered the collapse of Yggdrasil, and Heaven had almost been annihilated.

"B-b-but why?" His voice was slightly hoarse.

"Spending so much time in the presence of goddesses caused our energy to accumulate in your system, turning you into a singularity. As it continued to collect, it became so tremendous that it caused a relationship of mutual traction between you and Yggdrasil."

Keiichi was still a little hazy on the details pertaining to the system and the individual relationships involved, but he was blown away by the news of his own death and the universe's threatened collapse in its wake.

"It wasn't your fault, Keiichi . . . I should have been more careful."

Afterward, as a last resort, the goddesses had reset Yggdrasil, restoring Keiichi and the Heavenly Realm. Or so they'd thought . . .

The wind whooshed across the sky, passing between Keiichi and Belldandy.

In the brief silence that followed, Keiichi's thoughts raced. Even if there had been many mistakes in the past, they had been given a chance to start over. There had to be a way to make things work!

"In that case . . ." Keiichi said, with as much cheer as he could muster, "what if we're all just extra careful this time, so that I don't become a singularity again? Then everything should be okay, right?"

Belldandy gazed at him silently with her back to the setting sun. Then she shook her head. "That's what I thought, too. But . . ."

Belldandy told him how a major disturbance had been created by restarting only Yggdrasil. The backlash from the natural world was growing ever stronger, unleashing a corrective force to erase Keiichi's existence.

"I knew for sure after the disaster with the snow this morning—the reset universe is trying to repair itself. Even using all of my powers as a Goddess First Class, I won't be able to protect you from it. If you try to build something on an uneven foundation, eventually that structure will collapse. Because we didn't perform the reset correctly, this universe, and your life, are in danger."

The expression in Belldandy's amethyst eyes was poised and unwavering.

"Belldandy . . ."

Keiichi gazed at the goddess, sensing a change in Belldandy's demeanor. There was something unapproachable about her.

The sky was beginning to grow darker and the wind carried a new chill.

In all honesty, Keiichi hadn't understood about half of what Belldandy had explained. The part about the system and the relationship between the two realms was too abstract for him to really grasp.

Still, in the face of it all, there was one thing of which he was sure.

No matter what—I still want us to be together!—a voice screamed from deep within Keiichi's heart.

He had no memory of the previous four years; as far as Keiichi was concerned, his relationship with Belldandy was only just beginning. Even if there were a few risks—no, even if it meant his death—he would gladly trade his entire life for a single moment together.

The words were on the tip of his tongue . . . but something about the look in Belldandy's eyes prevented him from voicing them.

". . . I . . ." Keiichi croaked.

Belldandy nodded, her gaze serene. "The time has come to give this troubled universe a fresh start. We will return it to before you and I sealed our contract, and all of our memories will be reset."

Belldandy slid the ring off her left ring finger and placed it gently in Keiichi's hand.

"You were so sweet to give me this ring. Please forgive me the indiscretion of returning it to you now . . . I can't bring something that belongs to this time axis back with me to Heaven."

The beautiful afternoon they'd spent together on the beach seemed to crumble away.

With the return of one tiny ring . . . it seemed to Keiichi that their contract—that Belldandy would stay with him always—was finally over.

As he gazed at the sparkling golden tiara in his hand, Keiichi struggled hard to fight back tears. Watching him, Belldandy felt as if her heart were being ripped in two. She longed desperately to embrace his trembling shoulders and reveal to him her true feelings.

Ever since the system restore, her vigilant efforts to maintain distance between them had been hard on Keiichi . . . and now, even in their last moments together, she had to cause him further pain.

She hardened her heart.

But I am Belldandy, a Goddess First Class.

Her platinum blond hair shone in the warm glow of the setting sun. Holy Bell's white wings emerged and fluttered.

"Even without me—without the help of a goddess—you have the power to achieve your dreams, to find love, and to build a wonderful future . . . Take heart; you human beings are blessed with infinite potential."

"I . . ." Keiichi summoned every last drop of kindness and strength he could muster and gave Belldandy his brightest smile. "I still believe that we'll meet again."

As they gazed at each other, the wind was still and the moment seemed to last forever. The setting sun reddened, casting a rosy glow across the land.

"Goodbye . . ."

Keiichi's dark eyes widened.

"Keiichi Morisato."

He gasped, blinded by a sudden whirlwind of white feathers. He shut his eyes—it was almost like a blizzard.

After what was probably only a few seconds, the air grew quiet and Keiichi opened his eyes.

"Belldandy . . ."

The goddess was gone. All that remained was the darkening landscape and a smattering of white feathers.

"I won't stop believing . . ."

As he gripped the ring, the first tear landed on his fist. His smile crumbled and the tears streamed down his face. Now that the floodgates were open, there was no holding them back.

The sun continued to sink toward the ocean.

*　　*　　*

Sploosh!

A sudden column of water shot up from the still water of the bathtub.

The small, black-haired goddess who traveled by water gates sprang forth from the bathing area and hurriedly set the alarm on her watch. The sun would set in just thirty more minutes. She had until then to find Belldandy and bring her back to Heaven.

"We have to get back before Urd notices . . . Noble Scarlet—GO!"

With the assistance of her tiny angel, Skuld immediately began her search.

First the tea room . . . then the kitchen . . . she peeked into Keiichi's room, too, but no luck. After searching the house from top to bottom, Skuld ran outside to check the grounds.

"See? This is why I wanted to go back together!" she lamented.

After being thrust through the gate, Urd had given her a brusque explanation and then the preparations had begun, without even a moment to catch their breath. When things had finally quieted down a bit, Skuld had managed to slip away without Urd's noticing so that she could sneak back down to Earth.

"Belldandy . . . where are you?"

This time, when the reset was performed, their memories would all be erased. What if Belldandy was thinking of remaining on Earth for Keiichi's sake? Skuld was sick with worry.

Twenty more minutes . . .

The BMW was there, but Keiichi and Belldandy were nowhere to be seen. Skuld checked the Great Hall, and, though she knew it was a long shot, the storage shed. Still no sign of them. Her spirits sank—where else could she look? Just then, her angel tapped her on the arm.

"What is it, Noble Scarlet?"

The angel was pointing insistently toward the roof of the house.

Skuld squinted dubiously up at the roof—but there, right at the very top, a lone figure sat.

"Oh, no—Keiichi?! Is he stuck up there?"

Skuld didn't know what he was doing up on the roof, but there was no time to worry about that now. She had to act. "Keiichi, you're a pain in the neck, you know that?" she muttered.

Quickly, she returned to her room, dragged her Autonomous Sentient Walking Machine out of the closet, and brought it back to where Keiichi was. Unlike her older sisters, Skuld didn't have the power to levitate through the air up to the rooftop, let alone the power to bring a human being safely back to solid ground. She would have to use a machine.

"Keiichiii! I'm here to rescue you!"

A series of loud mechanical clanks approached the roof. When Skuld's head appeared suddenly at the edge of the eaves, Keiichi hurriedly rubbed his reddened eyes.

"What's up, Skuld?"

What kind of a question was that? Skuld's temper flared.

"What do you mean, 'what's up'? I came to help you because you're stuck on the roof!"

She didn't have a moment to waste, and she felt her irritation mount with every passing second. She extended a hand. "Come *on!* I still have to find my sister!" she urged.

"Oh . . . if you're looking for Bell, she went back to Heaven."

"When?"

"Just now."

"Whaaaaaaaaat?!"

They must have just missed each other! All of Skuld's worry and effort had been for nothing!

"I should have just waited for her in Heaven."

Now she had to help Keiichi get down, or her whole trip would be a complete waste. Still, he made no sign of getting up. She tried to grab his hand, but Keiichi declined her help.

"Thanks, Skuld . . . but I'm fine up here. Belldandy rejected me, and the world's about to be reset again anyway, right?"

"Huh?"

Skuld was bewildered for a moment to hear Keiichi speak of the reset—how did he know about that? But what really stuck in her craw was what he'd said just before that.

"She . . . rejected you?"

"Yeah. She gave me back my ring . . . and she said we'd never see each other again."

He gazed sadly at the shining ring in the palm of his hand.

"Keiichi, you stupid idiot!" Skuld shouted.

"What?"

"Don't you understand anything about my sister?!" The little goddess glared ferociously at Keiichi, her eyes welling with tears.

"Skuld . . ."

"You have no idea how anxious she was to receive that ring . . . how much she treasured it . . . how painful it was for her to say goodbye to you . . ."

Belldandy . . .

Suddenly, Keiichi finally understood the odd feeling he'd had when Belldandy had said goodbye. Her goddess-like composure—it had all been an act to spare his feelings. Meanwhile, he'd been so absorbed in his own feelings—and in his own conviction that a goddess was too good for him—that he'd done nothing but cry like a baby.

"Give it to me."

Skuld wiped her eyes and held out her hand.

"Wha—?"

"Give me the ring. I'll bring it to my sister."

When they implemented the reset, there was no telling how an object from Earth might affect the process. But because of who Belldandy was . . . and in order to preserve her memories of the time she'd spent with Keiichi . . . Skuld was filled with the desire to bring the ring back to her sister. She just had to!

"I'll take care of it." She snatched the ring out of Keiichi's hand and slid down from the walking machine.

"Skuld . . . thank you." Keiichi waved at her from his perch on the roof.

"Don't get the wrong idea, Keiichi," Skuld called over her

shoulder as she ran toward the house. "This isn't for you. It's for Belldandy."

Only fifteen minutes left.

The seconds were ticking away.

"Don't hassle me, Noble Scarlet!" Skuld rebuked her angel, who was tugging at her sleeve to remind her that they needed to return to Heaven soon. Skuld raced back to her room and began to scavenge for parts.

"I wonder if I can throw together a box able to transcend space-time with what I have on hand here . . ."

She'd delved into the project without looking back, but in fact Skuld was completely unsure as to whether or not she could build such a sophisticated contraption in such limited time. But there was no time for self-doubt, nor was there time to mull over the situation. She just had to do it.

"Here goes!" Skuld performed a series of rapid calculations. "Huh! Maybe I really *can* pull this off . . ."

Her uncertainty vanished into thin air. Even under severe time pressure, it was Skuld's nature to take pleasure in the invention process. She hummed to herself as she labored away at the speed of light.

In just a few minutes, her "Time-Space-Proof Mini Box" was complete.

"Lightning-quick implementation without sacrificing functionality or elegance! I really am a genius!"

She tucked the ring into the box and marveled lovingly at her creation. Noble Scarlet prodded her shoulder, interrupting her reverie. Less than five minutes left.

"Right! I'd better write a quick note now."

If she left a note inside explaining the situation, Belldandy would know what the ring meant even when her memories were gone. On a tiny piece of note paper, Skuld began to write.

My Dearest Sister . . .

Noble Scarlet fluttered over Skuld's shoulder, trying to get a peek at the note. A little white feather floated down, landing lightly on the box's lid.

Kchak! The box snapped shut.

"Wha . . . ?"

Startled by the sound, Skuld looked up. She gaped in disbelief.

"The Mini Box! It's closed!"

The crucial letter of explanation was not yet inside the box. The lid had shut on just a tiny corner of the page, the part that said *"My Dearest Sister."* Skuld cursed the safety measure she'd built in to her invention: once it was closed, the box couldn't be reopened until after the reset operation.

"Will she understand?" Skuld worried.

The little angel let out a voiceless cry, apologizing desperately. The angel wouldn't have blamed her mistress if she'd given her a good angry punch for this.

When Skuld's hand came toward her, Noble Scarlet squeezed her little red eyes shut.

But the hand pulled the weeping angel into a gentle embrace.

"...?!"

"It's okay, Noble Scarlet. I'm a genius. Even with our memories gone, I'll think of something. What's more important right now is that this time, I won't remember *you*. You're such a part of me, and I'm going to lose you!"

Skuld had been completely preoccupied with worry for Belldandy and her ring—but she, too, was about to part company with someone very special. When time was reset, Skuld would be returned to a time when she didn't have her angel yet, when Noble Scarlet had yet to be born.

"But we'll meet again . . . I'm sure we will. So I'm not going to say goodbye to you. We're just not going to see each other for a little while."

The angel smiled through her tears and kissed Skuld on the cheek. Reassured that they would be reunited, she folded up her wings.

"Noble Scarlet . . . I love you."

Skuld gave herself a little hug, sending waves of affection to the angel inside of her. Then she picked up the little box.

Three more minutes . . .

The rest is up to luck . . .

Using the part of the notepaper that protruded from the box to wrap it up, Skuld stuck the package in her pocket. Then she raced into the bathroom and plunged through her water gate.

As the sun retired from the sky, a quiet darkness settled over Tarikihongan Temple.

At that instant, the Yggdrasil system in Heaven and the Nidhogg system in the Demon Realm simultaneously gave off a luminous flash. The light poured down over the Earth, bathing it in the brightness of midday.

Keiichi gently closed his eyes as the warm brightness enveloped his body.

✎ ENDING ↷

Warm sunlight streamed down over the white-walled palace as a fresh breeze wafted through the deep, lush greenery and into the azure sky. The sunlight poured in through the windows, filling the white and beige room with a warm, bright atmosphere.

As she savored the beautiful afternoon, Belldandy stood in front of her mirror, wearing a comfortable robe. As a soft intonation escaped her lips, a burst of light immediately enveloped her body, transforming the robe into her official goddess uniform. Gently, the soft folds of the blue and white garment formed over her body.

Now she raised her right hand to the seal on her left ear and cast a seal spell.

The powers of a Goddess First Class were so great that at times they might wreak dramatic effects on another realm. That was why she was required to wear a power seal when entering the control room as an operator.

"Ah!"

The platinum blond locks streaming down her back turned chestnut brown. Belldandy pulled her hair up into a ponytail— now she was ready. She gave a gentle twirl in front of the mirror and nodded in satisfaction.

"All right, now!"

She glanced at the clock, making sure that she still had enough time, then quickly carried her tea set out to the table and sat down on the sofa.

"Today I think I'll have . . . this one."

She selected a Darjeeling tea from her collection and scooped it into the pot. Belldandy had discovered the British tradition of having afternoon tea once while she was researching Earth customs. For some reason, she'd fallen instantly in love with the idea, and now she made it a practice to enjoy tea time every day before work.

"Mmm, what a lovely fragrance!"

A rich aroma wafted out of the golden liquid in her tea cup.

Yggdrasil was as calm and quiet as ever.

"Oh . . . Urd did mention that there was another goddess-demon clash over market share on Earth . . ." Belldandy remembered, reaching for the information pad that had arrived that morning. A sort of Heavenly newspaper, it contained news of everything that transpired in the three realms.

Sure enough, the front page was emblazoned with a story about the ongoing raging conflict between Heaven and the Demon Realm.

"I thought so." Belldandy's lavender eyes clouded slightly.

*   *   *

Lately, the clashes on Earth had been escalating at an unusual pace, and they'd become a frequent topic of conversation in Heaven. Belldandy didn't like it one bit. For one thing, she'd never enjoyed that sort of gossip, and for another, it made her heart ache for her older sister, Urd.

"They'll probably be talking about it in the Operation Room again today . . ."

She let out a small sigh, just as a delicate melody filled the room, announcing the hour.

The high, domed ceiling made Belldandy's footsteps echo. She walked slower than usual today as she passed among the columns and arches of the sparkling white corridor. The light that poured down through the high, frosted windows was as lovely as spring sunbeams filtering down through the leaves of a tree.

Belldandy loved this long passageway that led to the operation room.

She held one of the most enjoyable jobs a Goddess First Class could perform—connecting to other realms by telephone and bestowing blessings upon the beings she encountered. As she walked down this corridor, she was always filled with happiness, her pulse racing at the thought of the people she would meet and the enjoyment that awaited.

I hope I meet someone wonderful today!

The gloom she'd felt just moments ago had vanished

completely, and the bracelets on her arm tinkled cheerfully, as if to reflect the joy in her heart.

Just as she began to quicken her pace, a voice from behind brought her to a halt.

"Sis!"

The shout echoed against the domed ceiling. Belldandy's little sister Skuld came racing down the corridor to meet her.

"Oh! What is it, Skuld?"

Normally, Skuld and Urd were busy with System Administration work at this hour. The buildings that housed the System Room and the Operation Room were quite a distance apart, at opposite ends of the corridor.

When the little goddess finally reached Belldandy, gasping for breath, she threw her arms around her big sister.

"Skuld, why the hurry?" Belldandy stroked Skuld's black hair, waiting for her to catch her breath.

Finally Skuld settled down, calmed by her big sister's sweet fragrance. Slowly, she pulled a tiny box out of her pocket.

"I found something of yours in my room!"

A small, silver box rested in the palm of her hand. But Belldandy had never seen it before.

"I don't think it's mine . . ."

"But there's a note inside!"

"A note?"

"See?"

Skuld opened the box, exposing a tiny scrap of paper that hardly qualified as a note. Barely legible, the letters "Dear Big

Sis" were scrawled across it, but the rest was torn away.

"But this is your handwriting, Skuld."

"Yes . . . that's a mystery, too."

It was clearly Skuld's writing, even though the letters were messy as if she'd written them in a hurry. That much was certain. But Skuld had no memory of writing such a note, and the tiny box was completely unfamiliar, too.

Belldandy took the box from Skuld and discovered something else inside.

"Oh!"

It was a lovely golden ring in the shape of a delicate tiara.

"This . . . belongs to me?"

"Sorry . . . I have no idea!" Skuld said helplessly, completely unsure of herself now. She'd hoped that by bringing the ring to Belldandy, everything would be resolved. But Belldandy was just as clueless as she was.

"What should we do?"

Belldandy smiled kindly at her flummoxed sister. Gently, she shut the box's lid and dropped it into her pocket.

"Thank you, Skuld . . . for taking the trouble to bring this to me."

"Huh?"

"I'll look into it properly after work. It might be something significant . . ."

"You're right."

Belldandy might be able to learn something through the system. There had to be a reason for the box's existence.

"I'll help you, too!"

"I'd appreciate that!"

"Okay!"

Her good cheer restored, Skuld waved, grinning, and raced off back down the corridor again. Belldandy watched her until Skuld disappeared from sight before resuming her own walk—this time at a hurried pace.

Ting! The lift chimed as it came to a stop.

Belldandy stepped out into the Operation Room. As she'd anticipated, it was abuzz with chatter like the twittering of song birds.

"Good morning, Belldandy! Did you hear the latest about the demons?"

". . . Yes."

The other goddesses flocked around her.

"Why, Belldandy! It's not often that you're the last one to arrive!"

"Yes! You're usually the first one here!"

"I know—were you talking with Urd?"

Just as Belldandy had expected, her half-goddess half-demon sister was a hot topic.

"No. I haven't seen her yet today. I was talking with Skuld . . ."

"Oh . . . Skuld . . ."

Clearly, they were disappointed by this. Once it was clear that there was no new information to be had, they returned to their conversations.

Belldandy let out a faint sigh of relief as she took her seat. The egg-shaped chair faced a workstation with an integrated control panel and phone. The chair's high back allowed her to concentrate on her work without being distracted by her surroundings.

Now I should have a bit of peace and quiet . . .

After a few moments, a gentle melody filled the operation room, announcing the beginning of the work day. All at once, the goddesses got down to work, and the Operating Room finally calmed down. Satisfied, Belldandy, too, began to set up her work.

Just then, the quiet was interrupted by a ringing telephone. The first call of the day.

"Hello! You've reached the Goddess Technical Help Line . . ." a goddess elsewhere in the room answered the call.

Belldandy's phone showed no signs of ringing yet. She savored the quiet while it lasted.

Suddenly, she remembered the little box in her pocket. She took it out and softly opened the lid. The tiny gold ring glittered proudly in its center.

I wonder where you came from!

The mystery of it made her heart race. Gently, she picked it up. As she gazed at it, an inscription caught her eye.

"To Belldandy"

Her own name was engraved in the ring in English letters.

This was a present for me?

The moment the thought popped into her mind, the ring gave

off a gentle, loving aura. Even though she'd never seen it before, Belldandy was suddenly filled with an overwhelming feeling of nostalgia. Before she knew it, she found herself slip it onto her left ring finger, as if succumbing to the golden tiara's wishes.

It fit her as perfectly as if it had been made for her.

This . . .

Riririririririri!—Just then, Belldandy's phone began to ring, signaling that somebody out there needed her help.

Her left hand reached for the phone as usual—but then stopped still.

Ririririririri!

The other goddesses began to shoot Belldandy curious glances as her phone continued to trill. Still, she remained frozen, her hand on the receiver.

The phone's persistent ringing filled the room.

Riririririririri!

The ring on her finger sparkled in the light.

❧ AFTERWORD ❧

YUMI TOHMA

I believe I first encountered the goddesses in the early autumn of 1991.

It was the first time I'd been called in to a recording studio for an animation audition (normally, they're held in sound studios)—and the first time I experienced a character audition in which song was the main component.

I still remember it clearly—I was told to sing Shizuka Kudo's *"Arashi no Sugao"* ("Face of the Storm") in Urd's voice and to shout "Lightning Bolt!" during the interlude.

As an actress, I was treated to all sorts of experiences through my involvement in *Oh My Goddess!* This year, after twenty years as a voice-actress, I was given the opportunity to express myself as a writer.

The transition from actress to creator wasn't an easy one, but I did my very best to pour my thoughts and feelings into my work.

I also tried something new—incorporating an opening and ending song into my novel. Back in my student days, my friends and I often had fun assigning songs to the illustrations in our favorite manga and novels. It's a mystery to me how just hearing a song from back then conjures up so many dear memories.

I chose Kazumasa Oda's "*Daisuki na Kimi ni*" ("For My Beloved") for Keiichi's eyes, and Keiichi and Belldandy's feelings during the final farewell scene are "*Memai*" ("Vertigo") by the band Dreams Come True. Since my relationship with *Oh My Goddess!* began through song, it seemed appropriate to assign theme songs to my imaginings. I wonder if this fits in with what you, the reader, imagined? I hope that you were able to intimately relate to the world of *First End*.

Finally, I would like to take this opportunity to express my gratitude to everyone who made this wonderful experience possible.

Many thanks to the great Kosuke Fujishima for kindly granting his approval for the novelization of his well-loved *Oh My Goddess!* series, and for taking the time out of his busy schedule to draw the cover art.

I would also like to thank the great Hidenori Matsubara for drawing all of the illustrations for the book despite his busy job as an art director.

I'd like to thank Shōhei Yoshida, the editor in chief of *Afternoon*, for approving the project and for accommodating me in so many ways. I owe thanks as well to Mr. Hiroshi Tada and Mr. Naoyuki Suzuki of *Afternoon*'s editorial department.

Thank you to Toshiaki Imai and Yoshikazu Yamada for your valuable advice.

I also want to extend my heartfelt thanks to you, dear readers, for picking up this book and reading it cover to cover.

I often think about what a personalized kind of entertainment novels offer.

I say this because the worlds described in novels, including the characters, places, and sounds, all take shape in the reader's imagination.

Naturally, detailed descriptions aid the reader's imaginings— but if a hundred people read a novel, they will come up with a hundred different ways of imagining the characters, a hundred different versions of the places and sounds and colors. This is what makes novels so enjoyable.

The reader can create his or her own image of a peerlessly beautiful woman, or of a landscape of unearthly splendor. Even though the reader is a passive participant, he or she also has a hand in the creative process.

There are few mediums of entertainment so wonderful.

When it comes to the *Oh My Goddess!* novel, the characters, voices, and places in the story already exist. At least, readers who have seen the animated series will probably imagine the characters looking and sounding as they do on the show. But beyond that, the expressions on the character's faces, their gestures, and the colors of the sky exist only in the reader's mind.

I hope you will enjoy your very own, personalized goddesses. The worlds you imagine may be more beautiful than the ones Ms. Tohma or I have envisioned.

Lastly, I would like to express my gratitude and admiration for Ms. Tohma, the novelist who created this world.

❧ ABOUT THE CREATORS ❧

As a voice actress YUMI TOHMA (*author*) is an international celebrity throughout the Far East, perhaps best known as the voice of the goddess Urd in the many animated incarnations of *Oh My Goddess!* Her animation credits also include the lead voice of Emma in *Emma: A Victorian Romance*, Deedlit in *Record of Lodoss War*, and Sylphiel in *Slayers*, among many others, but it is her close connection to the *Oh My Goddess!* characters and stories that have led to her writing this, her first novel. Equally in high demand for her distinctive voice in recording vocals for video games, live-action movies, and television, she can also be heard as the international voice of Sarah Wynter's "Kate Warner" in the television series *24*, Holly Marie Combs's "Piper Halliwell" in *Charmed*, Kate Winslet's "Rose Dawson" in *Titanic,* and Jessica Alba's "Susan Storm/The Invisible Woman" in *Fantastic Four*, as well as the voice of many characters in such popular games as *Soul Calibur* and *Tekken*.

Born in 1964, KOSUKE FUJISHIMA (*creator and cover illustrations*) began his comics career just after graduating high school as an editor for the comics news magazine *Puff*. After interviewing *Be Free!* creator Tatsuya Egawa for *Puff*, Fujishima soon became Egawa's assistant and, eventually, embarked on his own comics writing and illustrating career. Fujishima's first widely recognized series, *You're Under Arrest!* started serialization in *Morning Party Extra* magazine in 1986 and was an instant success.

In 1988, Fujishima featured the *You're Under Arrest!* characters in a four-panel gag strip which showed them praying to a goddess. That goddess became the inspiration for Belldandy and the creation of the *Oh My Goddess!* series in *Afternoon* magazine. It still runs there today, almost twenty years later. The series has been the basis for more than one hundred animated episodes, a motion picture, and numerous toys and statues. With thirty-four volumes in print in Japan and twenty-seven books in America, *Oh My Goddess!* is, as of 2006, the longest running Japanese manga series being published in the United States.

HIDENORI MATSUBARA (*interior illustrations*), Chief Animation Director and Character Designer on the weekly *Ah! My Goddess* TV series and the theatrical release motion picture *Ah! My Goddess: The Movie*, is perhaps the artist most closely associated with the development of the world of Belldandy, Urd, Skuld, and Keiichi aside from their creator, Kosuke Fujishima. An experienced and much sought-after animator and designer, Matsubara has also worked on the popular animated series and films *Sukeban Deka; Serial Experiments Lain; Gunsmith Cats; Sakura Wars*; and *Patlabor: The Movie*, to name a few.

DARK HORSE MANGA